William Beckford

The Lewis Walpole Series in Eighteenth-Century Culture and History

The Lewis Walpole Series, published by Yale University Press with the aid of the Annie Burr Lewis Fund, is dedicated to the culture and history of the long eighteenth century (from the Glorious Revolution to the accession of Queen Victoria). It welcomes work in a variety of fields, including literature and history, the visual arts, political philosophy, music, legal history, and the history of science. In addition to original scholarly work, the series publishes new editions and translations of writing from the period, as well as reprints of major books that are currently unavailable. Though the majority of books in the series will probably concentrate on Great Britain and the Continent, the range of our geographical interests is as wide as Horace Walpole's.

William Beckford
First Prime Minister of the London Empire

Perry Gauci

Yale UNIVERSITY PRESS

NEW HAVEN AND LONDON

Published with assistance from the Annie Burr Lewis Fund and the Louis Stern Memorial Fund.

Yale University Press books may be purchased in quantity for educational, business, or promotional use. For information, please e-mail sales.press@yale.edu (U.S. office) or sales@yaleup.co.uk (U.K. office).

Set in Fournier type by IDS Infotech Ltd., Chandigarh, India.
Printed in the United States of America.

Library of Congress Cataloging-in-Publication Data
Gauci, Perry
William Beckford : first prime minister of the London empire / Perry Gauci.
        p.   cm. — (The Lewis Walpole series in eighteenth-century culture and history)
Includes bibliographical references and index.
ISBN 978-0-300-16675-0 (alk. paper)
    1. Beckford, William, 1709–1770.   2. Great Britain—Politics and government—1727–1760.
3. Mayors—England—London—Biography.   4. Merchants—England—London—Biography.
I. Title.
DA501.B38 2013
942.1'2073092—dc23
[B]   2012044366

A catalogue record for this book is available from the British Library.

This paper meets the requirements of ANSI/NISO Z39.48–1992 (Permanence of Paper).

10 9 8 7 6 5 4 3 2 1

To Mum

Contents

Preface

Writing this book has been a great historical adventure. Having first stumbled across William Beckford in the context of a study of London merchants, I could never have guessed that it would lead to a full biography and to my most direct engagement with the Atlantic world.

Initially, I was puzzled by Beckford. Although listed as a merchant, he bucked every trend followed by the hundreds of other London traders I was studying. In particular, his apparently dramatic rise to political fame and immense wealth demanded an explanation. This book represents my response to that wonderful historical challenge. I found some aspects of his life to be stubbornly elusive, especially his relationship with his enslaved workforce, whose toil and suffering sustained his advancement. I have been much more fortunate when researching other areas of his transatlantic existence, however, and my appreciation of his importance as a British Atlantic figure has only grown as new materials have come to light.

It was clear that I needed a great deal of help if I was going to engage with Beckford's Atlantic world, and I have been deeply fortunate in receiving the advice and generous support of many fine academics, who have held my hand as I encountered the world of the eighteenth-century Caribbean. Trevor Burnard gave me a huge head start by providing me with research materials relating to the Beckfords and the "absentee" planters. Simon Smith and Nuala Zahedieh have been unfailingly enlightening in discussions of the Caribbean. James Roberston was just as judicious and generous in our conversations, and I can never repay his wonderful hospitality during my visit to Jamaica in 2007. James and Simon also bravely agreed to read drafts of this book, and the text has benefited enormously from their input. The anonymous readers for Yale University Press also deserve thanks for their thorough and supportive critique. Closer to home, Peter Thompson little realizes how much of a debt I owe to him for guiding me through the history of the Americas.

While this imperial terrain has been an exciting departure for me, I remain indebted to my fellow British historians for stimulating my thinking on metropolitan responses to the challenges of the eighteenth century. My Oxford colleagues, especially Jo Innes and Bob Harris, have contributed much to this work, and I would thank all the members of the "Regulating the British Economy" workshop for helping me to think through the interplay between social, economic, and political change. Laurence Brockliss, Steve Pincus, Rupert Mann, and Joanne Pearce have also been very supportive at key points. During the gestation of this work, I have also been lucky to have worked with an outstanding group of postgraduates, who will, it is hoped, see the imprint of their work here. The community of Lincoln College, with historians in its every pore, remains the rock and inspiration for all my historical endeavours.

My first biography gives me welcome cause to acknowledge many individuals beyond the halls of university. I would most readily acknowledge the members of the Beckford Society, especially Malcolm Jack and Sidney Blackmore, who have been incredibly supportive and informative. Philip Hewat-Jaboor has also provided me with huge encouragement, and I have benefited enormously from his knowledge of Beckford's cultural endeavors. I have also derived valuable assistance from those who can claim Beckford as a distant ancestor, amongst whom the Hon. Nicholas Assheton and Robin Merton deserve especial thanks for encouragement at an early stage of the project. Poppy and Eric Anderson allowed me to walk in the steps of William Thomas, and their support over many years is deeply appreciated. All these generous souls would join me in the hope that this work will see more Beckford materials emerge to paint an even more vivid portrait of this remarkable life. Another fellow traveler, Edward Pearce, has also been a great supporter of the project, and I hope that some of the joy of his writing will rub off on me one day.

As ever, this book would not have seen the light of day without a host of professional supporters. Every archivist and librarian I have come across in my Beckford-related labors has been both patient and extremely helpful with my enquiries, and I would warmly acknowledge the assistance of Alexandrina

Buchanan at the Clothworkers' Company at an early stage of my research. When I was finding my way in Jamaica, the staff at the National Library and the Jamaica Archives could not have been more supportive. I have also been particularly fortunate to have been able to call upon Louisiana Vernon as a research assistant in Jamaica, and I hope that she recognizes how important her work has been for the genesis of this book. Mike White, and Emma and Michael Page, provided expert technical help at key points. Funding for research, including trips both near and far, has been most generously supplied by the Michael Zilkha Trust at Lincoln College. I am also very grateful to all of the individuals and institutions which have granted permission for the use of images: Lord Margadale; the Worshipful Company of Ironmongers; the Courtauld Institute of Art; the British Museum; English Heritage (the National Monuments Record); the National Portrait Gallery; the National Library of Jamaica; the National Gallery of Art, Washington; the Museum of London; the Bodleian Library, Oxford. The sheer professionalism and enthusiasm of the staff at Yale University Press have made the end of this project a real delight too, and my particular thanks go to Chris Rogers, Laura Davulis, Christina Tucker, and Philip King.

I hope all these legions of supporters have already attained some sense of my gratitude. Friends and family have also helped to speed the adventure along, and I remain optimistic that Beckford will capture their general historical interest. Christina, Ella, and Sam have borne the brunt of Beckford and have repaid me with love and unquestioning support. He was not always left at the gateway to Kidlington, but I hope that they have not thought me an absentee. The dedication goes to my mum, who has always reminded me of the rewards of seeking the good in others.

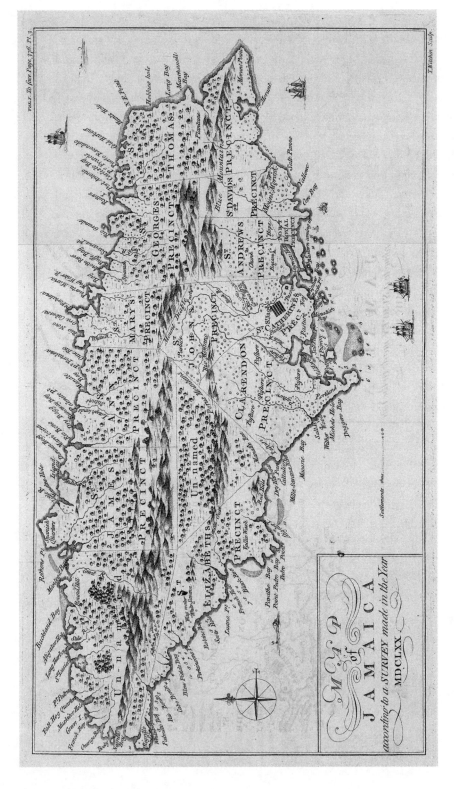

Map of Jamaica in 1770. (From Edward Long, *The History of Jamaica* [1774], vol. I, pp. 376–77, The Bodleian Libraries, University of Oxford)

Introduction

There was a singularity in the whole of this man's life which would
justify ample speculation. The different characters he affected to
possess, to reconcile with each other, and sometimes even to blend
in one motley mass, would furnish a most curious subject for the
biographer.

—London *City Biography*, 1800, on William Beckford

This book attempts to unscramble one of the most remarkable British
lives of the eighteenth century, that of William Beckford. As the epigraph
suggests, contemporaries were fascinated by the contrasts his career offered.
Born into the riches of the Jamaican plantocracy, he rose to prominence
in the mother country as a crusading lord mayor of London, even defying
King George III in an audience long remembered by London radicals.
Famous in his own time as a fiery speaker, he defended both the historic liberties of Englishmen and the colonists' right to enslave. A staunch critic of the
affectation and corruption of the aristocracy, he outdid most of them by
creating a mansion of remarkable splendor.

These contrasts reflected the dynamic and often-turbulent relations that
Britain experienced with its colonies in its first great age of empire. When
Beckford was born, in 1709, the colonies were largely confined to a collection
of small islands and narrow territories on the Atlantic rim. By the time of his
death in 1770, they loomed very large in the public imagination and were
widely viewed as the source of Britain's newly discovered global power.
Given these transformations, it was almost inevitable that Beckford's life
would be dominated by the opportunities and challenges faced by both
colonists and Britons as they adapted to this imperial revolution. As one of
the very few politicians to have experienced the growth pangs of empire at

first hand on both sides of the Atlantic, he offers a privileged view of the process at a key stage, presenting a most informed perspective on how empire challenged Britain's political, social, and cultural norms. His politicking in Britain and Jamaica made him a public figure, and in 1762 he was heralded as "the first prime minister of the London empire" to expose the novelty and pervasiveness of his influence. His supporters preferred to style him "the Alderman," to convey a more traditional status. No observer, however, could fail to ignore the ways in which his life transcended the ocean, bringing mother country and colonies into a closer engagement.

As we shall see, there was no shortage of contemporaries who sought to use him as a metaphor for the times. The upheavals of his final years ensured him a posthumous fame well into the nineteenth century, but his star was quickly eclipsed by that of his son William Thomas Beckford, the writer and collector, author of the novel *Vathek,* whose fabulous talents for both prose and expenditure have continued to enchant generations of readers and critics. William Thomas Beckford indeed venerated the memory of his father, but his own achievements and failures have overshadowed the importance of Beckford senior. As a reflection of this, historians have shown only a passing interest in the Alderman's life, and the dispersal of family records has also made it difficult to piece together his story. British historians, led by the eminent Dame Lucy Sutherland, have studied Beckford senior to cast significant light on the development of British politics in the eighteenth century. In this work, however, I offer the first full biographical treatment, committed to exploring the many sides of this multifaceted man.[1]

This study has been encouraged by recent achievements in the dynamic field of imperial history, which has inspired some of the most thought-provoking work on British development in this era. Once largely the preserve of economic, constitutional, or diplomatic historians, imperial history has broadened to encompass a staggering array of social, political, and cultural studies, leading to a fundamental reassessment of the character of exchange between Britain and its empire. The reconceptualization of the Atlantic world has been a prime driver behind this historical endeavor and, among other successes, has helped to identify a whole range of networks that sustained and widened Britain's transoceanic reach. The most recent surge of interest in global history has accentuated these scholarly trends, extending the agenda of historians in terms of space, time, and academic discipline. Consensus is rarely to be found amid such pioneering work, but there can be no doubt that these new approaches have rendered the empire as one of the liveliest topics in British eighteenth-century studies. The reanimation of interest in the development of the Caribbean colonies has been a most welcome result of this historiographical ferment, illuminating a field that had suffered comparative neglect when juxtaposed to the scholarship on their northern neighbors.[2]

The Atlantic paradigm has also renewed interest in the ways that imperial peoples helped to create and sustain communities founded in the name of European states. As one leading authority in the field put it, a study "unfettered by state borders . . . puts people at the centre." From metropolitan merchants to peripheral planters, and from the enslaved millions to the enlightened few, scholars have unearthed a vast array of imperial relationships, the intricacy of which were vital to the success of individuals, families, colonies, and the mother country itself. Although there can be no mistaking him as an elite figure, Beckford offers unrivaled opportunities to build on these recent scholarly advances, for his multifarious businesses led him to construct far-reaching networks that can illuminate societies on both sides of the Atlantic. As one of the largest sugar planters of his generation, he experienced slavery firsthand, influenced the fate of Jamaica in the island assembly, and encountered imperial conflict with Britain's rivals at close quarters. In Britain, he transcended traditional cultural boundaries by mixing in aristocratic circles and middling clubs, and by flitting between London and provincial societies. These networks brought him great personal wealth and influence, but they were also vital in helping to sustain the growth of the empire.[3]

It is Beckford's status as a "genuinely transatlantic" figure that has most absorbed my interest, and his life can cast important light on the relationship between mother country and colonies. Unlike the northern American colonists, significant numbers of Caribbean planters returned to Britain in the first half of the eighteenth century, and they have long been described as "absentees," often in a very pejorative sense. Castigated by many metropolitan critics as wasteful and extravagant, they have often been held to be a symptom of the moral malaise of the slave colonies and contributors to their long-term decline. As Michael Craton observed twenty years ago, however, "a general study of West Indian absentees as a class remains a great social history to be written." Excellent scholarship has revealed the ways in which these planters developed a highly lucrative sugar industry, and several key studies of their political role have highlighted their important influence within Britain. It is only relatively recently that scholars have begun to reconsider their crucial integrative role by in-depth study of their activities on both sides of the ocean, thereby linking their economic success to their impact on British society. As a key figure amid the most important wave of inward Caribbean migration in the second quarter of the eighteenth century, Beckford can illuminate the various roles the absentees played in the advancement of both Britain and its empire.[4]

Beckford's transatlantic status reveals much about the character of Britain's imperial enterprise overseas, but his experiences can also demonstrate how the mother country both influenced and responded to imperial growth.[5] The central importance of imperial development in the history of Scotland and Ireland has been widely recognized, and recent research has begun to argue that the colonies had a major domestic impact in England, ranging beyond the economic and the political to embrace sociocultural change as well. As Susan Amussen has argued with respect to Caribbean influences on English social and economic development before 1700, "the invisible trade in cultural practices and ideas is at least as significant as the visible trade." These imported influences have been highlighted by the study of print, goods, and cultural artifacts, and the presence of imperial peoples within Britain has gained increasing attention in recent years. Beckford presents excellent opportunities for evaluating the extent to which Caribbean figures may have influenced British society and how their views were conditioned by their experience of metropolitan society. Although they often met with outright hostility, the absentees represent an important case study of the ways in which imperial forces both succeeded and struggled to implant themselves in a metropolitan world that purported to be increasingly proud of its imperial identity. In this way, this review of Beckford's life seeks to contribute to the ongoing debate on the impact of empire sparked by scholars in Britain and America and to study these relationships across political, economic, and sociocultural themes.[6]

The book is structured with these scholarly debates in mind, although it retains a broadly chronological format through which Beckford's life is told. This narrative approach permits a greater appreciation of the various forces that promoted Beckford's advancement at different stages of his career, which correspond with key stages of British imperial development. In this way, Beckford's experiences can help us to understand the successes and failures of his family, colony, and nation. It is thus not a simple "life and times" biography but a study of an important agent of imperial exchange in his own right, whose transoceanic reach will alert scholars to new avenues of investigation on both sides of the Atlantic. Furthermore, given the importance of Beckford's associations, each section will seek to represent the perspectives of other absentee planters, thereby achieving a better sense of his representativeness as an imperial figure. As one of the richest men of his age, Beckford cannot be held to be typical in any guise. As a white, male Anglican, he shared little in common with the Caribbean masses. Nonetheless, as a transatlantic figure at the center of networks that helped to sustain imperial development at a critical stage, he demands our attention.[7]

The first three chapters examine his life at its most transatlantic stage, when he moved between the societies of Jamaica and Britain. The debts Beckford owed to his family for establishing the commercial and political foundations of his success are analyzed in the opening chapter. Right from the initial conquest of Jamaica in 1655 family members had employed a range of strategies to secure advancement both at home and abroad, and these networks helped them overcome the manifold challenges of building a transatlantic business empire. The building of a metropolitan interest was just as vital to the achievement of this goal as were their island activities, and the family exploited a host of informal agencies in London, encompassing government business contacts, the livery companies, and mercantile associations. Their prominence on the island was the reward for their industry on both sides of the ocean, and the more general success of the planter elite moved Jamaica from the perennial brink of disaster toward the prospect of real prosperity by the time of the Alderman's birth.

Chapter 2 studies Beckford's critical success between 1735 and 1745 as he battled to seize control of the great family fortune. This struggle took him across the Atlantic on several occasions and exposed him to public life on both sides of the ocean. It was also critical to forming his political outlook, for lifelong principles were forged amid civil and military duties in the Caribbean and in London. Recent scholarship has seen the period as vital for heightening British awareness of its dependencies, and detailed analysis of Beckford's political and socioeconomic strategies can also highlight the forces that promoted the settlement of absentees in the mother country.

Once he had gained a familial supremacy and secured an economic platform with which to attempt a return to Britain, Beckford could contemplate building a political interest in the mother country. How he sought to do that, both in the City of London and on the national stage, is the subject of Chapter 3. His spectacular rise illuminates the growing influence of the absentee planters but also acknowledges the difficulties they faced within British society. The adaptability of Beckford to metropolitan developments was critical to the success of both himself and his interests, which can be demonstrated by his parliamentary speeches, by his associational connections, and even by his choice of London residence. Taken together, these opening chapters highlight the seminal importance of family networks to colonial growth, demonstrating how transatlantic dynasties such as the Beckfords helped to stabilize these frontier societies and facilitated the social and political integration of the colonies with the mother country. Although Beckford spent the rest of his life in Britain, such absenteeism did not preclude his continued participation in a transatlantic community of associates. Nor did it undermine his commitment to the promotion of Jamaica amid debates vital for the future of both Britain and its colonies.

The remaining four chapters examine his British-based career after 1754, during which time the empire reached new heights of both real and rhetorical importance, particularly in the wake of the Seven Years' War. This stage of his political career is better known, but his actions deserve reassessment, in particular to consider how issues of empire and liberty were irrevocably intertwined with domestic and imperial agendas for reform. Beckford's political trajectory from 1754 to 1761, an era that has been widely regarded as pivotal for raising Britain's imperial consciousness, is examined in Chapter 4. In these years Beckford cemented his political connection with Pitt the Elder, and their oft-fraught relationship provides an excellent perspective on increasingly contested questions of empire. More important, his position within British politics continued to be influenced by Jamaican issues, most obviously the battle to retain Spanish Town as the island capital. Closer study of this contest reveals that Beckford's celebrated reforming instincts must be linked directly to growing Jamaican fears of executive influence, and his absentee circle became an important conduit for the dissemination of such views in the mother country. Chapter 5 analyzes how Beckford managed the difficult transition from war to peacetime, demonstrating that he was forced to reconsider his views on both Britain and the empire in the face of calamitous imperial reforms. Particular interest centers on the development of Beckford's views on liberty, which continued to be influenced by both metropolitan and imperial contexts. He also met with increasing censure as one of the most prominent colonial spokesman, and some critics even began to question the hypocrisy of this slave-owning friend of freedom. His political star continued its ascent in this period, particularly as a leading spokesman for the Chatham administration of 1766–68, but it is clear that he found it increasingly difficult to maintain a simultaneous interest in the City, the nation, and the empire.

Although politics dominated Beckford's metropolitan experience, his impact was not confined to matters of state. Chapter 6 reviews the public and private Beckford since his settlement in Britain, probing the ways he attempted to assimilate himself into British society through marriage, connection, and artistic patronage, as well as the economic resources that funded these strategies, which were critical in determining his transatlantic outlook and status. New evidence not only magnifies his reputation for profligacy but also highlights that even the richest absentee could not buy his way into some social circles. There is no doubt, however, that Beckford achieved great popularity by the time of his death, and in Chapter 7 its apogee amid the controversies associated with the American empire and John Wilkes in 1768–70 is examined. This section highlights how domestic and imperial crises presented him with a devastating personal dilemma, which he was unable to resolve. He was even prepared to contemplate alliances with political interests whom he mistrusted, such as the North Americans or the radical Wilkes, and he redoubled his efforts to exploit the City connections that had served him so well since his return to Britain. His significance at this time as a key figure in the first coherent movement for parliamentary reform has long been recognized, but he refused to become the darling of the mob, even though it appeared that the imperial system he had striven to maintain was increasingly untenable. Right to the end, he tried to make the most of his absentee status by acting as an imperial broker through both formal and informal channels, endeavoring to encourage metropolitan and colonial authorities to recognize common values and interests. His mediation, however, could not subdue growing differences both within London and across the Atlantic, and his passing was greeted with as much delight as lamentation.

Biographies always run the risk of presenting too narrow a viewpoint on wider developments, however important the subject. The temptation always remains to laud the achievements of the individual at the expense of others or to downplay wider forces of change. Nonetheless, Beckford's life offers remarkable access to Britain's eighteenth-century imperial experience. Beckford himself may epitomize the pampered and prejudiced outlook of the rich absentee, but his prominence ensured that those views were continually challenged by a wide array of critics on both sides of the ocean. Even though he often followed conventional paths to riches and influence, he was put on his mettle to keep pace with enormous changes throughout his imperial world, forcing him to develop connections and strategies that encompassed both formal and informal structures of empire. The detailed narrative reveals that at every key stage of his career he was forced to adapt to new challenges, and his absentee status rendered him particularly sensitive to the impact of metropolitan developments. The travails of his public life reflect the shifting power relationships within the growing empire most directly, and he expended enormous energy in the service of his cherished West Indian causes. Moreover, his transatlantic progress can be understood only with reference to a supporting cast of many thousands, who cut his sugarcane, shared his hospitality, and cast their votes for him. The biography of an elite figure may struggle to do justice to their role in his personal advancement, or in that of the empire more generally, but Beckford's imperial itinerancy encompassed a remarkable array of eighteenth-century interests.[8]

These perspectives could not have been re-created for Beckford without significant archival advances, which have revolutionized both the processes and possibilities of historical research, and which offer opportunities for maintaining the momentum of imperial and Atlantic history for many years to come. In Beckford's case, digitized sources have been critical in piecing his life together, enabling the study of the theory and the mechanics of empire in tandem. These are indeed exciting times for the study of national and transnational histories, and the field of imperial history promises a richer harvest than most. Arguments may still rage over the nature of authority and the origins of innovation within the empire, but all schools of imperial and Atlantic history have been empowered as never before to understand the complex interdependence of ideas, institutions, and individuals in determining change. Whether one conceives the empire as an authoritarian hub-and-spoke model or a more decentered spider's web, Beckford's life suggests that it must be seen as a mechanism in constant motion, and he clearly was one of the engineers who tried to make it work, if only for his own interests. Although more accustomed to classical or medical allusions, Beckford would have conceded that the empire replicated the intricacy of a clockwork movement, in which cogs of different sizes endeavored to play complementary roles to mutual productive effect. The teeth of the cogs could grind, and might not even connect in many instances, but it would be impossible to understand the workings of the empire without embracing the mechanism as a whole. Beckford himself was a small cog in this vast machine, but we can learn much about this expanding imperial leviathan from both his failures and his more successful strategies.[9]

The aim of this book is not to praise Beckford or to suggest that he bears the responsibility for transforming the British imperial polity. As the concluding coda will suggest, it is important to recognize that many of the contradictions of empire were never resolved, and that they were critical in sparking the revolutions that devastated several European empires after his death. Revealingly, amid this turmoil he retained a strong posthumous reputation on both sides of the Atlantic, but his legacy continued to be hotly contested in illuminating ways for our understanding of British society and culture. His struggles, and those of his Caribbean generation, are worthy of greater attention and can help us understand the development of both mother country and its dependencies as they faced the common test of empire.[10]

* * *

Note: Jamaican currency (J£) was rated at J£1.4 for every £1 sterling in the eighteenth century. For the conversion of eighteenth-century monetary values to modern-day equivalents, see the currency converter on the National Archives website (http://www.nationalarchives.gov.uk/currency).

CHAPTER ONE

The Torrid Zone

In common with many of the more celebrated architects of Britain's eighteenth-century empire, Colonel Peter Beckford met an untimely death. Although his life personified many imperial challenges and achievements, no artist thought to commemorate his dramatic passing in the manner of a Wolfe, Cook, or Nelson. Yet his last moments on the Kings Parade in Spanish Town, Jamaica, on 3 April 1710 just as surely reflected the troubled origins of Britain's global eminence.

As ever with such dramatic events, accounts of his death vary significantly in their detail, although the circumstances are very clear. Beckford was one of the leaders of a faction in opposition to the island's royal governor, Thomas Handasyd, whose actions over the preceding eight years had alienated many of the Jamaican elite. Clashes between the islanders and the agents of the Crown were standard fare by the early eighteenth century, but Handasyd had managed to stir up a hornet's nest of opposition, and members of the Beckford family were among his key targets as "the chief formentors" of his troubles. He had complained to his masters in Whitehall that the Beckfords were too powerful, and that two of Colonel Peter's relatives had escaped justice after killing fellow colonists. The Colonel's eldest son, another Peter, received particular censure for having stabbed a sixty-year-old judge before the latter could unsheathe his sword and then had used "interest" to escape prosecution. Even on an island whose lawlessness had become notorious, such actions were deemed unacceptable, and Handasyd was determined to bring the family into line.[1]

On the evening of 3 April, Peter Beckford junior was once again at the center of controversy. His connections had promoted him to the dignity of Speaker of the island's legislative assembly, but when it met at 9 PM there was a concerted effort to unseat him. There followed a huge commotion in the assembly room that "put the whole town in an uproar, and murder was cried in several places." The noise reached Colonel Peter in his home nearby, and he dashed toward the courthouse, loudly proclaiming that his son's life was in danger. He did not make it, collapsing en route. At the age of sixty-six, the excitement was clearly too much for him, and all attempts to revive him failed. He died within a few minutes, his end witnessed by a crowd of several hundred, who had gathered to discover the source of the commotion. Local doctor and historian Henry Barham recorded that his body was then conveyed into the courthouse, where it was greeted by "the great grief and lamentation" of two of his sons.[2]

The drama surrounding Beckford's demise was in many ways a fitting end to a remarkable life of political and commercial opportunism. Having first set foot on the island some forty years before as a young man of uncertain prospects, he rose to the pinnacle of Jamaican society, outsmarting and outliving the generation of adventurers who had arrived after the conquest of the island from the Spanish in 1655. He thus represented the great possibilities proffered by imperial expansion, and it is clear that the success of the Beckford dynasty owed much to his personal drive and abilities. As scholars now readily acknowledge, however, success in the Atlantic world was created and maintained by dense networks of support, and the most capable of individuals could not hope to advance without connections in both Britain and the colonies. How those networks evolved, recognizing not only the formal power structures that aided their advance but also the informal associations that developed through a variety of communities and institutions, is the subject of this chapter. The Beckfords highlight how enterprising colonists took advantage of every network at their disposal and adapted readily to changes on both sides of the Atlantic. The roles played by imperialists on the ground were clearly critical to individual and collective success, but the establishment of the Beckfords also demonstrates the importance of changing metropolitan networks of an economic, social, and political variety. Although the transformation of Jamaica was to prove more dramatic, both in terms of scale and character, developments in Britain were just as important for the family and put its members on their mettle to act as efficient brokers between metropolitan and colonial interests.

For certain, the Colonel's progress from young immigrant to island magnate represented remarkable success. Much myth and legend has surrounded Colonel

Peter's route to Jamaica, but most accounts agree that his early prospects were not encouraging. Tellingly, much uncertainty remains with regard to his background, although we can be confident that he was baptized at the church of St. James's, Clerkenwell, on 19 November 1643, the son of Peter and Philis.[3] Little is known of his parents, although his father may well have been the Peter Beckford of the Butchers' Company, who apprenticed his son Peter in the summer of 1658.[4] The rank of citizen was still regarded as a respectable station in life at that time, although the Butchers' Company did not rank among the elite liveries due to the nature of its trade, which forced it to the fringes of City life both politically and topographically. Nonetheless, his early career path in Jamaica does not suggest that Peter lacked substantial support, and his parents' proximity to more dynamic branches of the family on London's northwest perimeter would in time help him escape a tradesman's career.[5]

The modesty of his prospects at home remains the most plausible explanation for the decision of young Peter to embark on the hazardous voyage to England's new island possession. Although some accounts would place him on the island by 1661, the exact date of his arrival remains obscure. The first certain record of his presence comes in November 1667, when he bought a half-share of a sugar plantation in St. Catherine's for the considerable sum of £300. This first stake was subsequently consolidated by his securing of patents for a further 900 acres in the parish of Clarendon in September 1668 and June 1669, the deeds of which recorded in their accustomed fashion that he "hath transported himself together with his servants" to the island. According to the patent system at this time, the size of this grant suggests that Peter may have arrived with as many as thirty dependents, in the form of either family, servants, or slaves. These regulations were not strictly enforced, however, and we cannot be sure that he commanded such a significant entourage from the outset. Given his age and background, Peter must have received significant backing to have established this important stake on the island, but the identity of his sponsor (or sponsors) remains elusive.[6]

This estate immediately ranked Peter within the top 10 percent of the island's 700 white landowners. In common with many fellow planters, it appears that he did not have sufficient resources to become an independent sugar planter for many years. Even in the mid-1680s his Clarendon plantations were still listed as pens for livestock, provision farms, or cottonworks, all of which were less capital intensive than sugarworks. In time, this parish was to become very popular with sugar planters on account of its "healthy and pleasant situation, the fertility of the soil, and constant seasons." On the mountainous island, its hills were also lauded for their "gradual easy ascent," and it promised security from potential hostile invaders due to the narrow passageways through the parish. Although situated at least twenty miles from the coast, the estates were close to the source of the Minho and other rivers and were to form the core of the Beckfords' Jamaica holdings for 150 years. Young Peter had thus chosen well, and at a propitious time too, for within a generation the opportunities for such investment had shrunk considerably. While credit must be given to his perceptiveness and drive, his advancement cannot be divorced from the success of other family members on the island or back home in England.[7]

When Peter secured his first patent, the name of Beckford had been circulating in Caribbean circles for at least a decade, if not two. A ship captain, Edward, had transported and traded in West Indian goods and had received a land patent on the island in 1666.[8] More prominently, Richard Beckford, a member of the London Clothworkers' Company, had invested heavily in the island before the Restoration and could boast both the capital and connections to develop a substantial Atlantic trade.[9] He had first developed a considerable business in supplying the navy with cheap clothing (or slops), and in the late 1650s signified his increasing Caribbean interest by diversifying into more exotic products such as cacao nuts. His utility as a contractor also ensured that his business interests survived the Restoration unscathed, and he adapted quickly to the new political regime. Elected as a City alderman in 1667, Richard had close business dealings with some of the leading businessmen of Restoration London, and by 1670 he was held to epitomize the potential of the island, reportedly making £2,000 a year "clear of all his charges." In 1668 he built a splendid City townhouse to telegraph his status in the wake of the Great Fire, and his eminence ensured that its vicinity became known as Beckford Court. Although he remained an absentee landowner, his investment in the island's commerce was critical to the early development of the island and increased the likelihood that Jamaica might transform itself into as successful a commercial enterprise as Barbados. Furthermore, he personified the important link between the early stirrings of England's fiscal-military state and its colonial expansion.[10]

Although it is tempting to identify Richard as Peter's main sponsor, there is no evidence that he supported or traded with Peter in the 1660s.[11] Moreover, even though it is probable that Peter and Richard were related, they were not

Number 34, Great Tower Street, London, the imposing home and business center of Richard Beckford in the City. His investment in early Jamaica was facilitated by his success as a government contractor. (Reproduced by permission of the English Heritage Archive, National Monuments Record)

first cousins, as has often been suggested, and the former could not assume that these distant familial connections would be at his disposal. Indeed, it appears that Peter had to establish himself on the island before a transatlantic family connection could blossom. Accounts of his early years in Jamaica are colored by the factional politics of his later career, but it is clear that his advancement was based on hard work and resourcefulness. Disparaging reports suggested that he had arrived on the island shortly after the conquest with "two or three Negroes" and had made the "beginning of his fortune" by catching horses left by the vanquished Spaniards. A more admiring, firsthand account suggested that he was "bred a seaman" and then established himself as a merchant on the island by the 1680s. This version is also corroborated by later claims to "his great skill in maritime as well as land service." It also remains a more credible, incremental route to riches and is attested by his citation as a merchant of Spanish Town in 1681.[12]

The key to the family's longer-term advancement on the island was its landowning, however, and his trading was combined with increasing investment in planting. His first patents of 1668–69 were followed by a steady expansion of holdings to over 4,000 acres in the mid-1670s.[13] Connections with Sir Thomas Lynch, governor of the island in 1671–74, may have facilitated this speculative expansion and may also explain a decisive swing in Peter's politics too. In 1670 Peter had supported Sir Thomas Modyford, whose governorship of 1664–71 had witnessed an ongoing privateering war with the Spanish, much to the embarrassment of the English Crown. Modyford's replacement by Lynch saw the political tide turn in favor of the planting interest against the island's buccaneers, and Peter became a close associate of the new governor. His new lands placed him ever closer to the apex of the island elite, a status confirmed in 1675 when he first gained election to the island's assembly. Marriage into another leading island family, the Beestons, further cemented his island interest, and on these secure foundations of economic and political power he could hope to build stronger transatlantic connections.[14]

The London branch of the family also continued to prosper thanks to the expansion of Caribbean commerce and to their contacts with government. Richard Beckford remained the most prominent member of the London family until his death in 1679, but his younger brother Thomas was another key figure in the establishment of the Beckford empire. He emulated his brother by becoming an alderman of London and later outdid him by gaining a knighthood and election as lord mayor. These honors reflected an adept political mind, whose access to government was facilitated by his role as a naval contractor. Such dealings brought him into close contact with Samuel Pepys, who found Thomas a convivial yet canny colleague. At times the relationship became too close, for in February 1668 Pepys had severe qualms about accepting a gift of fifty guineas from Thomas, "telling him that it was not an age to take presents in." Pepys eventually relented, only to be further assailed with "a noble silver warming-pan" a few months later. The Beckford brothers were prepared to use any avenue to secure political preferment, including their membership of the City's Clothworkers' Company, where they wined and dined the then undersecretary of state (and honorary cloth-worker) Sir Joseph Williamson. Conscious of the importance of cultivating City contacts for his own political purposes, the undersecretary was ready to regale the clothworkers as his "brothers," thereby helping to cement the Beckford interest in governing circles.[15]

By the mid-1670s, with the Beckfords a rising force in both island and City politics, the first clear evidence appears of a transatlantic political interest. Significantly, the character of this association was informal, for neither the Jamaican nor the London Beckfords could boast access to execu-tive political favor on the basis of pedigree, government office, or wealth. Instead, both relied on their existing contacts, with Peter hoping that his distant London relations could secure him advancement through the offices of Undersecretary Williamson. Peter's appointment to the patent office of secretary of the island in late 1674 was a sign of his rising stock in London circles, and the strength of this transatlantic connection was further attested that year when Lord Vaughan was appointed governor of Jamaica. Williamson wrote to Vaughan on the eve of the governor's departure in December 1674, urging his support for Peter Beckford, "who is related to some very good friends [of Williamson's] in town." For his own part, Peter was on hand to read out Vaughan's commission on his arrival on the island in March 1675, thereby highlighting the growing political reach of the Beckford connection. Appropriately, the Clothworkers' Company later used a dona-tion from Richard Beckford to purchase a pair of silver flagons, as if to symbolize the importance the brothers invested in the conviviality of City culture. Agencies of varying formality powered and brokered the individual and collective success of both Britons and colonists, and however elevated a position the Beckfords enjoyed on the island, it was clear that their cause could be significantly advanced by friends back in Britain.[16]

Metropolitan connections did not render Peter Beckford immune to the uncertainties of island life and politics, and his ties with Williamson could not prevent his ouster as island secretary on the appointment of a new governor in 1678. Nonetheless, both his wealth and personal qualities demanded the increasing respect of metropolitan authorities. As island secre-tary, he had had frequent cause to report to government departments in London, and he had developed some intimacy with various officials. Furthermore, his bravery and military skills were in great demand in an era of constant threat from Spanish and French invasion. His appointment as

major of the island's forts in 1683 after the reinstatement of Sir Thomas
Lynch as governor was not simply a political favor, for by then he had established a reputation for action, with commendations as "singularly fit" for
the post, "having some knowledge of gunnery, and being very active, honest
and sober." In turn, his growing status on the island cemented his interest
with the City's commercial elite, who could provide vital services in the
metropolis. Sir Bartholomew Gracedieu was a key ally in London by
the mid-1680s, who signaled the bilateral benefit of their relationship by
empowering his "trusty friend" the Colonel to act for his interests in Jamaica.
Subsequently an MP and colonial agent (political representative) for the
island, Gracedieu was particularly well connected and later worked to
promote Jamaican interests with Gilbert Heathcote, the most influential City
figure of his generation.[17]

These links were tested by the stormy political world of the Restoration
era, both in England and across the Atlantic. On the island, Beckford
established himself in the 1680s as a leading supporter of Sir Thomas
Lynch, whose backing for the island's planting interest again brought him
into direct confrontation with Sir Henry Morgan's buccaneers. This factionalism threatened Peter's position on the island, and his prospects were also
imperiled by metropolitan divisions and crises. Although Sir Thomas
Beckford was prepared to trim his sails in accustomed family fashion during
the Whig-Tory battles of the late 1670s and early 1680s, on several occasions
he appeared more a liability than an asset, thanks to several clashes with
government departments over unpaid clothing contracts. Furthermore, the
bitterness of these party disputes inevitably resounded on both sides of the
Atlantic, especially after the death of Sir Thomas in 1685 left the family
exposed during the turbulent reign of James II. Colonel Peter lost his post as
major of the forts after the arrival of Governor Albermarle in 1687 and was
restored only after the Glorious Revolution after a volley of testimonies had
proclaimed his abilities and loyalties to the court. One petition mustered an
impressive roll call of eighty signatures, encompassing leading London
traders as well as planters and merchants from the island. Beckford could also
call upon Gilbert Heathcote to present it.[18]

This combination of colonial and metropolitan support provided a firm
platform for his subsequent success under the new regime. His growing
stature on the island was attested by his elevation to the island's twelve-
strong council, and he repaid the government's faith with sterling acts of

loyalty and courage as the island's English settlers faced its most turbulent decade. There was little he could do to ameliorate the devastation of the great Jamaican earthquake of 1692, but he proved his value when faced with man-made emergencies. His resoluteness in defending Port Royal against French invasion in 1694 was widely praised, and his stirring account of an expedition to Hispaniola the following year, which saw him in the thick of the action, confirmed his reputation as "a very loyal gentleman and a faithful asserter of the King's interest." His patriotism was again proven on 6 June 1695 when he was wounded by artillery fire while besieging the French stronghold of Port de Paix. With the threat of Spanish and French incursions looming, he found himself entrusted with ever greater responsibilities, and in November 1697 the metropolitan government honored him with the dormant commission of lieutenant governor of the island.[19] A painting of him as the heroic defender of the island survives and directly alludes to the ways in which his royal service and personal wealth advanced in tandem.[20]

Even though these appointments suggested that Peter enjoyed significant support in Whitehall, at times friends in high places were insufficient to guarantee support. As a sign of this, in the space of a decade the Colonel made three journeys across the Atlantic to pursue personal and island interests. In July 1689 he appeared at the Board of Trade to present a petition from the island and stayed on for several more months to aid his own political rehabilitation and to attend to private affairs, such as helping his eldest son settle in at the Middle Temple. In August 1694 he was sent over to London by the Jamaican assembly to represent the desperateness of its situation. Four years later he was again in the capital, this time charged with a more personal emergency, to defend his son against charges of murder. The importance of his metropolitan errands suggests that a trip across the Atlantic was not a decision taken lightly, but in each case his presence in London helped to cement the fortunes of both his family and the island. Amid the great wars of 1689–1713 the Jamaicans needed reliable allies in the metropolis, and the Beckfords continued to work hard to develop metropolitan connections to protect their interests on both sides of the Atlantic.[21]

The success of these strategies was signaled in 1702 when Colonel Peter became lieutenant governor of Jamaica on the death of Governor Selwyn, and in this dignity he proclaimed the accession of Queen Anne "with great solemnity" at Spanish Town. Although elevated to government office, he still felt the oppositional pull of the interest of crown and planter, and his speech

Colonel Peter Beckford, print published by Edward Foxhall in 1793. The original painting was probably executed in the 1690s and may have been commissioned to celebrate Peter's defense of Fort Charles (depicted in the background) against French attack in 1694. (British Museum, Chaloner Smith 2, © The Trustees of the British Museum)

on assuming the governorship sought both to allay the fears of his fellow Creoles and to defend the royal prerogative. "Your liberties shall never be struck at by me," he assured them, but in the same breath urged them not to press him to undermine the Crown's rights, for "I can no more suffer an encroachment upon his Majesty's prerogative than I would desire my own or your properties should be invaded." Humble and straight-talking before his political peers, he gauged the mood of the island elite and had the clout to ensure a peaceful transition to the new incumbent sent from England, the controversial Thomas Handasyd.[22] Renewed warfare turned the island into "a garrison colony" once more, however, causing much domestic upheaval and disruption of the island's trade. Governor Handasyd soon met serious opposition, led by the Beckfords. The Colonel did not hold back from causing him discomfort at every turn, leading Handasyd to conclude that "creolians . . . cannot bear English government." Beckford could have had few illusions about the risks of opposing the Crown's appointee, but he would not have anticipated a dramatic death on the main square in Spanish Town, in the epicenter of the government of the island. Even Handasyd was concerned by such violence, and he quickly moved to limit the damage to both himself and the island in the eyes of his superiors in London.[23]

Although alarmed by the threats to his son's life on his last day on earth, the Colonel would have been bullish about his family's prospects on the island. The furor surrounding his son's candidacy reflected fears that the family had become too politically powerful. In spite of their spirited service in the interest of the Crown, Handasyd was not alone in thinking that they might use their interest to frustrate metropolitan directives, and they were certainly well placed to influence island affairs. The proximity of Beckford's home to the Assembly House in Spanish Town reflected the Colonel's desire to influence the seat of government and to mingle with the other great planters. Most of the family estates were still to be found in the adjacent parish of Clarendon, some forty difficult miles to the west of Spanish Town, where several may have already boasted their own "great houses" for country visits. An active island politician like the Colonel, who had served in the assembly and council for over thirty years, needed a base in the island capital to broadcast and maintain their island status. Indeed, only six months before his death, his family had congregated at St. Catherine's Parish Church in Spanish Town to celebrate the christening of his grandson William, the subject of this book.[24]

As the second son of Peter Beckford junior (or the Speaker, as he was often known after being elected to that office in 1709), William's prospects were very bright. The Speaker was every bit as resourceful and determined as the Colonel and could also boast a legal training to bring to the family's political arsenal, having been called to the bar in 1695.[25] Aged thirty-five when he succeeded the Colonel, he was identified as a key figure "from his estate, capacity and great interest in the island," and he exercised those attributes to the full in a series of bitter disputes. He not only weathered the storm of 1710, but he saw off both Handasyd and his successors, Lord Archibald Hamilton and Sir Nicholas Lawes. In particular, Lord Hamilton felt the full weight of Beckford's influence on the island, with his rivals claiming that the Speaker had "a better estate in Jamaica than the Governor and Council . . . were all their estates computed together." Hamilton looked to London to provide him with the authority to tackle the local patriarch and his allies, but underestimated the resourcefulness of his rivals and their ability to wage a political campaign in the metropolis. These battles helped to promote metropolitan interest in colonial affairs, especially in the wake of the Peace of Utrecht, which had borne testimony to the increasing competition among the European powers for the spoils of imperial trade. Such significance did not mean that Whitehall was more responsive to the demands of the islanders, but the perceived importance of the colonies ensured that their interests would be subjected to ever increasing metropolitan scrutiny and to the influence of metropolitan partisanship.[26]

In the case of Hamilton, his machinations saw the battle spill over into an all-out pamphlet war lasting from 1714 through to 1717, which represented one of the most sustained debates on Jamaica in the London press to date.[27] Hamilton charged the Speaker with profiteering from his lucrative position as the island's collector of customs and accused other family members of corruption. The Beckfords counterclaimed that the governor had overstepped his authority and had used his position to overawe the islanders. In his own words, Speaker Peter saw himself as the leader of the "country" party in opposition to the "court" faction, although London-based supporters of the Whig government were ready to label him and his allies as Tories, thereby reflecting the differing alignments of island politics to metropolitan divisions. These battles also saw increasing coordination between the Beckfords of Jamaica and London, with the former's interests directly upheld in Whitehall by William Beckford, son of Sir Thomas, who had continued the family business as naval contractor and maintained the family's prominence in the City.[28] The conflicts only compounded the uncertainties of the island at the end of the wars of 1689–1713, and both sides claimed that their opponents imperiled the future prosperity of the island at a critical time. The Beckfords ultimately won, but only at the cost of confirming in the minds of many metropolitan observers that Jamaica was a factious and unpredictable colony.[29]

Having dispatched his enemies, the Speaker then extended his interests over the island still further, becoming a feared opponent in Jamaican circles and gaining riches that aroused the admiration of European observers. By a combination of shrewd purchases and mortgage defaults, Peter extended the family properties to cover seventeen sugar plantations and five pens for livestock, with major concentrations in Westmoreland in the west and in the family's traditional center of Clarendon. His wealth was said to have yielded him "many dependants, which gives him such a sway in assemblies," and a surviving list of over one hundred debtors (with liabilities totalling J£135,000) illustrates the extent of his local commercial empire.[30] Not only was he banker to a significant group of white settlers, but his legal expertise was often in demand from other leading planters, for whom he acted as a trusted confidant and attorney. Marriage ties further bolstered the family's position, most notably the Speaker's match with Bathshua, daughter of Colonel Julines Herring, and that of his brother Thomas to Mary Ballard, heiress of another planting family of St. Catherine's. By 1720, there was even a ship bearing the family name, plowing the seas between Jamaica and Britain, which the Speaker proudly proclaimed to be among "the best that use this trade." As his rivals admitted, he was the "famous" Beckford. One even dubbed him "the God of the Creolians," preeminent among those colonists born on the island. These "country natives" saw the prospects of the Speaker and the island as indistinguishable, his "many sugarworks and vast territories" ensuring that "for the good of his children 'tis impossible for him to do anything but what is the true interest of the country."[31]

Although few could match Speaker Beckford's success, his good fortune was shared after 1714 by other greater planters, who helped to turn Jamaica from an island perennially on the brink of disaster into a more settled colony. In part, this was merely the fruit of peace after a generation of war between France and England, but it also reflected a new stage in the island's history, as the greater planters further consolidated their supremacy on the island. The enslavement and transhipment of an ever greater number of Africans was a critical support of this development and increased the black-to-white ratio from a rough parity in 1673 to nearly 10 to 1 in 1739. With only some 8,000 whites on the island, fears of foreign attack or slave rebellions were never far from the minds of the plantocracy, and the Caribbean climate continued to supply periodic reminders of the fragility of the island's success. On 8 August 1712, "the greatest storm that ever the English knew in Jamaica" flattened St. Catherine's Parish Church, less than two years after it had witnessed William's baptism. Defiantly, the islanders rebuilt it at a cost of £6,000, proclaiming it as "the finest and largest church in the English colonies in America."[32]

Although ever resolute and resourceful in the face of adversity, Jamaica's white elite remained heavily dependent on the mother country, and the deficiencies of island society further strengthened their ties with the metropolis. European visitors to the island often remarked approvingly on Creole customs and could admire their hospitality, but Jamaica offered limited opportunities for self-improvement and civilized company. The dearth of schools and colleges was often identified as the root cause of the island's sociocultural failures and led an increasing number of planters to send their sons to England in the early eighteenth century. Even secondary schooling was little more than remedial, and there was little prospect of a local training for the law or medicine, increasingly the career options for the younger sons of the gentry in the mother country. Having benefited himself from the opportunities offered by Oxford and the Inns of Court, Speaker Peter recognized these shortcomings, and he later bequeathed a fund to endow a school in Spanish Town.[33] Nothing less than an English education would suffice for his own children, however. He had been schooled at the Merchant Taylors' in London, an establishment popular with leading City families, but William was destined for Westminster, a much more elite academy. It might have seemed harsh to dispatch a nine-year-old William there, but it increased his prospects of both advancement and survival. As one of his young school friends later put it, William and his siblings were now likely to have "not a common education but as genteel and polite a one as England . . . can give them."[34]

It is hard to fathom the impact that a rapidly changing London must have made on young William. Even visitors from the English provinces were staggered by the richness and intensity of daily life in the metropolis, whose population had swollen to nearly 600,000 by the beginning of the eighteenth century. Westminster perfectly captured the transformations of the mother country, its buildings and society bolstered by the political supremacy of Parliament and the success of the west end "town." Its genteel squares, conspicuous wealth, and sheer busy-ness must have offered a profound contrast to Spanish Town, and its attractions ensured that William would retain a residence within its precincts for most of his adult life. Not only did Westminster acculturate him into mainstream metropolitan society, but it also provided him with connections of lifelong significance. Admitted to the school in January 1719, he began to mix with the offspring of the country's leading families, thereby becoming "acquainted with many of the principal nobility and men of genius." In his six years there he made particular friends with young Scotsmen, including William Murray, the celebrated jurist and future Lord Mansfield. His willingness to befriend these Northern Britons reflected his family's associations with Scottish settlers on Jamaica, who had had an immediate impact there since the Union of 1707. The school also offered opportunities for cementing ties with other West Indian families, further enhancing the role of these elite schools in strengthening transatlantic ties. Beckford was thus exposed not only to the English upper classes but also to several innovatory influences within British state and society. In the course of his own advancement he would be called upon to play a significant role in integrating these forces.[35]

William did not regard Westminster as a mere playground or step on the social ladder, for the school succeeded in encouraging his scholarly instincts. Although friends of the Beckfords expressed concern that pupils at the school needed a private tutor to restrain them from "mischiefs in their hours of diversion," young William enjoyed Westminster for its academic rigor. Admired for the energy he brought to his studies, he was reported to have translated some of the classics while still at school. Particular inspiration for such application came from the guidance of Dr. John Friend, a leading classicist and later physician to Queen Caroline, who may also have awakened Beckford's interest in medicine. Judging by the family's decision to send four of his younger brothers to the school, they were happy with his progress there, although they doubtless suffered "the anxieties of the distant parent," as one Jamaican planter put it. Their concerns were eased by the family's City connections, which continued to serve their interests. The London merchants William and Thomas Beckford acted as informal guardians for the children during their first years in England, permitting them "at all times free access" to their home, "where they frequently came and resided for several days and weeks together." These two traders were based at Dunster Court in Mincing Lane, a stone's throw away from the great house built by Richard Beckford in 1668, and this arrangement ensured that the young Beckford experienced society at both ends of the capital and encountered a wide circle of British and imperial acquaintance.[36]

Although no direct reports of his schooling survive to judge the impact of Westminster School on his outlook, we can be certain that the experiences had not totally eradicated all marks of the Caribbean. He clearly retained some vestiges of the Jamaican accent, for his political rivals would continue to taunt him for his irregular cadence, especially when his spirits were roused. He also retained a ruddiness of complexion, which commentators continued to comment upon and which is even represented in sympathetic portraits at the very end of his career. Tall and thin in adulthood, he later proved a caricaturist's delight, and his family's prominent nose was latched upon as another distinguishing feature. These characteristics combined to render him a somewhat quixotic figure in English company, and a London education could compensate for such "otherness" only to a certain degree. Many West Indian parents hoped that an English education would cure their offspring of any colonial mannerisms and ensure their easy assimilation into British society, but metropolitan influences were often counterbalanced by preexisting island connections. Even at the heart of the empire Beckford could still mix within Caribbean circles, both planter and mercantile. Thus, even though fears were raised that Jamaica would be abandoned by its elite as the numbers of planter children in England increased mid-century, Beckford's schooling did not preclude his continued exposure to Jamaican influences. His education might have served to accentuate differences between Creoles and Britons, but it evidently did not present him with any acute crisis of identity, and it probably helped to confirm his trajectory as a transatlantic figure.[37]

The step up to Balliol College, Oxford, in December 1725 was a natural progression for a scholarly Westminster pupil. The college was a popular choice for medical students at this time, but the strength of its London connections may have been another argument for Beckford's admission. At this time the college was a tight-knit community of some one hundred students, presided over by the master and twelve fellows. Unlike many of his contemporaries, William was a hard-working student and subsequently rose from the rank of undergraduate commoner to fellow commoner, which denoted both increased status and higher fees. As evidence of his studiousness, in 1727 he composed a Latin verse to celebrate the accession of George II, which was published by the university:

> Per Mare, per Terras tandem Pax aurea ridet,
> Inviolata Deum semper in arce Manet.
> Illam Consiliis, Auguste, & classe dedisti,
> Ipse Tibi, Princeps, hanc Pietate petis.[38]

The scholarly, loyal, and pious character of this verse might seem to be at odds with the public persona which Beckford later attained, but there can be little doubt over the seriousness with which he approached his studies. In significant contrast to the Oxford experience of most gentlemen-scholars, he gained his B.A. in 1729, and his master's degree in 1732. His progress was mirrored by his brother Richard, who arrived in the college in December 1727 and took his B.A. in 1731. The evident closeness between the two brothers was forged by their school and university careers, even though their characters were often regarded as widely divergent. Brash and combative, William was often held to be the antithesis of the calm and conciliatory Richard, although these traits would later complement each other to mutual advantage.[39]

The early 1730s saw the brothers heading in different professional directions. His Balliol studies had firmly set William on a career in medicine, and in May 1731 he moved to Leiden to study under the eminent physician Herman Boerhaave. In this choice he may well have been guided by his family's connections with the Fuller family, another leading Jamaican dynasty with significant transatlantic interests. On the advice of the famed naturalist and collector Sir Hans Sloane, the Fullers had recently sent their son Rose to Leiden, with further directions to head to Paris thereafter to "study physic."[40] Beckford followed the same path, spending some two years at Leiden before heading for the Hôtel des Invalides. The Parisian hospitals offered excellent opportunities for medical students to gain surgical and clinical experience, and the Invalides could provide a wide range of conditions for the young William to study at first hand. Richard, on the other hand, was destined for the law and was admitted to the Middle Temple in 1730. But for a succession of deaths in the family, both of them may well have stayed in their professions and may even have refrained from setting foot in Jamaica again. William, in particular, retained a great interest in medicine throughout his life, and his advice was sought by family and friends.[41]

The professional success of his offspring doubtless warmed the heart of Speaker Beckford, who could regard their protracted education as a sound (though significant) social investment. News of their advancement was probably all the more welcome given the "undutiful behaviour" of his eldest son and heir Peter, who had run up significant debts by his mid-twenties. Some reports suggested highly erratic behavior, and the unpredictability of the Beckford heir clearly put the future of the great estate in doubt. There was little sign of tension when the Speaker granted the twenty-two-year-old Peter junior an interest in two Clarendon sugar estates in 1727. Four years later, however, the Speaker made provision for his great estate to be divided into two portions, reserving his British properties for Peter and the lucrative Jamaica plantations for his five younger sons. This division suggests little confidence in his heir's capacity to run the family business and presaged a much more important role for both William and Richard at the helm. By November 1734, the Speaker was prepared to show greater charity to Peter, earmarking some J£5,000 for the settlement of his debts, but the Jamaican plantations were still destined for the younger siblings.[42]

The question mark surrounding the succession of estates can only have sown uncertainty among the Beckford siblings, especially by compounding the perennial planter dilemma of whether to stay on the island. For all their success, and the island's steady economic progress, it was still unclear whether the Beckfords would rest there. Even Speaker Peter was not immune to the pressures of island life, and shortly before his death in 1735 an "old acquaintance" from his Middle Temple days in London sought to manipulate these anxieties in his own interest. William Byrd, now head of one of Virginia's leading tobacco dynasties, wrote in the hope of selling part of his estate to the Beckfords, and in doing so he seized on the inherent uncertainties in the white Jamaican mind, alluding to the oft-quoted status of the Caribbean as "The Torrid Zone." His summary of the superiority of the Virginia colonial experience encapsulated the core fears of the island's white planter class:

> We live here in health and in plenty and innocence and security, fearing no enemy from abroad or robbers at home. Our government too is so happily constituted that a governor must first outwit us before he can

oppress us, and if ever he squeeze money out of us he must first take care to deserve it. Our Negroes are not so numerous or so enterprising as to give us any apprehension or uneasiness, nor indeed is their labour any other than gardening and less by far than what the poor people undergo in other countries. Nor are any cruelties exercised upon them, unless by great accident they happen to fall into the hands of a brute, who always passes here for a monster. We all lie securely with our doors unbarred and can travel the whole country without either arms or guard, and all of this not for want of money or rogues, but because we have no great cities to shelter the thief or pawn-brokers to receive what he steals.[43]

Beckford could easily have contested the rural idyll painted by Byrd on every point, but he would have conceded that the Virginian's critique of Jamaica's shortcomings was all too accurate. With crippling rates of mortality, the constant threat of French and Spanish incursions, and an ongoing rebellion by runaway slaves (the so-called Maroons), Beckford had probably suffered from many of the sleepless nights to which Byrd alluded. Indeed, his Spanish Town home boasted a small arsenal of weapons along- side its planting equipment, with no less than seventeen muskets, ten "new guns," a pair of pistols, and as a stash of cutlasses. Byrd sensed that Beckford would "resolve to lay your bones where you first drew your breath," but he had hopes that one of his sons might be tempted to venture to the northern Atlantic colonies, where "you may make a prince of him for less money here, than you can make him a private gentleman in England."[44]

Byrd's pleas were futile, for the Speaker was dead before the letter ever reached Jamaica. His body was indeed laid to rest in the land where he had first drawn breath, in the chancel of St. Catherine's Parish Church in Spanish Town. He was interred in the same grave as his father the Colonel, and there could be no doubt that he had built on the foundation of that bold adventurer. The tombstone paid tribute to the family's success on the island, but it also indirectly acknowledged its parallel success in Britain, topped as it was by the heraldic arms granted to William Beckford of Mincing Lane in 1686. The monument thus symbolized the mutual strength which the London and Jamaica branches of the family had gained since their establishment on the island and which still offered rich possibilities for the Speaker's sons. On both sides of the Atlantic, government service and economic success had proved traditional paths to advancement, but the family's general stock was also raised by the exploitation of informal avenues of influence, ranging from the livery companies to the public schools. William and his siblings were clearly fortunate to have been sheltered from the island's inherent dangers by their education in England, and the commercial growth of the Caribbean in that time had built a firm platform for their subsequent success. Still, the challenges of life on the island could not be overlooked, especially when juxtaposed to the wider attractions of metropolitan society, but William's time in England had also strengthened his ties with other planting families and Caribbean commercial interests. He was thus very open to Jamaican influences and had had ample opportunities to build networks across the empire. It was still unclear whether his future lay on the island or in Europe, although the powerful symbolism of his father's grave suggested that he enjoyed the luxury of choice.

CHAPTER TWO

Transatlantic Man

We got within sight of Jamaica. . . . I was now to settle in a place
not half inhabited, cursed with intestine broils, where slavery was
established, and the toiling wretches worked in sultry heat, and
never knew the sweets of liberty, or reaped the advantage of their
painful industry, in a place which, except the verdure of its fields, had
nothing to recommend it.

—Charles Leslie, 1739

Even after six weeks of journeying across the Atlantic, travelers such as
Leslie could still find Jamaica a great disappointment. Leslie's oft-quoted
censure of slavery was somewhat ahead of its time, but even by this stage his
criticisms of Jamaican society were general themes of contemporary travel
literature relating to the Caribbean. When William Beckford returned to
Jamaica in late 1736, he doubtless shared some of Leslie's misgivings, particularly in the wake of his extensive education in Europe. Leslie's mournful
lament had indeed heralded Britain as "the seat of arts, the nurse of learning,
the scene of liberty, and friend of every virtue," and Beckford was clearly
facing a major challenge in resettling into Jamaican society. He may have
envisaged only a short sojourn on the island, but the ensuing decade would
see him fully incorporated into the island elites at a time when their relationship with the mother country entered a crucial stage of development. These
processes promoted Beckford as a key figure in imperial politics and would
lead to three more Atlantic crossings.[1]

On a wider plane, the experiences of Beckford and his family in this
decade merit great interest, beyond the prominence of his family and its ultimate success in the mother country. The steps taken by the Beckfords in

transferring their principal residence to England were contemporaneous with other leading planters of their generation and illuminate the development of the island at a key stage of its economic, social, and political evolution. Beckford also played a prominent part in extending the island's transatlantic interest, highlighted by the successful campaign for war with Spain in 1739. While elite Jamaicans could take much encouragement from these developments, the public and private challenges faced by the Beckfords demonstrate the difficulty with which "absenteeism" was achieved. Furthermore, relocation to Britain did not preclude constant attention to the island's affairs, whatever the problems of distance. As scholars have pointed out, colonists could become absentee landowners for a variety of reasons, ranging from the accidents of inheritance to a disdain for colonial society, but the actual processes of removal are less clear.[2]

The difficulties of these transitions also throw light on the important ways in which families helped to bridge the Atlantic world. The supervision of estates has rightly gained much scholarly attention, but the establishment of workable transatlantic networks, attuned to both the financial and broader ambitions of the British-based planter, remains more opaque. As we shall see, family attachments could easily founder in the face of personal jealousies, but dynastic considerations lay at the heart of the strategies of successful transatlantic figures. Given the demographic challenges of island life, and the dislocation of oceanic distance and travel, it was imperative that families resolve their differences, or else the maintenance of a transatlantic interest became highly problematic. In particular, the settlement of Jamaican interests was critical to the character and timing of the success of the Beckfords in Britain. Their personal advancement also dovetailed with that of the island. Increasing metropolitan commentary on the importance of the Caribbean and the wealth of the plantocracy highlighted the significance of the 1730s for reconfiguring Jamaica's imperial status. Closer inspection of William Beckford's progress demonstrates that the colonists themselves were increasingly convinced that a metropolitan presence was a vital precondition for making the British Atlantic support their interest.[3]

The principal objective of Beckford's Jamaica trip in 1736 was to settle his father's estate, a significant task given its sheer size and the number of claimants upon it. His father had taken the precaution of writing a will, but his last testament could not mask simmering tensions within the family. The unpredictable behavior of William's elder brother Peter remained a cause of deep concern, and of his four younger brothers—Richard, Nathaniel, Julines, and Francis—only Richard could be said to have reached an age of some independence. His sisters Elizabeth and Anne were unmarried and would soon reach the expected age of matrimony. Speaker Beckford had not been unmindful of these familial uncertainties or of the inherent difficulties of settling a transatlantic empire, and he had duly appointed his "cousin" Thomas Beckford, a London merchant, and George Ellis, a Jamaica justice, as executors of the estate alongside his widow, Bathshua. These precautions could not prevent a troubled succession.[4]

The Beckford estate was a testament to the commercial acumen and sheer ruthlessness of Speaker Beckford. In terms of fixed assets, at his death he owned or co-owned seventeen plantations and five pens, which were assessed at some J£204,000 (£146,000 sterling). This figure dwarfed the estates of the average Jamaican planter, whose median value was more in the realm of J£5,000. Beckford's property included 1,669 slaves, valued at nearly J£47,000 (£33,600 sterling), which comfortably established the family as the largest slave owner on the island. By the late 1730s these properties yielded sugar, rum, and molasses to the value of over J£40,000 (£28,600 sterling) each year. The inventories give no clue to the substantial outlay these plantations required every year for their maintenance, but these figures suggest a remarkable family enterprise by any contemporary standard. These enormous sums were supplemented by the aforementioned loans made by the Speaker to a range of Jamaican merchants and planters, which amounted to a further J£135,000 (£96,400 sterling). Such credit gave the family unparalleled influence on the island and had directly enabled the Speaker to build up his landholdings as debtors forfeited their estates to settle their liabilities. So great was this fortune that it was reported in the London press, with the *Gentleman's Magazine* estimating Speaker Beckford's wealth at £300,000 at his death, a sum that rivaled the estates of the greatest landowners among the British nobility.[5]

Although Beckford's return to Jamaica would aid his own claims to this vast fortune, his presence on the island also provided security for the family in general. He had been working in the family interest ever since his father's demise, liaising with his younger brothers to administer their estates during their minorities. As early as March 1736 Nathaniel Beckford had named William as one of his attorneys to protect his interests, and by the end of the year both Francis and Julines had yielded joint custody of their claims to him. His elder brother, Peter, remained beyond his control, and the timing of William's return to Jamaica may well have been prompted by Peter's decision to leave the island for London, a move that left the family's interests exposed at a crucial time. In June 1736, Peter gave power of attorney over his island affairs to three trusted family associates and left for Europe, probably with a view to establishing his claim to the family's English properties and their considerable business interests in the City. William also had the backing of brother Richard, who gave further testimony of their special relationship by granting him sole power of attorney to manage his affairs in December. William had thus established himself as de facto head of the family in Jamaica at the age of twenty-seven. The only real rival to his authority was his mother, Bathshua, who was taking steps to protect her rights, but there was little indication of the family rift that would develop over the next few years.[6]

Once established as the family's patriarch, Beckford could quickly assimilate into island society. He took up residence in Spanish Town, presumably at the family home, which had also served as the logistical base for his father's plantations. A reacquaintance with the Caribbean climate may have come as something of a shock to his system, but the Beckford mansion could offer every creature comfort available to the planter elite. At the death of Speaker Beckford, the household staff numbered twelve, and a further thirty-five slaves provided a host of skills from tailoring to bricklaying. The planter penchant for feasting was also attested by some J£1,000 of tableware. By the standards of the English gentleman, however, the house was sparsely furnished, with few items of value. The nerve center of the Beckford business, the countinghouse, or "long shade" room, was particularly spartan, with its fifteen "pictures, maps and prints, old and good for little." This lack of ornament was typical of planter houses, which were designed for shelter from the tropical climate and more noted for their fine mahogany woodwork than their material possessions. Rather than rely on excessive display, William knew that he could count on the fame and wealth of his forebears to gain him the respect of his new neighbors. One of the few items of value, a new "chariot" with harnesses for six horses, would have impressed in the streets of Spanish Town, although it would be too cumbersome for the serious business of touring his father's estates.[7]

A Spanish Town address gave William easy access to island society and politics. While William had been away in Europe the town had continued to suffer from natural disasters, including "the most dreadful storm or hurricane that ever was seen by the English" in August 1722, but the island's elite had rebuilt their shattered public offices to preserve its status as the seat of government. This role ensured the regular confluence of leading planters and merchants and presented William with excellent opportunities for establishing his reputation in island circles. Having mixed with other leading Jamaican families when in Europe, he would have kept abreast of the island's affairs, but he had much to learn about Jamaica's social and political networks, and he could not neglect them if he wanted to build a successful transatlantic interest. As the son of the God of the Creolians, there were few barriers to his political advancement, but he still had much to prove, especially at a critical time for white Jamaicans. In February 1738 he was elected to the island's forty-one-strong assembly as a representative for the parish of Clarendon and was plunged into discussions crucial to the island's future. On the day he took the oaths to take his seat the assembly learned of menacing reports of Spanish aggression and ordered that preparations be made to meet it. The arrival soon afterward of the new governor, Edward Trelawny, was greeted with great expectation, and Beckford doubtless took part in the entertainments to fete the royal deputy as he took up residence in Spanish Town. Trelawny subsequently paid tribute to the Beckfords' influence on the island by identifying Richard as a planter of "character and fortune" who might serve on the Jamaican council, but for the moment the family's political ambitions remained fixed on the assembly. William was one of the three assemblymen who drafted thanks to Trelawny for his first speech to the assembly on 15 June 1738, in which the governor did not shrink from the dangers facing the island, most obviously the "intestine evil" of the Maroon slave rebellion. These enormous challenges to the future stability and prosperity of the island put the white elite on high alert.[8]

To add to the island's woes, Beckford had more personal problems demanding his attention. He had hardly started the process of administering the family's assets when his troubled elder brother Peter returned to the island and committed unspecified "extravagancies" before his sudden death in August 1737. Only two months before Peter's demise, the family was rocked by the death of William's younger brother Nathaniel, who had established himself as a merchant in London. In essence, these misfortunes did little more than cement William's position as head of the family, but they further unsettled an already complex succession to the Beckford estates.[9] Also in August 1737, a new bombshell shook the family when a settlement made by Speaker Peter in 1722 was discovered, throwing doubt on the status of his final will. Under this newly discovered settlement, the lion's share of the Jamaica estate fell to Peter, leaving the other brothers to scrabble for the rest of the plantations in the west of the island. These events set in train a major clash between William and his mother and siblings, yielding numerous opportunities for contesting the distribution of the spoils.[10]

Beckford's position was further threatened by the summer of 1737 by his mother's return to England, where she was well-placed to attend metropolitan authorities to ensure her claims to Peter junior's estate, the bulk of which had been left jointly to her and William. She was named executor by Peter junior, and initially relations between mother and son remained good. In February 1738 she appointed her sons William and Richard to act for her in her dual capacity as executor for both Peter senior and junior. Trouble arose at the end of June, however, when William secured leave from the assembly to depart from the island for twelve months, a request reflecting his desire to protect his claims in person. His resolve to head for London was bolstered by the knowledge that his trusted brother Richard was on the way back to the island, where he was already "much praised." Even so, William still thought it prudent to appoint attorneys in Clarendon and Westmoreland to administer the family estates.[11]

Soon after William's arrival in England relations with his mother completely broke down. The trigger for this familial rift was his mother's decision to turn to law to settle the estate. In June 1738 Bathshua and the other executors of Speaker Beckford had filed a bill in Chancery asking the court to settle the estate in both England and Jamaica, valued at over £150,000, on his legal heirs, William included. This step might have appeared innocuous, but by October Bathshua had taken steps to replace William as her attorney in Jamaica, and early in the new year she filed a complaint against him over the settlement of the estate of her son Peter. She did not mince her words, arguing that William "doth sometimes pretend that the said Peter Beckford never made or published the said will," and that he claimed that Peter "was not of sound and disposing memory and understanding" to make such a will. William did not hold back either in his testimony of 23 March 1739, casting doubt on the authenticity of the will and insisting on full costs for the "many uncertainties, insufficiencies, errors and imperfections" in his mother's bill of complaint. The court took William's accusations seriously, and witness statements were ordered to test the authenticity of Peter's last will and his mental health at the time of its composition. Peter's physician testified to his disordered state in the final months of his life, with "his mind filled with strange and unreasonable fears and apprehensions of people's affecting him and endeavouring to destroy him by magic." Peter was capable of rational conversation but was also convinced that spells had caused his horse to collapse on the road and had affected his lungs. It was unclear whether these visions had been induced by an over-familiarity with the obeah beliefs and practices of his family's slave populations, but there was no doubt that battle lines had been drawn and that a settlement of the Speaker's transatlantic estate would not be easily achieved.[12]

The battle with his mother clearly consumed most of William's energies in the winter of 1738–39, but he did not neglect the wider interests of the island. In fact, his sojourn in London constituted a vital stage in his political apprenticeship, allowing him to participate in the most important metropolitan campaign launched by the West India interest to date. Although he had not been formally authorized by the Jamaican assembly to represent its concerns in the capital, he was quickly pressed into service by Caribbean absentees in their efforts to represent the deep uncertainties within the Jamaican assembly. Parliament had given them cause for encouragement by an increasing readiness to respond to Caribbean grievances, especially in the form of the Molasses Act of 1733, which sought to suppress the illicit trade between the French islands and Britain's North American colonies. The greatest priority of the West Indians, however, was to secure strong action against the Spanish, who had been accused of violently disrupting British commerce in the West Indies for over a decade. The Spanish could retort that they were merely protecting their colonies from illegal trade, yet they were fortunate that the government of Sir Robert Walpole was not keen to spark a war, however lurid the accounts of the so-called Spanish depredations. Such prevarication clearly fueled Beckford's dislike of the first minster and galvanized his efforts during his first Westminster campaign.[13]

The strategy of the Caribbean lobbyists was to join with opposition groups to stir up a wave of public protests for a war to restore British authority in the region. By Beckford's own later testimony, he was "a very active instrument in and out of doors," and later claimed some responsibility for bringing Parliament's attention to Captain Robert Jenkins, the most celebrated victim of Spanish cruelty. While this boast must remain suspect, as must his further claim that Jenkins's ear had not been severed by the Spaniards, he clearly took a leading role in this campaign. On 27 February 1739 he made his very first appearance in Parliament to make an impassioned plea on behalf of Caribbean merchants to the House of Lords, stressing "the great difficulties put upon them by the Spaniards." He then went before the Commons on 6 March, when several merchants and planters spoke out against the Anglo-Spanish convention that had been signed at the beginning of the year. Buoyed by the support of the parliamentary opposition and by a growing popular outcry against Spanish cruelty, the West Indians prevailed against the wishes of the first minister. Although Walpole's political position had been battered by a number of other crises in the late 1730s, the defeat over the Spanish war has rightly been seen as a significant moment for Britain's imperial expansion, and Beckford would recall it with fondness for the rest of his career.[14]

This campaign encouraged Beckford and his colonial allies to seek further legislative support at Westminster. In early June, he returned to the Upper House to back a bill to permit the direct exportation of sugar to Europe. On this occasion, he was examined on Jamaica's potential for sugar production, as well as on the sugar markets in Europe. He was also called upon to comment on French competition in the sugar trade, and again he received a positive response from parliamentarians, who passed the measure in double-quick time in the final weeks of the session. This second success was another encouraging sign of growing metropolitan sensitivity to the needs of the Caribbean islands and also of the political effectiveness of the West Indians themselves. Through these campaigns Beckford developed close ties with some of leading spokesmen from across the Caribbean, most notably John Yeamans of Antigua and his fellow Jamaican James Knight, who were crucial to the evolution of a powerful West Indian lobby over the next decade. He also aligned himself with key London-based politicians, such as the lawyer and general man-of-business Jack Sharpe. Just as important, he had also witnessed the political potential of an appeal to the national interest on behalf of the colonies, and for the rest of his career he would seek to harness this force for both personal and imperial benefit.[15]

The rumblings of war in the summer of 1739 counseled another return to Jamaica, but his contest with his mother in Chancery argued against it. His relations with some of his younger siblings were also strained, and several showed great impatience to enter into their inheritance. For instance, his brother Julines was married in January 1739 to a daughter of Solomon

Ashley, MP, an heiress reputedly worth £25,000. The attractions of the dowry were also bolstered by her father's connections, for he served as a director of the Royal African Company, and the newlyweds were even granted "a most gracious reception" by the king. Such contacts came at a price, however, for the Beckfords had to raise £25,000 to meet their obligations under the marriage settlement, a demand that further fueled the family feud. For the moment William remained intransigent, and in May 1739 depositions were taken at Dieppe to ascertain the sanity of his brother Peter at the time of the signing of his will. Furthermore, in October William insisted that the court take cognizance of over £20,000 worth of bank and trading stock overlooked by his father's will. His resolution suggested an eagerness to settle the matter while he was still in London and again highlighted the attraction of the metropolis as the locus of power.[16]

The urgency of Julines to marry stood in some contrast to William's personal circumstances, the unorthodoxy of which reflected the transience of this particular phase of his life. The first of his many recorded illegitimate children had been born in October 1736, and the mother Barbara may have been a long-term mistress whom he had met in Leiden and later settled in London. It was later claimed that this lover had borne another child after an affair with a mulatto servant during Beckford's absence, leaving William heartbroken and his friends in fear that the betrayal "would have cost him his life." Although no contemporary record survives of this distress, William continued to live the seemingly carefree existence that metropolitan observers increasingly associated with affluent young West Indians in town. Over the next fifteen years he would father another seven illegitimate children by at least two other partners. Scholars have highlighted how the harsh realities of Jamaican society affected male behavior, where the failures of white society and the temptations of masterly domination fed a voracious white male sexuality. In common with the experience of others in his social circle, Beckford's transatlantic existence may have encouraged this sexual incontinence. As he reached his thirties, he might have been expected to settle down like his siblings, but there was little chance of that while the family's affairs were so unsettled and with further transoceanic trips in prospect.[17]

Despite the contest with his mother, William did not tarry much longer in London, and by February 1740 he was back in Spanish Town, making preparations for war. He returned to an island buoyed by the recent peace established with the rebel Maroons but also daunted by the likely hardships engendered by war with Spain. Beckford achieved a heightened prominence in the island assembly on his return, which reflected his success as a spokesman for the island in London, as well as his growing ambition. Right from the opening day of the new session he was keen to play a leading role, gaining appointment as one of the three assemblymen to draft thanks to the governor for his speech. Over the next eight weeks he established himself as one of the most active assemblymen, serving on eleven committees and helping to develop policy in key areas such as the regulation of the militia, the encouragement of white settlers, and the raising of public revenues. In these tasks, he could welcome the direct support of his brother Richard, who was admitted to the assembly in April 1740. Their actions suggest that the brothers were determined to ensure that the island built upon the foundations of the Maroon Treaty, even if the wartime emergency was unlikely to promote fundamental reforms.[18]

By the testimony of one of his island rivals, Beckford's return to Jamaica saw him in no mood to compromise in his personal affairs. With legal proceedings in London still under way, Beckford was keen to stamp his authority over the family's Jamaica estates, and the widow of a Westmoreland planter, Jannet Hynes, bitterly complained of his ruthless pursuit of the family's creditors. In Beckford's defense, it could be pointed out that the Hyneses were his family's biggest debtors, with a massive mortgage of over J£38,000 lying on the Hynes plantations at the death of Speaker Peter. Hynes still thought William's haste to call in his debts was indecent, and even accused him of taking advantage of the death of his father's co-executor, George Ellis, by a private application to the governor before the body "was barely cold." Reportedly crowing "that he would have no mercy on his father's debtors that did not come into his terms," William insisted that plantation produce be sent to his nominee in London, thereby trumping his mother's orders. Hynes thought that such impetuosity had caused "a good deal of difference" within the family, and had damaged his reputation on the island, concluding that "it evidently appears in the eyes of all people that W[illiam] aims at all he can to the prejudice of his mother and brothers." Beckford was prepared to make the journey across the island to Westmoreland to put direct pressure on Hynes, and by August 1740 he had resorted to law, threatening an ejection to compel the family to follow his orders. In contrast, Richard was eulogized for his "good and honest intentions towards his mother and family" and appeared willing to act as a mediator between William and his relations in the still simmering family feud.[19]

It is fortunate that at this critical point for both Beckford and Jamaica we can understand Beckford's perspective on its own terms, thanks to a clutch of letters penned during this sojourn on the island. They were written to one of his London contacts, James Knight, an instrumental figure in securing the island favored status in a number of its commercial and military concerns over the preceding decade. The two were clearly close friends, and their shared commitment to the advancement of Jamaica's interests led them to range over subjects critical to the mutual benefit of mother country and colony. At root, Beckford saw no difference in interest or identity between mother country and colony, but he was all too aware that they could have different priorities and perspectives. In this knowledge, he was keen to relay to Knight the outcome of private meetings with leading Jamaican planters, such as Charles Price, in order that absentee Jamaicans were apprised of island views. Indeed, while still regarding Britain as "home," Beckford spoke of the island as his "country." His admiring verdict on the work of Governor Trelawny could even make this distinction: "zealous in his country's cause, and always attentive to everything that appears to be for the good of this country." His loyalty to the British Crown could not be questioned, but he betrayed a planterly suspicion of executive action, which convinced him of the need to maintain an effective transatlantic interest to protect the island. To this end, there were few topics that he was unwilling to vent, and although very much the junior of the two, Beckford felt able to discourse openly on his visions of the island's future in many key areas. In keeping with his public actions to date, he was not afraid to air his opinions and spared no individual deemed to have crossed his path. The Spanish threat fueled this personal urgency, prompting Beckford to review all aspects of island life and to conclude that the assistance of friends in Britain was critical to its longer-term future.[20]

Although the constant threat of their French and Spanish neighbors bore heaviest on all white Jamaicans, especially in a time of war, it is significant that Beckford's thoughts regularly turned to matters of internal security. In October 1740, he foresaw that an increase in the number of white settlers on the island was the most effective solution for a whole series of planter insecurities. Without them, the white minority would remain vastly outnumbered by black slaves, potentially productive land would be left uncultivated, and there would be fewer men to be trusted with the island's defense. He saw the answer to this white deficiency in the Scots nation, "men of strong, vigorous and goodly constitutions, and (if I am not misinformed) luxury has no great share in their education." After mixing with Scots in both Westminster and Jamaica, he was convinced of their loyalty and utility to the British Crown and shared none of the prejudices of the typical Englishman of his generation. "No man . . . ought to object to the country of a man no more than to his face," he mused, brushing aside fears that the island might become "a Scotch colony." Despite his unequivocal support, Scottish influence on the island remained a sensitive subject and one of the more obvious sources of division within white political culture. Nonetheless, in the ensuing decades Scottish settlers became an increasingly significant force behind the island's economic growth, helping to compensate for the largely static character of Jamaica's white population.[21]

As might be expected of one of the largest slave owners on the island, he did not suggest that the shortage of manpower be met by a more conciliatory attitude to the enslaved population. The current wartime emergency, however, led him to be more open-minded than other planters regarding the role of slaves in the military. He welcomed their use in the current war effort in supporting British troops, taking pride in having provided "25 able shots, as good men as ever smelt gunpowder," although he was predictably reticent to arm them directly. He also welcomed the recent peace treaty signed by Governor Trelawny with the rebellious Maroons and took evident pleasure that "they have a great confidence in us, and do everything to cultivate a good understanding." Such warmth had little humanitarianism behind it and was rooted in a brutal pragmatism. Not only would isolated plantations be free from Maroon raids, but the former rebels now patrolled the island forests for runaway slaves and returned them to grateful owners. Moreover, he hoped that their military experience would give "the rebellious as well as our own negroes a just idea of the force of the British nation." Although Beckford has left little direct commentary on his views on race, these observations suggest that he shared the common planter outlook on the inferiority of the Africans and also their innate fear of possible slave insurrection.[22]

Beckford also recognized that relations with the mother country had reached a critical stage and was particularly keen that he and Knight build on recent successes. He harbored a planterly suspicion of metropolitan intervention in island affairs, most obviously through the powers of the governor, but he was already casting his gaze to the imperial capital and envisioning for himself a much broader theater of political action. In particular, he saw the London planters' club as crucial for the island's future, reasoning that "it is very proper that a number of gentlemen should meet together in order to consult on everything that shall be thought for the good of the country, for in the multitude of councils there is wisdom." He also felt that the Jamaicans had a right to expect the support of the imperial Parliament, "considering of what infinite consequence we are to Great Britain." He sensed that Britain still underestimated the recent efforts of the islanders on behalf of the crown, which pains might "make us lookt upon to be of more consequence than formerly." Having recently sided with the opposition in London to press the ministry for war against Spain, he was naturally critical of Sir Robert Walpole's administration, but he was also wary of the impact of faction on the effectiveness of the island's metropolitan interest. Significantly, he betrayed concern that island divisions might lead to misrepresentations at home, and he wearily confessed to Knight that in the assembly "grumbletonians there are and always will be." Nevertheless, he had faith that the current governor would act as an effective conduit for the representation of the island's affairs as long as he listened to "the principal gentlemen of the island," in whom rested "the interest of the country."[23]

While these crucial issues of longer-term development were debated within the Jamaican elite, both resident and absentee, the ongoing war with Spain gained their immediate attention. After an encouraging start to hostilities with the attack on Porto Bello, the British had few victories to savor, and with fears of invasion very real Beckford expressed strong views on the correct strategy for success against the Spanish on both sea and land. In October 1740 he hoped that Admiral Edward Vernon would attack Cartagena on the Columbian coast, fearing that the Spanish commander stationed there (Admiral Blas de Lezo) could land at Jamaica at a week's notice. His work for the island assembly only increased his alarm. Having served on a committee of inspection in December, he anxiously observed that Port Royal "is a place at present of no great strength" and hoped that London would provide both men and materials to rectify this.[24]

The spirits of both Beckford and his fellow planters were raised, if only briefly, by the large amphibious force that arrived in the early months of 1741 to storm Cartagena. News arrived in Spanish Town in April of the first attack on the Spanish stronghold, and William and Richard were nominated by the assembly to draft a congratulatory address to Admiral Vernon and General Thomas Wentworth. It soon transpired, however, that the port had not been taken, and that the British had suffered a humiliating defeat, with the loss of thousands of servicemen and some fifty ships. Even though dispirited by this news, both William and Richard supported the assembly's ensuing proposal to raise 5,000 slaves to aid a now-beleaguered Vernon. The admiral's return to Jamaica preempted this initiative, but William subsequently supported the raising of 1,000 slaves for the next Vernon-led expedition to Cuba. Although supportive in public, Beckford soon voiced his misgivings to Knight about the campaign, criticizing the commanders for underestimating the difficulties of terrain in the region. He simply wanted his slaves back home and forecast little concrete advantage from the war, predicting that it would soon turn "piratical." He could scarcely hide his contempt for the commanders when the failure at Cuba was reported, scathingly observing to Knight that "an inglorious, inactive expedition of four months . . . always proves more fatal than the most bloody and vigorous engagements (thanks to our commander for it)."[25]

In contrast to Britain's lackluster war effort, William's protracted campaign against his mother and siblings came to a peaceful and successful conclusion in the summer of 1741. On 16 June, he was joined by his mother and brother Richard at Spanish Town and signed an agreement "for accommodating such disputes and preventing further such suits and expenses and for promoting harmony" between all the family parties. The armistice gained the support of Bathshua by increasing her yearly allowance from £1,000 (under Peter senior's will) to £2,500, with an additional sweetener of an immediate £1,500. These sums would assure her of a very comfortable widowhood, and she duly returned to England to live out her days in metropolitan comfort. On her return to London, it was reported that it was "her good conduct" that had ended the family feud, and she was quick to "silence the false report of her being injurious" to any of her children. It was certainly in the interest of all family members to preempt any continued ill feeling, but on a wider plane it was important to protect the good name of the Beckfords at a time when metropolitan commentators were all too willing to censure West Indians for greed and immorality. In his letters to Knight, William himself had demonstrated his sensitivity to attacks on the island's reputation, and he recognized that his success as a transatlantic figure depended heavily on the defense of his (and his family's) honor on both sides of the ocean.[26]

With their mother's consent secured by this financial settlement, the family plantations could be divided between the brothers. William retained the Clarendon lands, and Richard, Julines, and Francis divided the properties to the west. After three years of open warfare, Beckford had had to make significant concessions to strike a deal, but he could also take much satisfaction from a settlement that clearly established him at the head of the family dynasty, and with a considerable estate.

Even after ceding the western plantations to his brothers, Beckford remained one of the largest planters on the island (see table 2.1). He could not aspire to the standing of Speaker Beckford as a landowner, but few of his island peers could match his wealth. Assuming that he was an equal partner in the co-owned estates, his net earnings for 1740 were over J£17,000 (£12,100), and a workforce of nearly 1,000 slaves tended to his estates. By the end of the decade he would take decisive steps both to consolidate and extend these holdings, but his hard bargaining within the family had left him a

Table 2.1 William Beckford's Jamaica lands in 1740

Plantation	Stock value 1739–40 (J£)	Slaves	Crop returns 1740 (J£)
Full ownership			
Retreat (Clarendon)	5,156	139	3,337
Kay's (Clarendon)	3,934	139	1,952
Malmsey Valley (Clarendon)	1,835	45	2,504
Dank's (Clarendon)	[9,762]	—	2,943
Bodle's Pen (St. Dorothy's)	[964]	—	—
Co-ownership			
Lime Hall (Clarendon)	3,816	117	2,181
Rock River (Clarendon)	7,217	197	6,746
Croft's (Clarendon)	2,763	52	1,169
Seven Mile Walk (St. Dorothy's)	[2,255]	—	519
Esher (St. Mary's)	3,924	120	1,284
Guanaboa (St. Catherine's)	3,043	122	1,325

Sources: Most of the figures for stock values and slave numbers come for the second inventory of Peter Beckford's estate taken in the summer of 1740: JA, 1B/11/3, vol. 21, fols. 74–75. This is supplemented by the figures in brackets from an earlier inventory of Peter Beckford's estates, which generally gave higher estimates: JA, 1B/11/3, vol.18, fols. 200–202. Produce yields come from the crop accounts: JA, 1B/11/4, vol. 1, fol. 75. Bodle's Pen was used as a storehouse and distribution point for the Clarendon estates and therefore did not make a crop return.

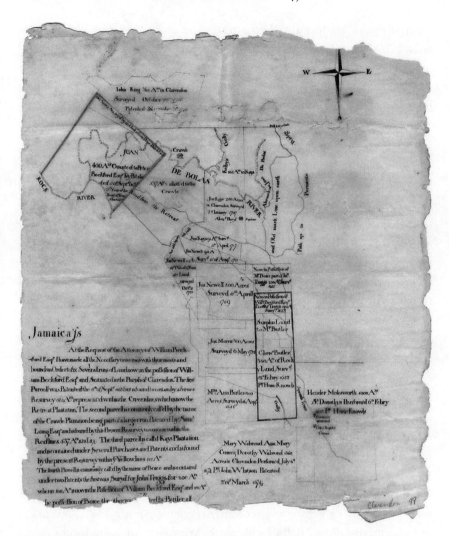

Plantation Map. Plan of several early Beckford plantations in Clarendon parish, Jamaica, probably commissioned by William Thomas Beckford. The Retreat and Kay's estates had a labor force of 380 slaves at the time of the Alderman's death. (Courtesy of the National Library of Jamaica, Maps Clarendon c. 99)

patrimony suitable to his station and his ambitions. It was a particular coup to have retained the family's oldest holdings in Clarendon, and their situation would also permit him to proceed with his political schemes in Spanish Town, which remained his residence while on the island. His brothers were also consoled by their significant holdings, although they chose not to base themselves on the distant Westmoreland estates. Most notably, Richard would also keep a Spanish Town residence to maintain his extensive legal and political interests.[27]

Beckford had thus achieved his principal goal since his return to Jamaica, but there was little else to brighten his mood, particularly with regard to the Anglo-Spanish war. After the disasters of 1741, he became more openly critical of both British military strategy and its leadership in the Caribbean, lamenting "our late state of inactivity, irresolution and want of harmony betwixt the general [Wentworth] and admiral [Vernon]." By the early months of 1742 he was also very despondent about news from Europe and the ineffectuality of Britain's attempts to protect Austria from French and Prussian aggression. His doleful prediction was, "I cannot conceive how we can prevent France being absolute unless other measures are taken, which I am afraid is almost too late to do." His spirits were briefly roused when word reached him of the fall of Sir Robert Walpole, which he regarded as the best news that Knight had ever sent him. He looked hopefully toward the Country Whig opposition for leadership, especially William Pulteney, whom he regarded as "a true and worthy patriot." No sea change in British military fortunes accompanied the elevation of the Country Whigs to power, however. In the spring of 1742 Beckford had opportunity to witness the feuding British commanders firsthand when he sailed with the abortive expedition to Panama. It is unclear why William accompanied this fleet, although his brother Richard's presence was seen as a "point of honour" in obligation to Governor Trelawny, who also traveled as "balance-master" between Wentworth and Vernon. After three weeks at sea, during which time Beckford was convinced that Vernon did not want to commit to any assault, they finally fell to attacking Porto Bello "with all the pageantry of a Spithead expedition." The Spanish defenders retreated to an unassailable mountain fortress, as had been predicted, rendering the campaign fruitless. Beckford suspected that General Wentworth was equally culpable of inaction, and only the governor showed "a true sense of honour" and acted "with a zeal becoming an Englishman." The experience confirmed William's hearty dislike of military commanders or politicians who balked at striking a decisive blow against the nation's enemies, which became a hallmark of his commentary on imperial affairs during his metropolitan career.[28]

In contrast to this national disgrace, which saw the recall of Vernon to Britain, Beckford's domestic affairs prospered, and their settled state may have encouraged him to consider a return to England. Relations with his mother continued to thaw, and he was prepared to show compassion to a creditor at her intercession in April 1742. In the same month, he advised James Knight that he intended to return to England "next spring," and although this proved premature, he was clearly planning to leave the island from this time. Business concerns were among the reasons that detained him in Jamaica, for at this juncture he redoubled his efforts to develop a direct trade in sugars from the island to Europe, taking advantage of the legislation he had helped to secure during his time in London in 1739. Resolving to drive this trade "to the utmost of my power," he sent a sugar shipment to Hamburg in 1743 and talked animatedly to Knight of the need to promote Jamaican exports to foreign markets. Although these hopes were not fulfilled, this enterprise revealed his determination to maximize the economic potential of his own estates. Without such improvement, his plans for relocation to England might founder, and his time in Jamaica could also be usefully spent in further cementing his status among the planter elite.[29]

Beckford's activity in the Jamaica Assembly in the sessions of 1743–44 does not suggest any urgent wish to depart, or that he was any less committed to the resolution of the island's major problems. In May 1743 he was again very active in proceedings to improve island fortifications. A year later, following Governor Trelawny's professed concern for the advancement of planting, he was named to the committee of inquiry to ascertain why the island's coffee, ginger, and pimento crops had declined. It was left to brother Richard to have the honor of presenting a bill to allocate an additional J£1,000 to establish a free school in St. Catherine's in accordance with their father's wishes. The introduction of the measure confirmed that the family rift had been healed, and the local vestry wrote to Bathshua Beckford in London to assure her of the full backing of her sons in Jamaica. Significantly, they also thanked her for promoting donations "among your Jamaica acquaintance that are now resident in England," highlighting how the family's wider networks were no longer threatened by internecine conflict. The letter also indicated that the mother country was now host to a sizable colony of Jamaican landowners, whose metropolitan presence was facilitated by the near doubling of London sugar prices in the preceding decade.[30]

The social success of his English-based relatives may well have clinched William's decision return to England. In March 1744 his youngest brother, Francis, married a sister of the Duke of Ancaster, demonstrating how the immense wealth of the family could secure connections in the mother country, if not social acceptance per se. Also in that year, preparations were in hand for the marriage of William's sister Elizabeth to the Earl of Effingham, another promising source of prestige and connection. A still significant aid to this union was the London branch of the family, who had established a modest country retreat at Ashtead, Surrey, where the Effinghams resided. Brother Julines, who had first proved the marital prospects for the family back in England, had also turned his back on the island by this time and was formally expelled from the assembly in March 1744, after a tenure of less than two years. Against this background of family advance, William's relations with the island assembly deteriorated in the course of 1744. His departure was presaged in June by his being taken into custody, if only briefly, for absenting himself from the assembly without permission. Only two days into the next session, on 20 December, the assembly resolved to expel him from the house, he "having departed this island without leave." Once back in Britain, the immediate cause of his departure became clear when he completed the purchase of the Fonthill estate in Wiltshire in January 1745, at a cost of £32,000, thereby establishing a permanent home in the mother country.[31]

Scholars have rightly regarded this purchase as a critical step and as symptomatic of a wider trend in planter absenteeism. Leslie's aforementioned critique of Jamaican society encapsulated many of the "push" factors encouraging white settlers to leave the island, and Beckford himself was painfully aware of the uncertainties of island life. Later that decade William would ruefully observe: "the climate of our sugar colonies is so inconvenient for an English constitution that no man will chuse to live there, much less will any man chuse to settle there without the hopes at least of supporting his family in a more handsome manner, or saving more money than he can do by any business he can expect in England, or in our plantations upon the continent of America."

Although William shared all the accepted misgivings of life in the tropics, his resettlement to Britain did not signal any lack of commitment to the future of the island. As his speech acknowledged, he was in the fortunate position of having the option of going "home" thanks to Jamaica's burgeoning prosperity, and his generation of planters were thus presented with opportunities to advance their interest on both sides of the Atlantic. In this light, the purchase of Fonthill should not be seen as a definitive rejection of island life but rather as part of a new chapter in the advancement of the

Portrait of Francis Beckford, Esq., attributed to Andrea Casali. The Alderman's youngest brother married into the aristocracy in 1744 and was often censured for spending his Jamaican inheritance. He epitomized the arriviste stereotype often associated with the absentee planters. (Photographic Survey, The Courtauld Institute of Art, London; Private collection)

West Indian interest. As we shall see, his responsibilities on the island were a continual magnet for his considerable energies, and these pressures required him to undertake another extensive stay on the island in 1749–50 and to contemplate further visits. Thus Fonthill should be seen as an important step in strengthening the family's transatlantic connection and not as a complete rupture of his Creole roots.[32]

If the timing of his departure was dictated by socioeconomic considerations, his subsequent actions revealed that its primary cause was political ambition. During an intermittent island residence of eight years, William benefited from his status as one of the big fish in the white Jamaican pool, but his experiences in the Caribbean and England had demonstrated that the fate of the island principally lay with the imperial Parliament. His correspondence with James Knight had hinted at this, with disparaging references to "our little island disputes." Shortly before William's departure, the assembly itself had acknowledged the importance of the metropolis when it voted to express gratitude to Knight for his "great and successful endeavours" in blocking the passage of an additional duty on sugars at Westminster, the prospect of which was deemed to be "so destructive and fatal to this island." William's unlicensed return to England had evidently ruffled assembly feathers, but his absence from Jamaica could work to their mutual advantage. In a more partisan vein, his return coincided with a difficult time for the Country Whigs he had supported since their anti-Spanish campaigns of the late 1730s, largely due to the continued mismanagement of the inconclusive war Beckford had witnessed firsthand. The current fluidity of British politics increased the island's need for friends in London, however, while also offering opportunities for the advancement of individual and collective interests. Thus after traversing the Atlantic for the fourth time in a decade, William Beckford still faced tricky political waters, but it would not deter him from the most ambitious course of any Caribbean politician to date.[33]

CHAPTER THREE

Fitting In

Tho' in general we consider those who leave us to be *civilly dead*, yet, not a year has expired since your absence in which we have not been very beneficially convinced that you are *civilly living*, and were I in the legislature again I would endeavour to get it resolved "that you was not an absentee," for those who serve us should always be deemed present.

—Thomas Harrison to Rose Fuller, 1775

When William Beckford arrived back in Britain for the first time in some five years, he could have had few illusions about the challenges of building an effective transatlantic interest. For all the recent success of the West India lobby in Parliament, and for all his personal advancement in Jamaican society, he knew that he would face many obstacles as he endeavored to fit into metropolitan society. He arrived at a key juncture, when other West Indian settlers also found opportunity to make an impact in the mother country. While the success of the plantation system would provide the greater sugar magnates with the financial clout to relocate to Britain, it remained to be seen whether political advancement or social acceptance would be accorded to Beckford and his fellow Creoles. His experiences over the ensuing decade in fact highlighted the differences that remained between colonial and metropolitan cultures, however much white Caribbeans sought to model themselves on the British. William was clearly a pivotal figure, and innovator, for his island's interest, but over the next decade he faced major challenges to ensure that his Atlantic connections secured both personal and collective benefit. Even though largely resident in London, he could not neglect the importance of Jamaican affairs, and the key to his success lay in aligning island interests with those of a fast-changing metropolis, where old and new channels of influence beckoned.[1]

The sheer speed of Beckford's political ascent in Britain has impressed both contemporaries and historians. With only a limited familiarity with British politics, he gained a parliamentary seat in 1747 (which he held for the rest of his life), an aldermanic gown in the City in 1752, and became MP for London in 1754. In part, this rise reflected the broader impact of the West India interest at this time, with Jamaica alone boasting as many as one hundred absentee proprietors in Britain by the third quarter of the eighteenth century. Beckford was both more resourceful and more successful than his fellow absentees. Like other planters, he sought political advancement through aristocratic connection and electoral bribery. More revealingly, he also espoused popular London politics, one of the most forceful interests to challenge the supposed age of Whig oligarchy. These influences highlight that Beckford was a key figure in adapting to metropolitan change, but they do not adequately explain his rapid advancement and overlook the importance of interlocking agencies between colonies and mother country. In particular, attention must be focused on Beckford's underappreciated efforts to secure alliances in the City before 1752 and on his dealings with Scottish interests.[2]

Although the metropolis was to be the scene of his early political triumphs, the purchase of Fonthill was the most important political signal that William could have sent to the established elite on his return. In many ways this was a very predictable move, for it established him as a country gentleman in a land where the gentry remained the social and political backbone of the state. In common with the self-fashioning of the great planters within the colonies themselves, Beckford wished to ingratiate himself with the English landed elite, and his Wiltshire estate was a first step toward broader social and political acceptance. It is important to note, however, that the house he bought from the Cottinghams could not match the fashionable grandeur of the aristocracy, described by its owners as "a handsome seat in good repair." Furthermore, his early remodeling of the house does not suggest any of the swagger of the later Fonthill Splendens. New evidence helps to explain the character of this important investment, for it is clear that Beckford could complete the purchase of the estate in October 1746 only with the aid of a £20,000 mortgage courtesy of Sir Jacob de Bouverie. It would take Beckford another four years to pay off this loan, encumbering

him with the debt problems faced by even the greatest of the planting families. The sale of several plantations in 1746–49 may well be linked to
Beckford's cash-flow difficulties and highlights the interconnectedness of his
ambitions in Jamaica and Britain.[3] In time, Fonthill would be developed as a
major estate of over 5,000 acres, and would be heralded for its opulence and
the cultural taste of its owner, but William showed discipline in his early
management. This caution came in contrast to the extravagance of his
youngest brother, Francis, who had already married into the aristocracy and
was censured by other Jamaicans as a "fellow that will spend five times his
income in one year."[4]

Not only were his estates linked by financial considerations. More significantly still, Fonthill was ideally situated for the preservation of his colonial
interests, as London was only an overnight journey away, and gave him even
easier access to Bristol and to the south coast ports, which retained important
commercial links to the West Indies. Thus although the purchase of an estate
imitated the landowner elite, the choice of Wiltshire highlighted his sensitive
reading of regional commercial networks, which in turn might help him to
secure political advancement in Britain. Although Caribbean purchases were
spread around the country, over time the strategic significance of the southern
and southwestern counties to the West India interest would become more
obvious in his lifetime and helped the development of an absentee social
network. In the very same year William purchased Fonthill, his brother
Julines established himself at a country seat at Iwerne Steepleton, Dorset.
The Beckfords can thus be seen as pathfinders in this regard, eager to translate regional connections with the colonies into a more permanent political
interest.[5]

London, however, remained the social and political center, and on his
return Beckford was quick to establish a metropolitan base. Somewhat
predictably, his choice was Westminster, the scene of his schooldays. His first
home was 12 Upper Brook Street, one of the most fashionable addresses in
the west end, only a stone's throw from Grosvenor Square in the Mayfair
district. Occupying one of the largest houses in the street, he was clearly
aiming to impress passersby in this genteel area of elite sociability. He could
also use this address as a base to maintain preexisting networks of interest.
For instance, from Upper Brook Street he could easily visit his brother
Julines in South Audley Street, as well as his mother, the first occupant of 1
New Burlington Street. He also could mix with a number of Jamaicans in the

parish of St. George's Hanover Square, whose plantations enabled them to live alongside the leisured classes of the west end.[6]

Beckford broke existing social and political molds, however, with his readiness to seek concurrent advancement in the City, an amphibian quality shared by few at either end of town. Beckford's success in the City was undoubtedly facilitated by his ability to strike a chord with the London populace, and he has been rightly seen in the same category as Sir John Barnard, the self-proclaimed City patriot and court critic, whose political star still shone bright when Beckford came back to London. In time Beckford has been seen to have usurped Barnard's role as the guardian against governmental corruption and tyranny, using the public sphere to compensate for the missing City credentials in his curriculum vitae. This image, however, does not adequately account for the importance of Beckford's London dynastic connections, and he recognized full well that he could not simply dazzle the City with gifts and promises in support of its imperial trade. Just as the capital had been instrumental in sustaining the family's colonial fortunes over the past eighty years, so he would seek to exploit this continuous Beckford interest in London for his advancement in Britain.[7]

Although no member of the family had held high civic office since the death of Sir Thomas in 1685, a continued City presence had been maintained until William Beckford's arrival in 1745. The son of Sir Thomas, William, had maintained important links with the government as a naval contractor and kept his father's business address at Mincing Lane, one of the most desirable addresses in the mercantile City, and still popular with Caribbean traders. William died in 1731, but his heir, Thomas, had also taken an address in Mincing Lane by 1730 and from there ran the London end of the family's Jamaica business.[8] It was under the watchful eyes of William and Thomas that the future alderman had first been exposed to City culture as a schoolboy and made aware of his family's importance within London. A personal appreciation of this dynastic sensibility came with one of the earliest documents to bear William's seal, a bond of October 1739, which displayed the Beckford arms granted to the aforementioned William Beckford of Mincing Lane in 1686. In common with his grandfather, the Colonel of Jamaica, the young William was keen to claim this connection, which would simultaneously gain him status within both the City and a wider social orbit.[9]

The personal significance of this City background is very apparent in the character of his political advancement after his return to England.

Although in most contexts he recorded his address as St. George's Hanover Square in the west end, his first major appointment on his return was very much as a City figure, as one of the sixteen merchant representatives chosen in February 1746 to remonstrate with the ministry over losses to the French and other privateers during the War of the Austrian Succession. His readiness to play this role suggested that right from the outset of his political career in Britain he was keen to stress his City roots. In this guise he could claim both a planter and mercantile character and thus ease potential tensions between the leading factions of the West India interest in the capital. A more direct recollection of his familial heritage came when he finally decided to embark on a civic career in 1752, for he chose to stand for Billingsgate, the ward in which Mincing Lane lay. Even though his main London residence was in Westminster, the press styled him as "an eminent merchant in Mincing Lane" when he gained the ward election. His actions thus reflect a deep appreciation of his family's prior success, as well as the inherent flexibility of his strategies for advancement within the metropolis.[10]

He was also using more innovatory channels of influence to secure an interest in Westminster, where his Scottish connections were particularly important. The critical role played by the Scots in the development of the eighteenth-century empire has become increasingly recognized, although it is only relatively recently that attention has focused on the metropolitan operation of Scottish interests. Beckford's early career highlights how important such connections were for the development of imperial interests in Britain. He had long expressed his admiration for the capacity of the Scots as adventurous and hard-working imperialists. It was thus only natural for Beckford to move in Scottish circles as he endeavored to establish a political interest in the 1740s.[11]

The more general importance of these connections for Beckford is highlighted by one of his first public pronouncements on his return to Britain, when he testified to a parliamentary committee in March 1745 on the likely success of British linen manufacture in the colonies. His recent colonial experience evidently promoted his appearance before the committee, but there were other political machinations at work. Only the previous year, one of the great early triumphs of the West India interest, the defeat of Pelham's sugar duty of 1744, was facilitated by the enlistment of Scots and Irish members in return for defense of their linen interests.[12] Beckford was clearly keen to exploit this alliance still further, for a leading witness at the inquiry was the

Scottish baronet Sir William Dalrymple, for whom Beckford acted as an agent to raise capital in the City. Other witnesses included John Yeamans and Samuel Martin, both of whom had worked alongside Beckford in the Caribbean lobbies of the later 1730s, and whose extensive interests in the Leeward Islands recommended them as intermediaries for Dalrymple. Together they raised some £3,700 for him, and subscribers to the loan form an impressive roll call of Caribbean planters at this time—Drax, Colleton, Pennant, Foster, Barham, Knight, and March. No fewer than five of these families were listed as residents of the parish of St. George's Hanover Square, and this loan highlighted the growing force of the planter interest at this time. The Scots were also prominent in the parish at the time, and such proximity was no mere coincidence of interest. Significantly, by 1746 Beckford had become one of the five directors in the newly created British Linen Company, whose London subscribers included Yeamans and Martin. For this enterprise, Beckford also called on an older, even more powerful friend in the shape of former classmate (and Scot) Thomas Hay, Viscount Dupplin, a member of the Board of Trade from that year until 1754.[13]

Thus in his first years back in England William had established firm networks of interest, and it was predictable that he would aspire to a parliamentary seat at the first general election to be held after his return, that of 1747. His first attempt, thanks to an insensitive intermediary at the Cornish borough of Penryn, ended in disaster and warned him of the difficulties of managing even small boroughs. These venal electorates might have appeared the surest routes to political favor under the Whig oligarchy, but they were not without risk for the parvenu. He thus turned his attentions to Shaftesbury, a pocket borough much closer to his Fonthill estate, and sought a by-election vacancy by a direct approach to the local patron, the fourth Earl of Shaftesbury. The peer clearly had little familiarity with Beckford but following a private meeting recognized that "he is determined to do extremely well and generously towards the town, and everybody knows he has the means amply in his power." In more partisan terms, they shared a mistrust of the Pelhamite Whigs, and the peer clearly warmed to Beckford's general political outlook. Beckford was commended for being "independent in his way of thinking, not being confined by particular attachments," and Shaftesbury was convinced that he had "the interest of the public" at heart. This political independence was important for gaining the peer's support, but Shaftesbury did not back William with money, for Beckford "was prepared to do everything of that kind fully, and I dare say he is." These exchanges suggested that the political investment in Fonthill was already paying encouraging dividends, impressing upon the local magnate Beckford's wealth and his commitment to the area.[14]

Even with the enlistment of aristocratic support, Beckford met significant opposition to his candidacy, and his original hopes of gaining the seat without expense foundered in the face of a determined opposition from London banker Fraser Honeywood. The catalyst for Honeywood's candidacy remains unclear, although it does not appear to stem from party difference and was probably largely opportunistic, for many local observers considered him as much of an outsider as the Jamaican. Beckford was certainly vulnerable on account of his prominent backing for the linen interest, which may well have alienated local clothiers, who had campaigned vigorously against recent parliamentary initiatives to favor linen manufacturers. Beckford was also let down again by the inexperience of some of his electoral agents (who included Yeamans), with one report highlighting the "ill-blood" arising from "the indiscretion of some of Mr. Beckford's friends." In the short term, this cost Beckford dearly, for £1,000 was deemed necessary for gaining local support. Lord Shaftesbury's subsequent support for the establishment of a monthly club in the town composed of townsmen and local gentlemen, including Beckford and his brother Julines, may have aimed to heal differences caused by such insensitivity. In fact, Beckford's colonial background was not openly attacked until the early 1750s, which again highlights his sensitivity to integration, rather than confrontation with British political interests. His money and friends prevailed to win the seat, but for the self-styled principled patriot this method was clearly hypocritical, if not genuinely distasteful, and may well have convinced him of the need to maintain several concurrent channels of interest.[15]

Once Beckford had taken his seat, political commentators were keen to track his political opinions more exactly. As a lobbyist for Caribbean interests he had gained some publicity and had proved a thorn in the side of the Pelhamite Whigs, who had reasserted their dominance at the 1747 general election. True to his principles, he became associated with anti-court figures, a political trajectory aided by his social connections in Wiltshire and Dorset, especially his links with Lord Shaftesbury and George Bubb Dodington. Many contemporaries and historians have duly identified him as a Tory or as an independent Whig. While the latter seems more appropriate, it was easy for opponents to bracket him with all enemies of the Pelhamite Whig interest, and his bitterest critics even branded him a Jacobite on occasion. Beckford realized full well that he was taking risks by associating with oppositional figures, but he evidently gained political capital out of these links, and in common with other resourceful Jamaicans, he was prepared to play the metropolitan political field for personal and sectional advantage.[16]

Although successful in his pursuit of a place in the Commons, Beckford did not cut an active figure straightaway. In his first session he was appointed to only three committees, two of which predictably related to mercantile or colonial affairs. There is also little evidence that he made any significant contributions to Commons debate, although on 8 February 1748 he made a spirited defense of the sugar interest when opposing an additional levy on merchandise. Beyond this, it is hard to trace his political imprint for the ensuing two years, and it is easy to assume that he was consolidating his position quietly within the Westminster establishment. In fact, Jamaican records confirm that this relative obscurity was due to a return to the island. In December 1748 he was in Bristol, eagerly awaiting the first fair wind to take him to the island, and by the following May he was back in Spanish Town, where he would remain for at least another year.[17]

A variety of matters took him back to Jamaica, although the timing of the visit was probably suggested by the ending of the War of the Austrian Succession. Judging by his extensive business in the island's Chancery, the main reason for his return was the settlement of his estates, as he sought to bring his liabilities on both sides of the Atlantic into equilibrium. The £20,000 mortgage on Fonthill was clearly a major preoccupation, and while back on the island he sold two major properties, which raised J£28,000 (£20,000). He also spent considerable effort in collecting debts, although he found that he could "recover but little" of the "very great sums due to me." In order to maximize the productivity of his existing estates, he oversaw the purchase of significant numbers of recently imported slaves to work on his plantations. He did not play any formal role in the island assembly, but his return was anxiously monitored by the island's governor, Edward Trelawny, who, acknowledging that William's "interest and that of his family are very powerful," was sure that he aimed at nothing less than making the "country subservient to his designs." In this trip, however, William was content to reacquaint himself with the island elite and made no overt move against the governor in his current battle with the faction of Rose Fuller. Beyond these political divisions, Beckford found the island in a very distressed condition in the aftermath of a long war, reporting to one of his Scottish contacts, "There is an uncommon want of money and credit at present, and I see no prospect that things will be better." These bleak conditions argued for a more prolonged stay on the island, but with considerable momentum behind his metropolitan political career, and the reassuring presence of brother Richard in Spanish Town, he returned after an absence of little over a year. It is clear that Beckford did not regard the trip to the island as his last, and that he recognized the importance of an island presence to his ambitions on both sides of the ocean. As one Jamaica resident advised an absentee on the benefits of a yearlong stay on the island, "You will find work [a]plenty and see things in a different light to what you possibly can now." Beckford would have readily acknowledged the wisdom of this counsel, even though it became increasingly difficult for him to retain a transatlantic character in person.[18]

It was inevitable that William's absence caused some neglect of his British interests, and he did miss opportunities to build upon his success to date. For instance, Friday, 8 September 1749, should have been a red-letter day for him, with the consecration of the new parish church at Fonthill Gifford, all paid for at his expense. The ceremony represented the culmination of eighteen months of planning and construction, William having led the call to replace the dilapidated church with a new building for the benefit and convenience of the parishioners. He had laid the foundation stone of the church in May 1748, but he was not there to play the role of the beneficent patron at the consecration. Although the church itself would gain few admirers, the ceremony marked an important local occasion, for it was presided over by the bishop of Salisbury, who led prayers for the absent Beckford before a congregation of his employees and tenants. On their own, neither the church nor the congregation would suggest that Beckford could be ranked among the county's leading magnates, but such acts of local patronage were significant markers of status, and William could ill afford to pass up chances to raise his domestic stock. On the other hand, the benefits of his Jamaica trip were revealed on his return in August 1750 when he was able to pay off the mortgage on his Fonthill estate.[19]

After a year's absence Beckford attended to his political duties with renewed gusto, eager to promote his continued advance in the metropolis. The parliamentary session of 1750–51 saw a notable increase in his activity in

Fonthill House, known as Fonthill Redivivus, painting by Arthur Devis, c. 1750–55, depicting the Alderman's remodeling of the house and grounds, including the new bridge and the new church consecrated in 1749. (Fonthill estate, courtesy of Lord Margadale)

the Commons, with no less than twenty-four committee appointments. Many of these bills related to schemes for the improvement of roads and rivers and mirrored the concerns he had shown as an assemblyman back in Jamaica. Perhaps motivated by his recent experiences of island hardships, he was also prominent in colonial affairs. On 10 June 1751 he acted as a teller to counter the delaying tactics of opponents to a measure to regulate the use of paper credit in New England. Although the Caribbean islands maintained extensive links with the mainland colonies, commercial tensions remained, and the session ended with another standoff when the West Indians warned the government of the smuggling of foreign sugars through the British Virgin Islands. This issue managed to unify the London-based Caribbean politicians and produced a particularly intense bout of politicking which highlighted the central role Beckford had assumed by this time. In the course of agitating the measure, he even managed to solicit the advice of Prime Minister Pelham, who directed the West Indians to broadcast their concerns by a petition to the Commons. Although Beckford was still learning the political ropes of Westminster—and had frequent recourse to legal expertise in the course of this campaign—Caribbean politicians eagerly pressed him for his views, and he in turn sought to coordinate and galvanize their efforts. On this occasion, the West Indians ran out of parliamentary time, but Beckford could take some comfort from their growing efficiency as a political lobby.[20]

It was at this stage that Beckford took a series of significant decisions, which dictated the character of his contribution to British politics for the rest of his career. Evidently the settlement of his Jamaica affairs enabled him to undertake new political strategies, and early warnings of the sheer metropolitan ambition of William and his allies had been relayed from Jamaica to London by Governor Trelawny. As he informed Premier Pelham, "There is a scheme, or I am greatly mistaken, among the West Indians to make themselves formidable; as many as can are to get into the House and keep together." The imperiled governor foresaw this influx of Caribbean MPs as a prelude to the complete domination of the assembly over the colonial governors, which would cause serious problems for Pelham himself: "Of what ill consequence this may be to his Majesty's affairs and the ministry, how easily the City inflamed, [I] need not mention." Warming to this theme, he was convinced that transatlantic interests could easily bridge the worlds of island and metropolitan politics, enabling the divisions of the Jamaican assembly to "fire the clubs in the City, till the City itself is in a blaze, and Westminster, even to the very palace, under the greatest alarms." Trelawny's fears were clearly stoked by the resoluteness of his Jamaican rivals, but he later had cause to be thankful for the influence of the Beckfords. In particular, the brinkmanship of Richard Beckford was crucial in brokering a political accommodation between the governor and the warring factions in late 1751. Richard's "disposition for peace" was heralded as a precondition for the "happy reconciliation" of the island parties through the signing of an "Association," the benefits of which would be welcomed by politicians on both sides of the Atlantic.[21]

Although there is no proof that the London-based West Indians were pursuing the coordinated strategy that Trelawny suggested, there can be little doubt that Beckford himself saw the wisdom of strengthening his formal influence in the capital. The first sign of his renewed effort to build an effective metropolitan interest was a change of address in 1751. To date, he had based himself in Mayfair, and although claiming political associations with the mercantile City, he had few direct ties there beyond his distant relations. His recent skirmishes with the North Americans revealed, however, that he was keen to maximize the potential support for the Caribbeans throughout the capital. West Indian merchants could usually be found at the Jamaica coffeehouse in Cornhill, which had long served their social and professional needs. For the planters based in Westminster, the Bedford Head Tavern in Bedford Street was a regular resort, and Beckford's correspondence reveals that it was used for meetings of the planters' club at this time. Thus, in order to maintain political interests at both ends of the metropolis, he decided to relocate from Mayfair to Soho Square in 1751. The latter was by this time a less fashionable locale than the squares farther west, but it allowed him to move more easily between both ends of town and served as a prelude to a broader civic strategy that was unveiled the following year.[22]

His decision to pursue advancement in the City corporation was certainly one of the most momentous in his life. In many ways it went against the political tide, for since the later seventeenth century the City had expressed continued concern at its failure to retain the services of its most prominent citizens. This trend, however, had not prevented Sir John Barnard from using the City as a platform for establishing himself as a government critic of truly national significance. Beckford could have had few doubts that the senior officers of the corporation were burdened with significant and onerous duties, but the City's voice had proved a powerful force in recent national debates, and even ministers could not ignore London's views on the future of

Soho (or King's) Square, print by Sutton Nicholls, c. 1725. Number 22 was the Alderman's principal London residence from 1751 until his death. (British Museum, Crace XXIX.2, © The Trustees of the British Museum)

a commercial and imperial polity. Thus, in the summer of 1752 Beckford was formally admitted to the civic community in a hectic series of inaugurations, which has been rightly seen as a deliberate attempt to build up his City profile, especially with oppositional elements there. While partisan considerations were important, his choice of livery company and ward was probably influenced as much by his family and West Indian connections as they were by his party leanings. For instance, his preference for the Ironmongers' Company over the Clothworkers', the livery of his ancestors, may well have reflected the recent success there of another Jamaican, the recent lord mayor Sir Samuel Pennant. Furthermore, his family's enduring attachment to Mincing Lane meant that the ward of Billingsgate was his natural choice and anticipated possibly damaging attacks on him as a carpetbagger or outsider. His subsequent success in the City suggests that he had to be sensitive to such considerations, for money alone could not win sufficient support to command a longer-term civic or popular interest.[23]

Alongside this more traditional route to City influence, William also attempted to cement his interest by supporting more novel associations, such as the patriotic Society for the Free British Fishery. Not only did this society provide him with further opportunities to mingle with the City's elite, but it also confirmed his Scottish connections and maintained his links with new allies within the ranks of the parliamentary opposition. The society had first met in January 1749, led by a mixture of London mercantile and Scottish interests, and had sought to raise funds for the advancement of the herring fishery, long regarded as an excellent nursery for mariners and a source of employment for the poor. Beckford appeared at its general court at Mercers' Hall in December 1751 to argue that the society's pickled herrings would be very welcome in the West Indies and stressed that his own subscription "was to serve the kingdom." Two months later, doubtless aware of the advantages of envisaging public affairs "in a mercantile light" before a City audience, he appeared again to praise the society "as a new branch of commerce." His commitment to the society was signaled by his election to its council in September 1752, when he took the oaths of office alongside one of his key agents, Thomas Collett, an experienced Caribbean ship captain and merchant. In the ensuing months, a host of other Beckford contacts joined him on the board, including Sir John Phillips in February 1753, George Bubb Dodington in August, and Lord Shaftesbury himself in the final month of the year. The recent City popularity of these patriotic societies was an obvious spur to his participation, and he clearly aimed to emulate the public profile achieved by Londoners such as Slingsby Bethel and Stephen Theodore Janssen, both of whom were Fishery members. He also mixed with gentlemen with strong metropolitan links, such as the Middlesex MP George Cooke, and with Admiral Sir Peter Warren, the hero of Louisbourg in the last war, who had served in the Caribbean under Vernon while Beckford had been based in Jamaica.[24]

While keen to exploit the commercial patriotism of the day, Beckford also began a broader public relations campaign in the City, using his wealth to curry favor with a range of metropolitan interests. Again following the fashionable tide, he acted as a steward for a number of philanthropic associations such as the Lying-In Hospital (at Shaftesbury House), the charity schools of London and Westminster, and the Society for the Support of the Sons of the Clergy. These commitments were particularly welcome for the busy Alderman, offering maximum publicity with a minimal outlay of time. He also confirmed his growing reputation as the "opulent" Beckford by one-off, striking moments of generosity, such as the gift of a turtle of "near 200 weight" to the officers of his Billingsgate ward on the occasion of his election as alderman. In turn, he received a rich return for his investment, for all these City occasions presented him with opportunities to build bridges with leading metropolitan politicians and to enhance his popular support. The City corporation itself had taken significant steps to broadcast its national importance by the building of the Mansion House to a magnificence suitable to its dignity as the greatest commercial center in the world, and Beckford was keen to take advantage of this self-promotion for his own interest.[25]

His advance in the City certainly helped him to garner political capital in opposition circles in the west end of town. As his involvement in the Society for the Free British Fishery revealed, he was able to use his Wiltshire and metropolitan connections to promote national schemes that would enhance his credibility in Westminster circles. In turn, his new allies could rely on him to criticize the ministry at every opportunity, but he could do little to improve the fortunes of a divided opposition. Opponents of the court were increasingly ready to take his counsel, as revealed by the efforts made by Dodington and Shaftesbury to sound him out on a projected union of independent Whigs and Tories on the death of the Prince of Wales in 1751. Nonetheless, such confidence could not translate into political advancement while the Pelhamite Whigs retained royal favor and a powerful Commons majority.

Beckford's activity in the City demonstrated that he was willing to build up his interest patiently, but the tempo of his politicking had increased by the summer of 1753. With the prospect of a general election on the political horizon, he was ready to make a much more significant move by forging an alliance with the Duke of Bedford, a true political grandee who had left the ministry in 1751. As a former secretary of state for the Southern Department, the duke had plenty of experience of Jamaican politics, and Beckford sent him a turtle to acknowledge his "high opinion of your abilities and way of thinking in public affairs." Their rapprochement also saw Beckford embark on new political territory with his backing of the anti-court newspaper *The Protestor*. It proved a short-lived affair, and his alliance with Bedford would not endure long either, but these political machinations hinted at the growing ambition of the Alderman. They also reflected well on his success in establishing wide-ranging and mutually enforcing networks of interest.[26]

By the time Beckford announced his candidacy for London in 1754, he was no unknown political force, and he did not simply rely on the sugar interest, ideology, or the profits of slavery as his route into British politics. His rise shows how imperial wealth still had to be mediated through traditional channels of influence, and that even the super-wealthy of the Caribbean had to work patiently to build up an interest of any significance or permanence. Equally, Beckford's connections highlight how developments in Britain provided increasing openings for the imperial politician and suggest that he had timed his return well. This cautious integration of colonial and metropolitan interests can also be detected in the ways in which Beckford represented the empire in his speeches in the 1747–54 Parliament.

There has been surprisingly little study of Beckford's contribution to public debate on the empire, largely on account of his contemporary reputation as a poor speaker. Nonetheless, he probably made more speeches in the imperial Parliament than any other eighteenth-century Creole politician, and doubtless with his connivance, several of his earliest orations were reported in extenso.[27] His standard political position at this time was that of government critic, and he was fairly predictable in terms of his partisan views. In fact, on one occasion Premier Pelham testily advised him that "if he would praise oftener where it was deserved, his reproofs would be more regarded." The arguments, and especially the identities, adopted by Beckford are of much greater interest, however, as he tried to adapt to this metropolitan political arena. His tactics suggest that he could not merely rely on his connections or on the putative "rise of empire" to achieve his goals. Instead, he had to work hard to take full advantage of the metropolitan interest secured by Caribbean politicians by this point. As he had confided to James Knight prior to his return to Britain, Jamaica had "been grossly abused and misrepresented by a pack of scoundrel writers, who know nothing either of our situation or constitution." In this way, he echoed the caution of other West Indian leaders such as the London-based Henry Lascelles, who was convinced that "the accumulated weight of all the people of this great city is nothing in competition with the influence of the ministry." Beckford fully recognized the difficulties the imperial politicians faced and tailored his rhetorical strategies accordingly.[28]

The sessions of the 1747–54 Parliament, which saw Britain undergo the difficult transition from war to peacetime, gave ample opportunity for the discussion of imperial affairs. Beckford cut a forthright figure almost straightaway, and when discussing imperial matters most directly in connection with foreign policy or taxation, he left his fellow members in no doubt of the importance of the West Indies to the future of Britain. In one spirited exchange he identified the Caribbean as the place "where all our wars must begin and end." He appreciated the need to present an integrative picture of empire, however, and did not lecture his domestic audience too harshly. He always portrayed the colonies as indivisible parts of the mother country and continually stressed the common cultural and material links between them. Moreover, he was also very transparent about his imperial connections, recognizing that identification with a vested interest would not have unduly worried a Parliament which had become increasingly familiar with the tactics of rival economic interests since the time of Glorious Revolution.[29]

His first published speech, that of 8 February 1748 on a proposed 5 percent levy on all merchandise, can at one level be read as a very predictable defense of the sugar islands. He opened his speech somewhat combatively, alluding to the commercial ignorance of the Commons with the observation that "there are not many gentlemen in this House well acquainted with the facts relating to the sugar trade." More amicably, he went on to align the interests of the planter with the domestic elite by comparing how an increase in duty would hit the producers of wheat. Beckford painted a gloomy picture of how small farmers would be incapable of passing the costs on to consumers in the short term, forcing them to abandon the crop or even give up their calling, thereby ensuring that "one half of the arable lands of England have been deserted, or converted to some other use." He even displayed some awareness over the possible insensitivity of the sugar lobby, pointing out that the importance of the sugar trade "has been so fully done upon many former occasions, and is so well known, that I need not trouble you with anything upon that subject." This showed some apprehension of possible backbench ennui, but it also permitted him to gain an unargued assumption in favor of his interest. His stridently anti-French line was also sure to win over a British audience, although the urgency and directness of his attacks suggest a Creole-bred fear and impatience. His backing for a "blue water" strategy foresaw particularly chilling consequences for the French, for with naval mastery "we may conquer from our enemies, they can conquer nothing from us, and our trade will improve by a total extinction of theirs." In lieu of the proposed duty he advocated a tax on court pensioners, thereby displaying his oppositional credentials, but he had served his colonial interests by a range of rhetorical devices.[30]

Similar sentiments and tactics are evident in his speech of 22 January 1752 on a proposed subsidy to the elector of Saxony. He opened with a defiant statement of interest as a warning to any who might promote foreign rivals: "I sit here as an English gentleman." There was also another bold declaration of support for blue water warfare, in the course of which he claimed that it was only the vulnerability of the French colonies to British naval power in the last war that gave the country any leverage over its Gallic rival. Two months before, he used a speech on the British militia to talk proudly of the importance of the New England militia in the recent war against the French, lionizing their part in the seizure of Cape Breton. Warming to his theme, he then embarked upon a proud defense of the capacity of trading peoples to acquire military discipline, pointing to the Dutch and the Swiss as proof of their resilience against despotism. Furthermore, as in so many of his speeches, he left the audience in no doubt of his thorough grasp of British and European history and showed off his schooling in the classics.[31]

The militia speech also highlights another of Beckford's favored presentational techniques, for he linked imperial issues and perspectives to recent developments in Britain and adopted domestic discourses to stress the common cause of metropole and colony. He clearly harbored doubts over the potential receptiveness of the landed elite to imperial demands, recognizing that Caribbean interests had to be portrayed as British concerns. For instance, in order to combat a bill to prohibit the insurance of foreign ships, on 25 February 1752 he took on yet another political persona—"I am one of those private merchants"—to challenge the East India Company. Adopting a firm anti-monopolist stance, he rhetorically questioned whether "a wise, trading nation" should leave one of the richest sectors of world commerce to "a few interested, spiritless directors in Leadenhall Street." This position might be interpreted as an echo of long-standing opposition to company interference in the Atlantic colonies, but it also rehearsed recent domestic attacks against the remaining monopolies, which had fired City politics for the preceding two or three years. Significantly, the following speaker, Alderman Baker, one of the most respected Londoners in the House, endorsed his stance and commended Beckford as a member whose "knowledge and integrity are so well known." Later that year Beckford intervened in a debate on the import of French cambrics to portray himself as the concerned magistrate, defenseless against a rising tide of smugglers. In this guise he echoed wider backbench fears over the failings of the Bloody Code, observing that "when you by statute inflict too severe a punishment upon some small crime, you can never get a jury to convict the offender." A mercantilist desire to undermine French rivals might underlie his position on this issue, but he skillfully adapted it to encompass matters of domestic concern.[32]

Taken together, these strategies demonstrate how imperial spokesmen had to adapt their appeals to a parliamentary audience. All his pronouncements suggest that he had to acknowledge domestic models of argument and interest if he wanted to gain his point, even if he was convinced that the Caribbean was sufficiently important to fix the attention of the metropolitan Parliament. His readiness to align himself with oppositional leaders did threaten to jeopardize these endeavors, but even his rivals did not think that he had undermined his colonial political interest by backing the opposition to the Pelhams. To the contrary, by 1753 he had been signaled out on several occasions as a key figure in colonial debates. A tract of 1753 calling for the increased production of sugar even recalled the testimony of "a worthy planter of Jamaica" at the bar of the House in 1739, when Beckford had boasted that Jamaica alone could supply all Britain's needs if thoroughly cultivated. More combatively, in that same year a friend to the grocers and sugar refiners of London attacked the self-interest of the planters for underproduction and thought that their extravagant profits would encourage "still more of them to quit their plantations for the pleasures of the capital," singling out Jamaica as especially vulnerable in this regard. His position in the limelight invited such criticisms, but he did not flinch from such public debate, even when he contemplated his greatest political challenge to date, the storming of the capital at the general election of 1754.[33]

Beckford had shown himself to be a resourceful politician since his return to England, and his second general election revealed just how ambitious he was for himself and his familial interest. With some experience of British politics now behind him, and a more certain domestic political profile as an anti-court spokesman, Beckford sought seats for family members at no fewer than four boroughs—London and the Hampshire borough of Petersfield for himself (with the reversion of Petersfield for brother Francis); the nation's second port, Bristol, for brother Richard; and the Wiltshire borough of Salisbury for brother Julines. Although Governor Trelawny's dire warnings of a Creole Parliament proved unfounded, William gained a seat at all four constituencies, although eventually yielding Petersfield to his ally Sir John Phillips. He was also successful in securing the return of James Dawkins at Hindon, the parliamentary borough closest to Fonthill, thereby accounting for five of the thirteen West Indians returned at this election. This was a great personal triumph, especially the success in the capital, for the London election was always deemed a true test of any politician, widely regarded as a weathervane of popular opinion by dint of its large electorate, its proud traditions of independence, and its central importance to the national economy. As Beckford surveyed his electoral prospects there in the spring of 1754, he could not fail to see that the City poll would spark the most thorough review of his political character, in which his claims, and those of the interests he represented, would be minutely scrutinized. He had worked tirelessly to secure connections since his return to Britain, but his appearance at the hustings would reveal the real political progress he had made.[34]

As with all London elections of this era, there was extensive newspaper coverage of the campaign, especially from the announcement of the candidates on Valentine's Day, some ten weeks ahead of the poll. Beckford prudently and predictably styled himself as the City patriot, determined to oppose "every measure that may affect either the religion or liberties of this kingdom in general or the rights and privileges of the City in particular." He also aligned himself with patriots of a more established pedigree, such as Sir John Barnard. The importance of having such backing is reflected in his

first published image, *The City Up and Down*, which pictured him alongside
Barnard and Slingsby Bethel. Beckford was depicted as saying, "it becomes a
man of character to keep good company," a satire on the novelty of his candidacy and on his relative lack of a natural power base in London. He knew
that the City had always favored candidates with long civic careers behind
them, and he had to work hard to compensate for these missing credentials.
He certainly worked his constituency hard, and he redoubled his efforts to
exploit his recently acquired associational connections. He duly appeared as
one of the stewards for the anniversary feast of the London Hospital at
Merchant Taylors' Hall and took a prominent part in debate at the Society of
the Free British Fishery alongside Lord Shaftesbury. Many publications were
active in broadcasting the benefits of the society at this time, especially
through depictions of its current president and Beckford's running mate,
Slingsby Bethel, who was often shown with herring barrels. It was also no
mere coincidence that a report of Beckford's mercy to a petty criminal
managed to make its way into the papers.[35]

As poll day drew closer, the first major attacks appeared against him, his
enemies deliberately targeting his status as a newcomer as his vulnerable
flank before the livery. On 12 April, a broadside discussed the ideal character
of the London MP and concluded that long-serving officers were best suited,
those who by their efforts had earned themselves the repute of being "a good
citizen in London." Later that week Beckford acted as steward for another
City feast (this time on behalf of the London Lying-In Hospital for poor
married women), but the pressure on him only mounted. Attacks on his political principles were common, and he was accused of enlisting Whig support
for his brother's candidacy at Bristol while acting himself as "a nominal
Tory" at London. The only conclusion to be drawn from this was that he was
a "person of interested principles," whose values "appear to be thus conven-
iently suited to the interest of different places," a charge to which the colonial
broker was naturally susceptible.[36] Recent enemies in colonial debates also
surfaced to question his patriotism, with one tract roundly censuring him as
"the Great Jamaica Planter," who had worked tirelessly in his own interest to
defeat reform of the island economy. His supporters quickly hit back,
declaring his speeches as a member to have shown that "his abilities, his
public spirit, his importance as a merchant well versed in the commercial
strengths of England are so thoroughly known." The emphasis on England's
benefit was clearly deliberate here, for as the poll began his rivals renewed

The City Up and Down, or the Candidates Poiʒ'd, a print satirizing the candidates at the London parliamentary election of 1754. Beckford sits in the topmost carriage with fellow candidates Sir John Barnard and Slingsby Bethel. The artist appears to have taken some care to record the Alderman's features. (British Museum, Satires 3265, © The Trustees of the British Museum)

their endeavors to portray him as a self-interested outsider, going to the lengths of publishing his attendance record as alderman, an underwhelming 24 percent in fifty-four courts. He was also attacked for his borough-mongering in other constituencies.[37]

Beckford had done enough, however, and came home in fourth place, clinching a seat ahead of two fellow aldermen of longer standing. He thanked his supporters for doing him "the greatest honour," and while admitting that they had known him only a "short time," he rejected fiercely "the prejudices that have been injuriously raised against me." On 31 May, he processed with his three fellow City representatives to the House of Commons and took one of the privileged places on the right-hand side of the Speaker, doubtless content that he stood poised on a platform rich with possibilities for the advancement of his personal and imperial interests. Significantly, his supporters had not sought to raise his colonial character to boost his campaign in any printed works, which suggests that neither they nor Beckford thought it a vote winner. In fact, there is evidence that Beckford had to mollify an individual who sought to expose Jamaica's failures to encourage white settlement on the island by publishing "an account of the miseries, wants, insults, disappointments and deaths." Instead, Beckford's supporters concentrated on issues that resonated strongly with the constituency, such as Jewish naturalization and the building of Blackfriars Bridge, for the electoral appeal of the empire was as yet unclear. Broad claims to the defense of commerce were sufficient to appease City opinion without drawing him into unnecessary and distracting battles between rival sectional interests. It is perhaps more surprising that only one of his rivals sought to exploit his imperial background as evidence of his non-Londoner status, especially given later attacks. His detractors probably thought it sufficient to provide evidence of his "outsider" character, especially his lack of civic commitment and his provincial political interests, without developing specific critiques of colonial interference. All that would come later, when he became a leading critic of imperial policy and the ally of the Elder Pitt.[38]

The sensitive, almost evasive manner in which Beckford supporters tackled questions of empire before a metropolitan audience was vindicated by the family's electoral experience at Bristol. With its own political traditions and strong partisan interests, the nation's leading provincial port was always going to present a mighty challenge for its would-be MP Richard Beckford. These difficulties were multiplied by his absence from the country and the lack of any familial interest in the City corporation. Moreover, in significant contrast to London, where the sheer multiplicity of sectional interests often stymied debate on particular economic matters, the predominance of the West India trade in Bristol saw Beckford's rivals eagerly seize opportunities to demonstrate how the Jamaicans might undermine the values and interests of the borough. Attacks on Richard suggested that Bristolians were familiar with developments in Jamaica and were very aware of how they might influence domestic English affairs. In this way, the Bristol election anticipated many of the difficulties the Beckfords and their fellow West Indians would face as they strove to create a more efficient transatlantic interest.[39]

William's political skills and reputation were closely tested due to his prominent role as Richard's electoral agent at Bristol. The first overt sign of their familial ambitions had come in March 1754, when the town's Tory Steadfast Society admitted Richard as a member and recommended him as one of the town's MPs alongside Beckford ally Sir John Phillips. Within a few weeks, William, Julines, and Francis had also become members of the society, and on 9 April the Alderman made an election tour of Bristol, making "a handsome speech" to the corporation. He then impressed the citizens with an oration at the Exchange in which he demonstrated his "spirit of liberty" by his opposition to monopolies and his support for their trade. In the wake of this visit, opponents of the Beckford-Phillips ticket were much readier than their metropolitan counterparts to besmirch the West Indian by reference to his actions in the Caribbean. In an all-out attack on 12 April, a Whig writer likened a pro-Beckford journalist to a master "tyrannically dictating to his negro slaves in Jamaica." William himself was likened to a West Indian hog—"large and tall (tho' not very fat)"—whose departure from Bristol had robbed local Tories of the chance to hold an election-day entertainment "peculiar to the Jamaican taste call'd Barbequed Pig." Within a week the attacks broadened into a wider censure of the family's insidious influence in Bristol's Atlantic hinterland, with stories circulating of their economic coercion of Jamaican merchants and their opposition to the removal of the island capital from Spanish Town to Kingston. The Beckfords constituted a "mighty Leviathan" whose influence could crush Bristol's traders, and all four brothers had to be stopped to foil the "arbitrary deeds of this overgrown arbitrary family." These colonial themes were grafted onto preexisting religious and political divisions within the Bristol citizenry, highlighting how profoundly imperial expansion had influenced the political culture of communities directly tied to the Atlantic by the 1750s.[40]

This bitter contention ensured a hard-fought poll, and all of William's efforts could not prevent Richard from trailing for most of the week of voting, although a late rally saw him pip his running mate Phillips to the second seat. Newspapers speculated that it was only the detestation of Whig supporters for Phillips that ensured Beckford the seat, and there could be no doubting that the new member would still have to win over his new constituency when he arrived back in England in late June. The ferocity of the attacks on his family advised him to publish an open letter ahead of his personal appearance, in which he promised to support "the public good and the trade and interest of the City of Bristol," but his presence did little to curb factious exchanges in the local press. More senior political observers were just as censorious of the family, with the Duke of Newcastle prepared to prefer the "broken Jacobite" Phillips over the "wild West Indian" Beckford, a view shared by the king himself. In the wake of the family's electoral success, the verdict on William was also still out, with one of the duke's contacts reporting: "People are so divided in their opinions of him that very few think so well of him as he seems to value himself, and that in reality lessens him in the breasts of many who thought better of him before. He mimicked the man of importance, and his very advocate can deck him with nothing higher than that he is rich in fortune and will be as troublesome to the court as he can." Thus, for all their advancement, questions remained concerning the true political interest of the Beckfords in the mother country, and their familial success only placed their transatlantic networks under closer scrutiny.[41]

The general election was thus not a complete triumph. Beckford had proved himself endlessly resourceful and tireless in taking advantage of every possible avenue for political advancement, and he had exploited both his island interests and his metropolitan networks in order to strengthen his transatlantic powerbase. He had achieved much by 1754, but as he clambered the slippery pole of political favor his family and his island were exposed to closer critical review. The candidacy of his brother Richard at Bristol had highlighted this fact of transatlantic political life most explicitly, where the rumblings of discontent over such issues as the fate of Spanish Town had reverberated across the Atlantic and would pose ever growing challenges for imperial brokers on both sides of the ocean. Equally, the importance of such issues would counsel the Jamaicans to continue to strengthen their metropolitan presence, convinced as they were of the importance of British power for the future of the island. While nonresident, however, William and Richard were not absentminded. Their colonial perspectives would continue to play a key role in shaping their thoughts and actions as they sought to respond to the challenges of mastering a fluid metropolitan political world, which was on the verge of the greatest global war it had ever fought.

CHAPTER FOUR

Empire and Patriotism

I had much rather shew all the respect and regard in my power to a lover of liberty and his country (although poor) than to the first nobleman in the kingdom who had barter'd away the freedoms of the people and his own independency, for the sake of empty titles or the lucre of place, pension or employment. . . . I am perfectly convinced from my own experience that the middling sort of people are the most uncorrupt and consequently the most to be depended on in case of danger either from our enemies abroad or from our own intestine commotions.

—William Beckford to John Kirke, 1754

Beckford's words of reassurance to a humble Bristol voter highlight how profoundly he had been influenced by his early experiences of British politics. His embrace of the language of independency placed him firmly in the ranks of opposition, and his respect for the virtue of the middling classes echoed a brand of patriotism that aimed to rid the country of the corruption of government contractors, libertines, and Francophiles. Given the metropolitan currency of Beckford's views, it was predictable that he would rise to a new stage of prominence in British society, capped by his political alliance with William Pitt beginning in 1756. Not only was this era of key personal importance for Beckford, but scholars have identified the 1750s as critical for Britain's engagement with empire, as the onset of the Seven Years' War tested its imperial visions as never before. Both Beckford and Pitt have been seen as principal agents in popularizing the empire as a force within British politics and society, especially in London itself, thereby helping to promote the colonies as integral to the interests and values of the mother country.[1]

These developments clearly mark out the 1750s as a critical era for Beckford and the West India interest, and in this chapter I will demonstrate that it is impossible to understand their responses to these imperial challenges without an Atlantic lens. The global war encouraged Beckford and his allies to strengthen political ties between colony and metropole, and there can be no doubt that they consolidated their influence within the corridors of power during this decade. Less obviously, their impact in London was conditioned by events in the Caribbean, and their outlook was profoundly influenced by the battles they fought to secure their interests on both sides of the ocean. In particular, little attention has been paid to ideological forces emanating from the colonies at this time, even by historians who have highlighted the importance of metropolitan forums for the political development of the island. Jamaican concerns, particularly the battle to move the island capital from Spanish Town to Kingston, highlight how Caribbean politics remained a critical influence on the orientation of the absentees within the metropolitan arena and on their general views toward the mother country. Significantly, these battles heightened Creole sensitivities on key issues regarding the liberties and security of the islands in the mid-1750s, which were ultimately to influence the thinking and allegiances of the absentees within metropolitan politics. In common with Beckford's statement above, the West Indians were often careful not to draw attention to Caribbean events and ideas, sensing the need to pitch their thoughts for a metropolitan audience. The private letter to Kirke captures this innate caution; in it the Alderman adopted a language of middling independence that would have little direct resonance in Jamaica itself. Thus, even though Beckford could regard this period as a new apogee of influence for himself and his interest, he remained wary of British politics and of an appeal to the public. Even his much-vaunted alliance with Pitt came at a price and was not without its tensions.[2]

For all his personal success at the 1754 election, Beckford could only regard the metropolitan political world as a continuing challenge. Most obviously, the election confirmed the dominance of the Pelhamite Whig government headed by the Duke of Newcastle. After several years of flirtation with opposition groups, this was not an encouraging prospect for Beckford, and as MPs gathered for the autumnal opening of Parliament, most political observers expected him to remain firmly in their ranks. His recent alliance with the Duke of Bedford clearly influenced these verdicts, but Beckford's political allegiance remained a matter for speculation. In early

November 1754 Newcastle was informed of "a great secret," that Beckford and ally Sir John Phillips were likely to fall under the command of Sir John Barnard, Beckford's City running mate, but there was no obvious concert between the two London MPs in the early parliamentary skirmishes. Notice was taken of Beckford's recent electoral success, however, highlighted by a testy exchange between Beckford and Old Horace Walpole, brother of Sir Robert. Having spoken to "our American concerns" in the Commons, Beckford took Horace to task for smiling and nodding during his oration, challenging him to tell "if I have revealed any absurdity." An experienced diplomat, Walpole assured him that he had "the highest opinion of the value and consequence of our American colonies," but he instanced this with the observation that "we import everything from [there]; nay, we have lately imported a new commodity: Political Geniuses, for which we cannot make them a proper return." Such ridicule suggested the Beckfords had enhanced their political profile, but also hinted that they were still cast as political outsiders whose cause had considerable obstacles to surmount.[3]

Although William was baited in the Commons, his electoral success had clearly confirmed his status as the most powerful of the absentee planters in the capital. The civic advancement of Richard Beckford, who emulated his elder brother by becoming a London alderman within months of arriving in England, underlined the family's political momentum.[4] Their influence was attested most graphically by the testimony of Rose Fuller, who, writing from Spanish Town in the summer of 1754, warned his brother Stephen in London to cultivate the friendship of William and Richard as much as possible. Even in private affairs, "they have the greatest power of any persons in or belonging to this island to serve you, and without them nothing can be done." Coming from one of the most prominent families in Jamaica, this praise was significant, and many islanders recognized that such influence was of acute necessity at this current juncture. The rumblings of war in the Americas remained an established concern, and in Jamaica the actions of the new governor, Admiral Charles Knowles, gave rise to growing fears for the island's liberties. As had been shown at the Bristol election, the clashes of Knowles with the planter elite over a proposed move of the island capital had already threatened to spill over into domestic British politics, but Creole alarm reached new heights when he set up camp in Kingston in the spring of 1754. The Board of Trade embarked on a long series of hearings on the matter from July, and opponents of Knowles turned to their metropolitan contacts to represent them in Whitehall, thereby ensuring that this battle would be the most significant test of the Jamaican interest to date. It certainly influenced Beckford's political pathway in 1754–58 and further developed his thinking on pan-imperial rights, which in turn were to have wider implications for him and his interest.[5]

Beckford's published speeches for the 1754–55 session were notable for their urgency and for their warnings of sudden imperial change. His speech on the Address on 14 November took particular issue with the threat of Spain, arguing from historical precedent that Britain's appeasement only encouraged "the natural haughtiness of that nation . . . to run into an insufferable excess" and was unbecoming of "the imperial crown of Great Britain." He implored members not to be distracted from their true interest through fear of French ambition in Europe, arguing that the last war had shown that the way to defeat France was by subduing its colonial trade. Lauding the blue water strategy of Elizabeth I, he urged an attack across the Atlantic, where British colonists (although recently mistreated) would render "the utmost assistance." Beckford left open a door to negotiation and spoke feelingly of the cost of recent conflict, including his own, but only a change of ministry would convince their rivals of Britain's resoluteness in the current international crisis. In response, Old Horace Walpole took a swipe at Beckford's "private interest," while his nephew Horace recorded the Jamaican's observation that "Queen Elizabeth in her distress did not go about begging and buying alliances." Young Horace thought Beckford peculiarly sensitive to claims that France's colonies and commerce had grown faster than Britain. The ministry easily rebuffed his objections, but he had further opportunity to advance imperial concerns on 9 December, when the House debated the extension of the Mutiny Act to cover the American colonies. Rhetorically declaring whether "gentlemen who were born, or have lived many years in America are the best judges" of such matters, he launched into a defense of colonial loyalty and of colonial rights. He heralded the colonial forces as a volunteer citizen force and defied anybody to contest that "our people in America forfeited their right to any privilege they are entitled to as Englishmen by going to settle, or by being born in that country." In a notable show of unity with his northern colonial brethren, he also urged the Commons to listen to similar concerns from "the gentlemen of New England," only to meet another rebuff.[6]

This sensitivity to the free-born rights of white Jamaicans can be linked directly to the battle with Knowles, and it was this same language of citizen rights and responsibilities that dominated his interventions in the Commons in the early months of 1755. Teaming up with brother Richard, on 15 January William attacked a measure to reform the Bristol night-watch, characterizing it as a move to invest urban magistrates with new powers to subvert citizens rights. His position was influenced by the recent opposition of the Bristol corporation to his family's political interest, but he took the opportunity to expound his political philosophy on a range of constitutional matters. Significantly, he did not hesitate to see this modest measure as a move toward a form of servitude, observing that "slavery may be as absolutely established, and tyranny more cruelly exercised, under a republican form of government than ever it was under the most despotic." In passing he also alluded to the corruption infesting "too many of our little boroughs" and showed a wider concern for the autonomy of urban government, instancing historic challenges to urban independence such as the quo warrantos of the late seventeenth century and Walpole's "famous act" of 1725, which regulated City elections. This criticism clearly placed him alongside those who declaimed Pelhamite political management, but Beckford was no democrat, and he also echoed fears of the dangers of popular elections. Nonetheless, his confirmed belief was that the people must share in the government of the nation, and thus he insisted that the watchmen be both nominated and paid for by the citizens themselves.[7]

Eight days later Richard also ransacked British history to support the cause of the anti-government candidates at the inquiry following the fiercely contested Oxfordshire election. Ranging from Tacitus to Paul de Rapin's *History of England*, he argued for a limited franchise to support the independence of the electorate, fearing that the poorer sort would soon fall prey to the influence of the great. In common with his brother he had no hesitation in engaging with the concept of slavery, observing, "Thank God, we have no slaves in this kingdom: I mean, slaves to their masters; for I fear we have too many slaves to their passions, and I do not know how soon they may make us all slaves to our government." No opponent sought to expose the hypocrisy of the Beckfords as major slaveholders, but the brothers elicited incredulous responses from the government benches for the ways in which they had attempted to portray these issues as major constitutional crises. Lord Barrington rebuked the Beckfords in the debate on the Bristol watch, lamenting how "our constitution and liberties" were too often "hooked into a debate," and never more arbitrarily than on this issue. Henry Fox was equally dismissive in his response to Richard's Oxfordshire election speech, remarking that "the question before us is a very short and a very plain one; I have no occasion to enter into an examination of remote antiquity." The Jamaicans thus gained little political capital from the language of rights, and in the eyes of many observers they had confirmed a growing reputation for overblown oratory. These interjections were still highly significant, linking as they did the traditions of English urban independence with leading Caribbean voices. Furthermore, it soon transpired that this language encapsulated their wider transatlantic concerns in the mid-1750s and presaged their future contributions to the domestic political agenda.[8]

The first session of the 1754 Parliament had thus given ample testimony to the Beckfords' opposition to the current Newcastle administration, but the political priorities of the Jamaica interest directed them to maintain effective channels of communication with those ministers who had power to influence crucial decisions on the fate of the colony. The mounting crisis caused by the actions of Governor Knowles, which had led to the dissolution of the island assembly in November 1754, was clearly the greatest priority of the Jamaican absentee circle. The anti-Knowles faction even renewed the Association of 1751, declaring their resolution to restore harmony and good government to the island by defending "undoubted" liberties, such as the assembly's right to determine its own elections. Knowles counterchallenged that the people's freedoms might be lost through "the tyranny of a decemvirate," thereby raising the constitutional stakes to new heights. Richard Beckford led the metropolitan campaign, and in March–June 1755 attended the Board of Trade to argue against moving the capital from Spanish Town to Kingston. Although the board showed sympathy for the association's cause, Knowles successfully schemed to produce a subservient assembly, which backed the moving of the capital to Kingston. This battle was to seesaw for another three years, during which time the Beckfords had a central role to play, Richard as the initial coordinator of the legal team, and William as the political strategist for the cause of Spanish Town. The continuing "strange political odyssey" of Beckford in the mid-1750s can be understood only in the light of this vital struggle for supremacy on the island.[9]

The battle for political interest continued on several fronts in the summer of 1755. Beckford maintained the momentum of his London advancement in

August when he was elected London sheriff, and he confirmed his reputation for hospitality with a series of expensive entertainments. More significantly, in the same month appeared the first issue of the weekly *Monitor, or British Freeholder*, the Beckfords' second journalistic venture. "Originally planned" by Richard, the *Monitor* became the mouthpiece of William's political views over the next ten years, and it immediately embraced the language of independency and liberty the brothers had maintained in the preceding parliamentary session. Proffering a stark choice between freedom and slavery, the very first issue warned that the corrupting influences of the times were just as sure to enervate citizen rights as the more overt challenges offered by the prerogative in the past, for "the condition of a slave is not defined by the stripes he receives, but by the power of inflicting them." The editors thus set themselves up as the guardians of the constitution, and although the content was pitched for a domestic audience, they did not miss any opportunity to broadcast the common challenges facing Britons and colonists.[10]

Irrespective of their efforts, the summer's headlines were dominated by the failures of British colonial forces in North America, putting the government on the defensive. Increased speculation on the political orientation of the Beckfords on the eve of the 1755–56 session reflected the gathering sense of crisis, as political leaders sought to solidify their positions in anticipation of difficult ministerial times. William's links with the Duke of Bedford were still seen to have some force, and the duke's recent shift toward Henry Fox inclined some to predict that William would follow suit. Rose Fuller, who had only recently arrived in the capital, confirmed that the Beckfords were still likely to favor Fox over Newcastle. Fox's appointment as secretary of state for the Southern Department later that month raised speculation that Beckford might even be reconciled to the administration, but Newcastle himself was more inclined to align William with the increasingly disgruntled Pitt. The early stages of the session proved Newcastle's forecast more reliable, with William listed alongside Pitt as one the speakers on 13 November against a motion to support Hanover. A mere eight days later, however, when Pitt launched into a furious assault on the rudderless state of the government, Beckford was more moderate in his critique of the ministry and professed "he had a great opinion of the abilities of Mr. Fox, which, if exerted well, would have his support." He chorused this approval the next day, thinking that "we have a better chance with a man of sense." He did so in accordance with his expressed wish to regard "only measures and not men," but it may also have served notice of his desire to build bridges with the administration in readiness for the next London hearing of the Knowles affair. A few months before the Board of Trade had recommended that the Jamaican government return to Spanish Town, and Rose Fuller also detected signs that the ministry was showing signs of tempering its support for Knowles. Planter hopes were thus raised, but it was clear that the West Indians still needed political contacts, especially at such a delicate stage of international relations. As fellow associator Edward Clarke commented to Rose Fuller, "We are not insensible . . . how much the restoration of this country will be owing to you and to your family as well as to the diligent application and address of the Beckfords."[11]

Although conscious of the benefits of ministerial support, in his subsequent Commons interventions Beckford betrayed growing unease at the conflict developing in the colonies. On 2 December 1755 he urged the government to show leadership by either securing "an honourable peace or a declaration of war," adding that "he preferred war to uncertain peace." He took the opportunity to highlight the vulnerability of the merchant marine in the current climate of uncertainty and claimed that the colonies accounted for no less than three-quarters of national trade, "which shows us how much it imports us to take all possible care of our colonies and plantations in America." Three days later, he again took issue with the indecisive and incoherent policy of the government in North America, and he even took upon himself the mantle of "representative" of the Americans, although he had shown little previous inclination to conflate the interests of the continental and island colonies. He continued to speak and vote against the government for the rest of the year, although it was still far from clear whether he had thrown in his political lot with Pitt.[12]

Significantly, even as caustic a critic of the Alderman as Horace Walpole the Younger could recognize that the turning point in Beckford's politics was the first parliamentary hearing of the Knowles inquiry in January 1756. With news reaching London that the rival factions had sparked a riot within the Jamaican assembly, in the wake of which Knowles had imprisoned twenty assemblymen, the colonial battle was seen to have reached the boiling point. On 24 January Beckford took the opportunity of the Commons inquiry to tear into Knowles, "whom he abused immeasurably." The Alderman's diatribe might have been expected in the wake of a series of speeches which had been widely regarded as hymns to colonial self-interest, but Walpole freighted it with especial significance. He interpreted it to be the moment when Beckford moved decisively from Fox to Pitt, with Fox defending Knowles while Pitt "paid great court to Beckford, who till now had appeared to prefer Mr Fox." For its own part, the House expressed its concern at these imperial upheavals by addressing the king for all the papers relating to affair, which the Spanish Town group regarded as a victory in their efforts to outmaneuver their opponents. They were also encouraged in that month by a Board of Trade recommendation that Knowles be removed from the island. The credentials of his successor, Henry Moore, were much more appealing to the planter interest, and Moore could boast strong personal connections with the Alderman, they having been students together at Leiden. In turn, Moore recognized the need to cultivate allies in London and sought to play on this long-term friendship in his letters to Beckford, vowing that "as it was begun in the early part of our lives it will continue to the latest." Although the recall of Knowles was a significant gain, island leaders recognized that the campaign had a long course to run, and William could have no doubt that the Knowles affair would continue to influence his standing within metropolitan politics.[13]

At this promising juncture came the severe blow of the death of his brother Richard in March 1756. Richard had not enjoyed good health since his arrival in England. He had visited France in hopes of a recovery but succumbed at Lyon, aged only forty-four. William's growing prominence as spokesman for the Spanish Town interest can be plausibly linked to his brother's ill health, and his passing certainly robbed the Jamaicans of a firm but diplomatic agent. As the prime mover of the *Monitor*, he was the family member with the greatest pretensions to the status of ideologue. Given his industry since his arrival back in England, there is no doubt that he planned to make as great an impact as his elder brother in metropolitan politics, including as a City MP. William's other brother Julines, the Salisbury MP, had not been politically prominent since his return to Parliament, and William would now face even greater pressure to represent island interests. Richard's passing also brought William into a closer working relationship with the Fuller brothers, who has previously worked more directly with Richard both in Jamaica and Britain, and spurred him to seek further metro-politan allies. This political determination was signaled by the *Monitor*, which vowed to continue its weekly publications in honor of the life of "so public-spirited a man" and to maintain "the same generous design, which he thought too important to be rested upon the contingency of a single life." Only a few months later, the Beckfords could delight in William's marriage to Maria March, the widow of a London-based Jamaican, but the family's political prospects appeared much more uncertain.[14]

Barely had the mourning for Richard ended when the inevitable official declaration of war against France was announced in May. William showed little or no inclination to court either Fox or Newcastle, and he spared the ministry no criticism of its early failures in the war, launching a scathing attack on 11 May to bemoan Britain's lack of preparation. He expressed deep alarm that the French had sent 2,500 men to the Caribbean and placed the blame for the catastrophic loss of Minorca squarely on the ministry, insisting that "12 sail would have saved Minorca." This stance was consistent with his averred principles and priorities for some years, but in common with his fellow MPs, for Beckford the war heightened the significance of any personal strategy in such fluid political times. His Jamaican allies left their London agents in no doubt of the need for extra diligence, with Rose Fuller being reminded in June that the Spanish Town group had "no other hopes than from yours and Mr. Beckford's interest at home." Others lamented that they "would imagine Jamaica was of very little consequence to Great Britain from the situation we are in" and implored their London allies to "remember Jamaica." Leading planter Charles Price wrote directly to Beckford to urge him to "to do justice to your injured country," promising that the islanders would provide the "materials" for him to represent their concerns effectively.[15]

It is in the context of this desperate need for political capital that Beckford's increasing solicitation of Pitt in the winter of 1756–57 must be understood. In many ways, it is surprising that a closer alliance had not already occurred. Since the late 1730s Beckford and Pitt had shown a general mistrust of the Old Corps Whigs, and both had expressed their aversion to Britain's seemingly pro-Hanoverian foreign policy, which was held to be inimical to the nation's true colonial interest. They even shared a common heritage of family colonial endeavor, with the latter's grandfather Thomas "Diamond" Pitt every bit as much the imperial adventurer as Colonel Peter Beckford, albeit in an oriental theater. Their failure to unite sooner can be attributed to the flaws of both politicians. Pitt's mercurial political career, which had seen oratorical brilliance matched by personal inconsistency and ill health, rendered him an unpredictable ally of often dubious value. Beckford's political star was rising in Britain, but he could not as yet bring any commanding political interest to the table to bargain for the support of a frontline politician of genuine quality. As evidence of this, in the early months of the war, Beckford and Fuller still made approaches to Newcastle or to the Earl of Halifax, suggesting that the desperation of their position argued for a multi-frontal assault in a factious political world. In this way, they differed from their North American counterparts, who were much less prepared to engage with partisan politics, but this risky strategy might yet bring significant reward.[16]

The delicacy of the situation, both for Beckford and the wider Jamaica interest, is highlighted by the intense politicking which surrounded the appointment of a new colonial agent for the island in the autumn of 1756, occasioned by the death of long-term incumbent Jack Sharpe. Stephen Fuller, brother of Rose, immediately set about making interest for himself, enlisting his brother to canvass key figures in both London and Jamaica. Although the formal nomination rested with the island assembly, the Fullers acknowledged the key influence of London power brokers in this matter and applied themselves to Halifax and Beckford for their support. In this suit, the Fullers gambled that the earl would be elevated to higher office within days, but they were wrong-footed in October by the ministry's collapse and the appointment of the Pitt-Devonshire administration. In fact, Stephen Fuller was castigated for indolence by one of his London colonial contacts for not coming to town to witness "the revolution of our grandees, and how very great, and triumphantly, the new ruler [Pitt] drives all before him." Beckford himself made evasive noises on 6 November, revealing that he was already engaged to support the rival candidate Lovell Stanhope, and referred Stephen to his brother Rose to explain why he could not say more on the matter at this difficult political juncture. At this point, Stanhope was most likely a protégé of the Duke of Bedford, and thus Beckford can be seen as repaying political favors from earlier alliances. In common with other Jamaicans, the Alderman recognized the dangers of permitting the court or other political grandees to influence an appointment of such importance to the interest of the island, which might be tantamount, as one observer put it, to "leaping out of the frying pan into the fire." In the current wartime crisis, however, Beckford evidently thought that it was a risk worth taking.[17]

On the very same day that Beckford poured cold water on Fuller's hopes for the agency, he wrote a letter to Pitt himself, which remains the earliest surviving correspondence between the two men. With a new administration about to take the reins, Beckford clearly thought that the time had come to strike a closer association with the politician who had championed the cause of empire for a generation. Far from suggesting any prior familiarity, Beckford's tone suggests some distance between them, although he was clearly trying to adopt a political style and persona that might appeal to Pitt. He opened deferentially, entreating the minister to "let my esteem and regard plead an excuse for the impertinence of this letter," which he attributed to "the melancholy prospect of public affairs." He was quick to disown any responsibility for this to Pitt, blaming "the old leaven" of the cabinet, which corrupted the impact of new ministerial appointments and denied them any real power to fulfil their patriotic duty. He was equally keen to declare his own political independence and, in keeping with the times, made a virtue of his colonial background and his prior service in the national interest: "In the militia of Jamaica I was no more than a common soldier: in our present political warfare, I intend to act as one of your private soldiers without commission." Above all, in this capacity he hoped to defend "the cause of liberty," a rhetorical flourish consonant with his recent defence of Anglo-Jamaican freedoms and to Pitt's thunderous speeches in the Commons in recent times.[18]

There is no record of any direct response from Pitt, but on the eve of the session Beckford seemed excited by the prospect of his leadership of the Commons, enthusing to one of his circle, "I have a real good opinion of him." He did, however, appear to harbor reservations about Pitt's ability to surmount the formidable challenges ahead, expressing the hope that "he may be able to do as much good as he seems to [be] inclined to do for his country." When the session opened, it was clear that a distance between the two men still remained, for in the debate on the Address Pitt was reported to have "poured cold water on the head of Alderman Beckford, who had vaunted in his usual style on the grand strength of England." Possibly as a means to demonstrate his loyalty to the new leader, Beckford channeled much of his efforts into attacking the Duke of Newcastle, whom he continued to blame for Britain's weakness abroad. It was reported that Beckford "grossly abused" the duke both inside and outside the House, and that the Alderman had even labeled him "the head of a smuggling county [Sussex]." The continuing difficulties of the war may have led William to target the rotten part of the constitution, but it was still unclear whether such vituperation would win him the trust of the hard-pressed minister.[19]

Once again Jamaican affairs would help to forge the Pitt-Beckford alliance. Amid the growing military crisis in Europe and North America, Jamaica's domestic discontents had been largely overlooked in Westminster, leaving the resolution of the fate of Spanish Town and Kingston unresolved. The enforced return of Knowles to London may have represented a victory for Spanish Town, but his determination to clear his name sustained the contest. The rival factions had submitted petitions from the assembly and council, respectively, and by the early weeks of 1757 the new ministry appeared increasingly resolute to settle the matter. Beckford and Rose Fuller were two of the three-man team appearing before the Board of Trade to make final pleas for their respective causes before the Earl of Halifax. Confessing that "he had never studied a point so laboriously in his lifetime," Halifax then made the landmark ruling that the courts and records of Jamaica should stay at Spanish Town, while reserving the right of the governor to appoint the location for his residence and the site of the assembly. The associators were jubilant, expressing their "entire approbation" for this arrangement, and their opponents could find no immediate grounds to contest the judgement. The Kingstonians subsequently attempted a rearguard action to secure parliamentary support for their cause, with Admiral Knowles himself to the fore, but Halifax's ruling of 8 February was widely regarded as a decisive turning point. It also made the London delegation heroes in the eyes of the leading planters and confirmed the value of ministerial support in the eyes of those London agents.[20]

Beckford's subsequent actions in the Commons gave further proof of his swing to Pitt. Although he had been highly critical of Newcastle's handling of the Minorca crisis, he sympathized with Pitt's position on the trial and execution of Admiral Byng, the scapegoat for the military disaster, whose punishment Beckford thought "cruel." Amid these heated debates he also appeared keen to protect the reputation of George II from public censure, focusing blame squarely on the Commons. On 18 March 1757, he launched into his first public attack on Fox, dismissing him as a self-seeking supporter of Crown rights. The dismissal of Pitt in early April, however, highlighted once again the difficulties Beckford and his allies faced in an unpredictable political world. Pitt's fall also appears to have encouraged Beckford's Jamaican adversaries to continue their fight in the parliamentary hearing of the Knowles affair. The Kingstonians managed to score a victory late in the session by gaining a ruling that the Jamaica assembly had acted illegally in one of its earliest clashes with Knowles. There was insufficient parliamentary time for resolutions on the many other points of difference, and thus this ruling permitted Knowles and his allies to claim official exoneration for their actions. Although Knowles proved that he had no stomach for a further contest, the Beckford group could not rest and continued to seek ministerial authorization for the return of the capital to Spanish Town.[21]

Beckford's political trajectory invited the most open attacks to date on both him and his interest, with the appearance in April 1757 of *The City Farce*. This work introduced the sobriquet of Alderman Sugarcane and sought to expose the politicking behind the alliance of Pitt and Beckford. Clearly aiming at a London readership, where both politicians had made strenuous attempts to curry support, the author characterized their partnership as a mercenary pact of convenience. The satire of Pitt was more conventional, with his quest for power ridiculed by such devices as the title of William IV. The attacks on Beckford were more novel and sought to expose him as "the king of negroe-land" who had brought Jamaican customs to England. In this guise, the Alderman was able to reassure Pitt of the loyalty of the citizens, for "they're all my Negroes." Pitt responded gleefully to this news, praising Beckford's "great creolian soul" and proceeded to advise how to rouse the citizens against his rivals and the Hanoverian interest. Significantly, Beckford's rewards were to be the governorship of Jamaica and other perquisites lately held by "the admiral." The new allies were to be thwarted in their designs, however, for "the people were not us'd to be spoken to by a creolian," a sign that Beckford was still seen as an outsider. Further trouble for their common London interest was also anticipated, leading Beckford to encourage Pitt to play the great man to impress the citizens. This exchange highlighted that Beckford had entered a new stage of political advancement in Britain, and that his rapprochement with Pitt would be scrutinized with ever greater vigilance. Just as one of his enemies had formerly vowed to "lower the topsail of Jamaican popularity," so Beckford had to be careful not to undermine his island's interests through his metropolitan associations.[22]

Beckford's solicitation of the metropolitan grandees was watched with some uneasiness in Caribbean quarters, whatever the potential benefits that such alliances might bring to the island. The backing of Governor Henry Moore gave the Spanish Town party plenty of cause for optimism, but a flurry of exchanges in the spring of 1757 suggested that the unity which the

anti-Knowles campaign had brought to the planter interest might soon
unravel. In particular, the Fullers were clearly piqued by the passing over of
Stephen Fuller as agent and demanded explanations of conduct from their
supporters on the island. While their correspondents relayed effusive decla-
rations of loyalty and thanks to the Fullers, they pointed to the pro-Stanhope
testimonies which had arrived from Lords Halifax, Holderness, and other
peers, as well as to the "letters from the Beckfords warmly recommending
Mr. Stanhope." Not wishing to offend such powerful forces "to whom we are
so immediately indebted for the late change [of governor]," they had thus
backed Stanhope, irrespective of the claims and abilities of Stephen Fuller.
More evasively, they chose to blame delays in the postal service, which had
supposedly caused pro-Fuller testimonies to arrive months after those
backing Stanhope. While some expressed sympathy for Fuller's treatment,
sarcastically labeling it as "a remarkable instance of creole steadiness and
gratitude," they were clearly looking to the future and regarded his hopes as
a sacrifice worth making in the longer-term interest of the island. Probably
in the hope of salving the Fullers' pride, several contacts were quick to talk
up Rose Fuller's qualities and to extol his success in gaining the support of
the Duke of Newcastle, "from which this island has reason to hope for great
advantages in having the power and influence of so able an advocate and
friend to support its true interest." As one put it, "the friends of liberty" had
every expectation that their metropolitan allies would continue to defend
their interests. Desperate to avoid a damaging rift, the leading planters sought
to refocus the London agents on the island's pressing needs in the acute
wartime crisis.[23]

The advent of the Newcastle-Pitt coalition in June 1757 clearly boosted
Jamaican hopes that the politicking of the Fullers and Beckfords might be
richly rewarded, and the Alderman's subsequent relationship with Pitt
suggested that he needed to demonstrate the value of his political alliances to
the islanders. The planters could conjure the most bleak of predicaments to
fire their representatives:

> high taxes, low price of sugar, high freights, high insurance, and hoops
> and staves very dear, the merchants calling in their debts to keep up
> their credit at home, and no money in the country, even for the common
> occurrences of life. Our Treasury exhausted and the public credit very
> low. When you add to this an unsuccessful war against a potent enemy,
> I believe you will think our situation very bad.

It was thus incumbent on the likes of the Beckfords and Fullers to play the political system for all their worth and to put aside any simmering personal discontents. Over the next two years Beckford would play his part by taking every opportunity to praise Pitt's leadership of the war effort, while gently exerting pressure for his Jamaican interests. This essential tension ensured that the two men shared an often uneasy relationship until the war swung decisively in Britain's favor in 1759. Fuller's brief was to gain the support of Newcastle for the island, an alliance deemed to be equally important to their future. If the absentees could work together, the Jamaican interest could represent a formidable force, but even as it rose to new heights of influence, this Atlantic connection continued to discover new challenges to test its unity and effectiveness.[24]

While Jamaica affairs demanded their attention, Beckford and Fuller also had to demonstrate their utility to their London masters. For instance, on 20 September, Beckford wrote to Pitt to report that on a recent trip to Norfolk he had sought out a dissident George Townshend to reconcile him to Pitt's cause. "I have presumed to be your guarantee to him and many other very worthy gentlemen," Beckford loyally declared, and he added that he hoped that success overseas might soon ensure "that the people . . . have one huzza." Yet even in the course of mundane matters of political management, he could not miss an opportunity to alert Pitt to brewing disquiet in Jamaica. On this occasion the island was unsettled by reports of the imminent appointment of a new governor, Colonel George Haldane, and Beckford assured Pitt that his concern was shared by "many of the most sober and thinking planters and traders." Beckford's correspondence with Rose Fuller revealed that both men feared that Haldane would arouse as much acrimony as Knowles, and there appeared a growing animus among the planters over the metropole's favoritism for military men as governors. Beckford was at pains to stress that Fuller's thoughts on the matter "correspond exactly with my own" and appeared keen to mend fences with his fellow Jamaican, reminding Fuller how "all animosities began to subside under the present governor." Fuller was prepared to overlook recent events and directed Beckford to apply to Pitt on the matter; in turn, Beckford encouraged Fuller to approach Newcastle. The Alderman had already sought assurances from Halifax and could enthuse that the earl had informed him that the next governor would be a man of "une grande calibre." However, in this instance the politics of Whitehall worked against them, with Newcastle taking advantage of

Halifax's temporary withdrawal from office to ensure the appointment of his nominee Haldane. It was evidently a setback, but the working accommodation evident between Fuller and Beckford presaged better times for the Jamaica interest.[25]

The winter of 1757–58 proved an important test for both Beckford's public profile and his relationship with Pitt, for he felt increasingly able to communicate his thoughts to the minister in private correspondence. On the eve of the parliamentary session Beckford wrote to Pitt to express his concerns at the unpatriotic tone of "certain personages of some distinction," who ridiculed all recent measures in the war and argued that peace would have to be sued soon "since we had starved the cause in Germany." Although expressing his full support for ministerial policy, he did not shrink from offering pointed criticism of the recent failure of an amphibious attack on Rochefort. With memories of 1741–42 very much in mind, he declared that "I have often lamented the fatality attending conjunct commands" and argued that such squabbling between officers might be averted by the clear hierarchies of command employed by the French. His priority was an attack on Cape Breton, "the only port the French have in all the Atlantic," and vulnerable if the right commanders could be found. Also keen to emphasize his credentials as an ally in the capital, he also reported that the City was "very uneasy" at French success in their invasion of Hanover. These concerns were not guaranteed a ready welcome in Whitehall, nor were his pronouncements in the House in the session of 1757–58. On 1 December he returned to the anti-Hanoverian sentiments of his earlier career, criticizing the employment of so much money in sustaining the German electorate. These attempts to rebalance Pitt's overall strategy were born out of increasing frustration at the progress of the war, but Beckford's impatience did not presage a rupture between the two.[26]

Continuing concerns over the vulnerability of Jamaica clearly preoccupied the Alderman and his allies, but they recognized that they needed to tread warily for fear of appearing insensitive to the global reach of the conflict. They also needed to preserve a united front to secure their interests and to avoid, as one planter put it, "the character of a turbulent, ungovernable people, which in England 'tis said is given us." Endeavoring to put past divisions behind them, in February 1758, Beckford and Fuller appeared before the Board of Trade to argue for more troops to be sent to the island, and subsequently they expended every effort to fete the new governor

Haldane before he left Britain. In a notable show of unanimity between the merchants of the City and the planters of the west end, a "grand entertainment" for Haldane was held at the King's Arms Tavern in Cornhill on 13 June, to which some sixty leading politicians were invited. Although it is unclear whether Pitt himself attended, the Jamaicans welcomed a glittering array of peers and MPs, many of whom had served on the Board of Trade. The organizers reasoned that "unless we have a genteel appearance we had better have none at all" and accordingly put on a magnificent show, including over two hundred dishes and desserts. They were careful to set the right political tone, raising healths to commanders in all arenas of conflict, including Germany, but ending with charges to the sugar colonies and the commercial prosperity of London. Newspaper reports suggested that no fewer than eighty-seven leading Jamaican landowners were present, testifying to the growing influence and visibility of the Jamaica interest in the metropolis. The gathering clearly achieved its immediate aim of ensuring cordiality between Haldane and the planter group, but it also highlighted the considerable political resources at the disposal of the island in the capital.[27]

Fortunately for Beckford and his allies, the summer of 1758 would mark a remarkable turnaround in the fortunes of British forces, initiating a run of unprecedented military success, which would turn the war decisively in their favor. Predictably, these victories transformed the fortunes of Beckford and Pitt, and they were crucial to the establishment of a truly enduring political relationship. Whereas Beckford liked to congratulate himself on the astuteness of his reading of events in the Atlantic theater, to the extent of seeing himself as a prophet, it is hard to credit him with any real responsibility for Britain's success. In truth, he had to follow his leader and compromise on long-held principles in order to secure political access. More encouragingly, he became a confidant of Pitt's at this time, for a letter of 10 July 1758 yielded the first indisputable evidence that the minister had been discussing policy with him. On the other hand, it also reveals how much ground Beckford had to give way on to secure a sympathetic hearing from Pitt, for Beckford not only commended colonial advances, such as the seizure of Senegal, but also engagements in Europe, most notably in the Rhine and at Saint-Malo. Beckford still endeavored to stiffen Pitt's commitment to a blue water strategy, recommending attacks on the French coast or on French naval squadrons ahead of any campaigns in the Low Countries or Germany, observing that these expeditions might divert French attacks on the continent. Nonetheless, he approved of the sending of cavalry to assist Prince Ferdinand of Brunswick, whose skillful leadership had checked the French threat to Hanover.[28]

Even in the Atlantic theater, Beckford had to work very hard to ensure that he achieved success for his interest. Although his letters to Pitt yield a very clear picture of Beckford's vision of the pathway to British domination of the Atlantic, he had to be sensitive to Pitt's global schemes if he was to achieve a positive response. For certain, every word of advice was laced with West Indian interest, and Beckford provided a very good service for his Caribbean allies by highlighting strategies that might serve mutual metropolitan and West Indian interests. Thus when news reached Britain of the seizure of Cape Breton in August 1758, Beckford not only celebrated it as "the key to Canada" but sought to tap into the mind-set of a minister responsible for the war effort by heralding the importance of the region's fishery, which he boldly described as "a standing nursery for 20,000 seamen." He was also keen to move Pitt onto the next objective, fixing his gaze on Martinique, "that most opulent island," in order to urge a winter campaign while the North American theater took breath. The following month he was prepared to praise Frederick the Great for his resolution under heavy attack, but he swiftly returned to the question of Martinique, offering his opinion as "a volunteer in the last war." The island's stock was represented to be £4 million, "and the conquest easy," although speed and secrecy were vital. In this instance, Beckford's influence on the subsequent war strategy can be detected, although his predictions of easy conquest proved illusory. In September came more unmistakable proof of the benefit of the Pittite alliance when wild celebrations in Spanish Town greeted news that formal permission had been given for the governor to return to the old capital. Pitt's actions had not always pleased the Jamaicans in this protracted campaign, but Beckford's patient courtship of the great commoner clearly helped to facilitate their ultimate victory.[29]

Amid these grand schemes, Beckford was wary of placing too much pressure on Pitt or on their developing relationship. In a most revealing extract in July 1758, he warned Pitt of the fickleness of popularity, especially in wartime, and cautioned him not to rest upon it politically to too great a degree, for he feared that rivals would attempt to undermine his public support. Even while the country rejoiced at the succession of British victories, Beckford remained wary of public opinion, advising the minister that it was unwise for either politician to get carried away by success, or to be duped by the apparent support for sustaining major campaigns across the empire. The onset of a new parliamentary session in November 1758 highlighted, however, that Pitt retained the greater public composure and that he was ready to rescue his ally from his wilder speeches. For instance, in response to the Address on 23 November, an excitable Beckford suggested that the Duke of Marlborough's victories had never achieved the "superiority" now attained by British arms. Uncomfortable with such extravagant flattery, Pitt corrected him to disclaim the standards of achievement set by the duke and took the opportunity to warn that the peacemakers of Utrecht had squandered these advantages. Only four days later, Beckford again showed himself a less reliable ally by labeling George II as "the King of Resources." In their private exchanges, Beckford appeared to acknowledge his own impulsiveness, observing after an impassioned call on 18 December for an attack on Quebec that he would not broach the question of Corsica for fear of trying Pitt's patience. Nonetheless, the session of 1758–59 provided the most credible evidence of the value of the Pitt-Beckford alliance.[30]

The dawn of the Year of Victories saw the prospect of the most dangerous rupture between the two allies to date, as the government sought to maximize its revenue from one of the nation's richest trades. With the national debt spiraling to over £120 million, Chancellor of the Exchequer Henry Bilson Legge targeted sugar as capable of a substantial increase in duty but was amazed to find that Beckford was able to count on Pitt to block the measure on 9 March. Not only did Pitt overrule his own chancellor to move instead for a broader tax on all dry goods, but he then launched into

> an extravagant panegyric on Beckford, who he said had done more to support government than any minister in England: launched out on his principles, disinterestedness, knowledge of trade, and solidity and he professed he thought him another Sir Josiah Child. The House, who looked on Beckford as a wild, incoherent, superficial buffoon, of whose rhapsodies they were weary, laughed and groaned. Pitt was offended, and repeated his encomium, as the House did their sense of it.

Not only was this oration "mortifying" to the chancellor, but Beckford continued to thwart his plans for the rest of the session. The slighted chancellor was forced to acknowledge Beckford's political and commercial standing by sounding him out on likely City responses to the new subsidy on dry goods. Beckford did not mince his words, rejecting "these hackneyed expedients" as inimical to the principles of all commercial nations. Toward the end of the month, the Alderman was just as active in trying to thwart Treasury plans to withdraw the drawback on re-exported sugar. On 24 March he contacted Pitt directly on the matter, although stressing that it was "with reluctance [that] I am obliged to be this troublesome on affairs relating to the sugar colonies." A delegation of colonial agents had visited Beckford to warn him that Legge would rob them of their drawback, a move deemed to be "contrary to all the rules since the Revolution" by discouraging the export of a manufactured or refined commodity. Once again, Beckford prevailed, much to Legge's ire. Critics such as Walpole might sneer at Pitt's declaration of respect, but that was a small price to pay for a very major concession to the West India interest, and Beckford had proven his value to his allies in both the metropolis and in the Caribbean.[31]

This blatant favoritism could not go unnoticed, however, and in the wake of these exchanges there was a notable backlash against the perceived partnership of Pitt and Beckford. There had been disquiet expressed over the ministry's partiality to Caribbean interests following reports of a new excise on tobacco in February, when the *London Chronicle* speciously asked: "What means this bold pernicious measure, either with regard to the minister or his West Indians, but gross and palpable corruption?" Pitt's subsequent defense of Beckford then led the paper to feign admiration for the minister's "eulogium on the merits of his new friend, Mr B***d, equally unnecessary as unexpected (for surely Mr. B***d's merits were not unknown to the public) . . . his oratorical distractions between corn and sugar, all these were subjects proper for panegyric." It is significant that this paper could still recall Beckford's speech from a decade earlier, but beyond the ridicule both Beckford and Pitt recognized that these attacks could be damaging. For all the euphoria of recent imperial campaigns, the sheer scale of the war effort placed huge demands on the Treasury, and the perceived wealth of the absentees, so much more evident thanks to the visible spending of Beckford himself, made the government vulnerable to charges of cronyism. As long as the war went well, then Pitt could protect his political allies, but the West Indians could not count on his favor indefinitely.[32]

The sheer scale of the victories of the summer of 1759 left Pitt's opponents with few opportunities for attack. As news flooded in of British success in Canada, the Caribbean, and India, Pitt reached the zenith of his power, and for a time there could be little room for doubters, whatever the cost of these global campaigns. Beckford predictably reveled in this success, and it firmly cemented his relationship with Pitt. Moreover, having "enlisted" under Pitt's command some three years before, Beckford was keen to play his part in furthering the nation's military glory. In August, Pitt and Beckford headed a list of subscribers to a fund to encourage enlistment in the army, and in the late summer the Alderman was able to play out his patriotic dreams as a militia captain, commanding a battalion of Wiltshire volunteers stationed at Winchester to repulse a possible French landing. Such was his confidence with Pitt that he took him to task over Whitehall's treatment of these bona fide patriots. Heralding service as a "severe duty," he mused that "a secretary of war who sleeps on a soft downy bed and lives luxuriously every day, may have forgot that we poor militia men sleep on the cold ground, at a time of the year when Phoebus is withdrawing his kind influence." Pitt demurred in his response, leading Beckford to renew his complaint, stressing that other units had been much better treated and that "the poor solider is my object." With brazen confidence, he was sure that "when all circumstances are considered, our sentiments will be the same," although he later tempered his tone to suggest that the two men could never disagree "so long as my object is the good of my country." Deeply preoccupied with the challenges of directing a worldwide theater of war, Pitt could have been forgiven for reprimanding his self-appointed lieutenant, but there was no sign of any cooling of relations. As proof of this, shortly afterward Edmund Burke observed that Beckford was seen to have "great weight" with the national hero, even though "it is not very easy to have access to Mr. Pitt."[33]

The victories of 1759 emboldened Beckford to express ever more ambitious schemes for delivering a fatal blow to the imperial pretensions of France, forcing Pitt to intervene to curb his enthusiasm. On 13 October, Pitt jumped in to save Beckford from a "nonsensical speech," and he was again called into action during the debate on the Address on 13 November, after Beckford had made "a very long speech on his having foretold all the victories that had happened." Beckford was insistent that France must concede to a lasting peace settlement and boldly asserted that the nation could sustain another decade of war, extolling the recent role of the militia into the bargain. Pitt rose reluctantly to suggest that a decade was an exaggeration and that he was conscious of the strain public credit now labored under, hoping thereby to dampen the prospect of endless campaigning. A week later, the two were more in concert when discussing the funeral honors for General Wolfe, Pitt wiping away tears while Beckford "cried too, and wiped with two hanker- chiefs at once, which was very moving." The debate on the war had clearly entered a critical stage, and the contrasting tones of Pitt and Beckford on the Address highlighted the anxieties that unparalleled success had brought the nation's leaders—how could they craft a peace which would appease domestic and colonial expectations while ensuring tolerable Anglo-French relations in the longer term? After years of public denouncements of France, Beckford's hawkish stance was widely recognized, Elizabeth Montagu iden- tifying him as one of the leading voices "exhorting Mr. Pitt not to muzzle the dogs of war." She also strenuously rejected Beckford's characterization of France as ready for ruin, sarcastically commenting: "indeed, Mr Alderman, if you can persuade France to lie still, we may trample on her at pleasure; but she will move an 100,000 legs and as many arms before she will suffer it." Thus, if Beckford could rejoice in the confusion of his foreign enemy, it was still unclear whether the metropolitan authorities would provide him with the longer-term settlement he and his Jamaican allies desired.[34]

Almost inevitably, the euphoria of 1759 was transformed into more sobering political realities in the early months of 1760. Beckford's outspo- kenness amid the nation's finest hours and his singular intimacy with the mercurial Pitt duly earned him increasing criticism. By February 1760 he could lament, "I am the object of envy, hatred, malice and all uncharitable- ness." More worryingly still, he came under increasing pressure to provide political services for Jamaica in the wake of a number of crises. As the war entered its fifth year, further pressure from the Treasury might have been expected, and he once again suspected Legge of planning to undermine the sugar colonies. Despite previous assurances, the West Indians were alarmed when moves to encourage the export of spirits appeared to show greater favor to corn-based spirits over molasses and rum. As in the previous year, Beckford lobbied Pitt directly as the "the only protector" of the colonies, predicting that the Caribbean lobby could expect little sympathy in the Commons without his intervention. He thus implored Pitt to attend to the matter in person, sensing that the minister's absence was felt by "no set of men so much as those concerned in the West India colonies." Pitt's tempo- rary indisposition did not aid the West Indians on this occasion, but their interest again prevailed in the form of a measure to encourage the export of Caribbean rum and molasses-based spirits.[35]

Compounding these metropolitan concerns was news of worrying developments on Jamaica itself. Governor Haldane had fulfilled the hopes of the planters by acting as a unifying mediator between the island's factions, but his sudden death in August 1759 had reignited party tensions, which the returning lieutenant governor Henry Moore struggled to contain. Even more disturbingly, the spring of 1760 saw a series of slave revolts on Jamaica, commonly known as Tackey's rebellion. This uprising was one of the most serious of the whole century, and it resulted in a death toll of some 50 whites and 500 slaves. The disorder even reached one of Beckford's estates, at Esher, where at least two white employees were murdered, including the overseer. Several of Beckford's slaves played a crucial part in thwarting the revolt by alerting the authorities to the insurrection, but the bloodshed underlined the brutalities of plantation life. The news clearly shocked the Alderman, for his wife commented in June 1760, "I never saw anything so hurt as Mr. Beckford." This calamity spurred the absentee planters and merchants into a new campaign to secure a permanent garrison of 2,000 regular troops on the island to deter further rebellions. It also brought about a renewed accommodation within island politics, for it was clear that Tackey's revolt had touched a raw nerve, reminding islanders and absentees alike of their vulnerability and dependence on the metropolis.[36]

Despite all these challenges, relations between Pitt and Beckford remained good. As a measure of this, when William Henry Lyttelton was appointed the new governor of Jamaica, he was assured that "Mr. Pitt . . . will make Beckford your friend, or at least keep him quiet." The birth of the Alderman's first legitimate son in September bore further testimony to their closeness, for Pitt became godfather to William Thomas. Their private exchanges in the wake of this event were particularly warm, and Beckford expressed increasing confidence in the direction of the war. On news of the fall of Montreal, he even broached the prospect of securing "a safe and honourable peace" with an exhausted and humiliated France. He still reveled in the role of Pitt's militia officer, passing on detailed accounts of his experiences and proclaiming the Wiltshire regiment "as well appointed as most regiments in his Majesty's service." The death of the monarch in October 1760 offered no immediate threat to their partnership either, and the session of 1760–61 began very much as had its predecessor. Horace Walpole espied some tension in Beckford's response to the Address on 18 November, when the Alderman labeled recent military endeavors as "languid," although even the hostile Walpole admitted that this barb was not aimed at Pitt. Although the strength of their alliance was not in doubt, both men could not fail to sense the growing political tensions at the new court, especially amid an increasingly fraught public debate on the likely peace settlement with France.[37]

It was a measure of Beckford's perceived standing with Pitt that he was targeted by leading politicians as they jockeyed for influence at the new court. George Bubb Dodington recorded in February 1761 that Beckford had been in conversation with the king's favorite, Lord Bute, who reported that the Alderman "wish'd to see the King his own Minister." Bute retorted that "his great friend Mr. Pitt" thought very differently, and that Beckford could report Bute's sense of this to Pitt. Bute's account, especially at such a politically sensitive juncture, must be regarded as suspect, but it demonstrated that the Alderman was still regarded as an important confidant of Pitt's, whose views had to be taken into account. More positively, Beckford may have wanted to keep the doors open to an alliance with Bute, whose political star was clearly in the ascendant. Furthermore, although it is unlikely that he would have broached the controversial notion of the king playing a more direct political role, he bore no obvious animus against the new monarch. In the early stages of the reign, Beckford's pronouncements suggested that, in common with most observers, he shared the optimism that George III would personify the patriotic credentials that the first two Georges were seen to have lacked. The future confrontation between Beckford and George III should not cloud earlier signs of entente, such as the appointment of the Alderman's sister Elizabeth as a lady of the queen's bedchamber by the summer of 1761. Bute's report may have been little more than mischief-making, but if there was little prospect of a Bute-Pitt alliance, it was just as unlikely that Beckford would have deserted Pitt or have formed an immediate antipathy to the new court.[38]

The uncertainty of court politics formed a troubled backdrop as Beckford campaigned to retain his seat at the City's parliamentary election of April 1761. The great victories of the war may have cheered many commercial interests, but it remained unclear whether they supported Pitt's bellicose stance toward Spain, or if they were prepared to give credit to Beckford for his political role over the previous seven years. Significantly, at a meeting of the livery to choose candidates some six weeks before the poll, he began most defensively, attempting to clear himself from charges that he had neglected his aldermanic duties. While admitting that these criticisms were "just," he pointed to the superior importance of his role as an MP and then launched into his most explicit attack on the representativeness of Parliament to date. By his calculations, "this great City" paid one-sixteenth of the land tax and one-eighth of taxes in general but elected only 4 of the 558 MPs. At this stage, he was not prepared to broach any specific reforms to rectify this injustice, and the observation simply aimed to justify his claim that his parliamentary duties were a "more essential" service for the London citizenry. Warming to this theme, he then defied anyone to contest that he had not done his utmost "where the trade, liberty and franchises of the City were concerned," taking particular pride in his role as a militia captain, where he had "done his duty as an officer and a soldier." His protestation evidently struck a chord with the electorate, for he finished third in the poll, nearly 500 votes above fifth place. His victory speech again suggested his sensitivity to his critics, who had labeled him as either despotic or arbitrary in his principles. He remained defiant, however, insisting that his independence mirrored that of the City itself and that he remained loyal to a patriot minister and a patriot king.[39]

Although the poll had confirmed his standing in his London constituency, Beckford's subsequent speeches revealed that the pressures on his position were steadily growing and that his partnership with Pitt had not been an unalloyed boon to his interests. In particular, in the wake of the election renewed attacks were launched on the pervasive influence of the West Indian interest, sparked by continuing debate on the likely territorial settlement with France and the prospect of a war with Spain. The most notable of these assaults came in a September issue of the *London Chronicle*, in which a provincial correspondent argued for the retention of Guadeloupe as a means to lower sugar prices and defeat the schemes of monopolizing "overgrown sugar-planters." The article not only dwelt on economic arguments, but attacked the absentees for their influence in Britain, suggesting that the current sugar market "served only to mount several planters in gilded coaches." These riches permitted them to flit between Britain and the Caribbean as their extravagance dictated, only to "appear again in Old England as comets or blazing stars." If Beckford had any doubts about the target of such abuse, the author concluded that high sugar prices should be attributed to "the cunning management of our rich planters, the Jamaican planters in particular." Other critics vented their spleen against the number of West Indians absentees returned at the general election, and these pressures would grow while key questions regarding the fate of the American empire remained unresolved.[40]

While assailed for his Caribbean interests, Beckford faced growing political uncertainty on account of his alliance with Pitt. The new king's animus against Pitt was becoming more evident, particularly with the elevation of Bute as secretary of state on the eve of the general election, and it was increasingly hard to see how Pitt and the royal favorite could be reconciled. If Bute had ever seriously entertained a political accommodation with Beckford, there was little sign of any rapprochement in the wake of the election, and the Alderman did little to endear himself to the new court when the City welcomed the newly crowned king in September 1761. Although the City spent lavishly on the event, several observers remarked on a clash between Beckford and the king's steward, Lord Talbot, after the former refused to cede a place of honor at the celebratory banquet to the Knights of the Bath. Beckford reportedly "bullied" the master of ceremonies, reasoning that "it was hard to refuse a table to the City of London, whom it would cost £10,000 to banquet the King, and that his lordship would repent it, if they had not a table in the Hall." "This menace prevailed" in favor of the City and doubtless played well in civic circles, but it only served to highlight the increasing fragility of Beckford's position.[41]

The political storm finally broke the following month with Pitt's resignation from office, ostensibly over his failure to secure backing for a preemptive strike against Spain. Given their close political relationship over the previous four years, it was inevitable that this event would be seen as a devastating blow for Beckford, and the press response can be read as a summary of the successes and failures of the Alderman to date. Beckford's cause was not helped by the public letter of self-exculpation issued by Pitt within weeks of his resignation, *A Letter from a Right Honourable Person, to ——— in the City*, in which he offered the Alderman "sincere acknowledgements for all your kind friendship." Although not all opponents of the Spanish war were censorious of Beckford or saw his actions as determined by his political interests, his most bitter enemies delighted in his political confusion and sought to expose the self-interestedness of the absentee planters. Philip Francis was the most cutting critic, spuriously attempting to preserve the public pronouncements of Pitt and Beckford for posterity, lest they be "lost to remembrance, or be sent, in their newspapers, perhaps to Jamaica to exercise the criticism of sugar-planters, Negroes, and Creolians?" In some of the most direct personal attacks on Beckford to date, he sought to expose the unpatriotic nature of Beckford's position, even to the extent of highlighting the otherness of the Alderman's skin color:

> Then should creolian B———d, like himself,
> Start from the Canvas in his Native Hues,
> The bronze tartarean, and Jamaica Tint,
> Sun-burnt and deep enamell'd.

These personal reflections were a natural product of Beckford's political prominence at a time of intense factionalism, but they did little to deflect him from his current political path, even after his ally accepted a pension on exiting office. The attacks, however, did serve as a reminder that there were political costs to the advancement of the West India interest.[42]

Significantly, while Pitt had gone on public record to acknowledge his debt to Beckford's support, in private he demonstrated some hesitancy regarding their future political relationship. Pitt had gained much political capital as the darling of the City and as the champion of empire and commerce, and Beckford had played a key part in currying that favor. When Beckford pressed him to accept an invitation for a celebratory reception at the Guildhall in early November, however, Pitt expressed reservations to his immediate circle. He eventually relented, but Hester Pitt suggested that her husband regretted yielding to his friend's plea and that his acceptance proved "against his better judgment." The event passed peacefully, although critics sneered at the public demonstrations of support for the ousted minister and portrayed Beckford as reduced to the roll of cheerleader, having "visited several public-houses overnight" and then "appointed ringleaders to different stations, and had been the first to raise the huzza in the hall on the entrance of Mr. Pitt." The demonstrations did little to raise the immediate political stock of either Beckord or Pitt or to suggest that public support would be sufficient to lead them out of the political wilderness.[43]

Although both men faced a very uncertain political future, there could be no doubt that their political accommodation had facilitated the integration of the empire into British politics. Beckford personified all the turbulence of these changes, his national political standing having reached new heights and new lows. He had certainly established a strong metropolitan interest and had used it most effectively to win the favor of a leading minster. This partnership had proclaimed the common interests of mother country and

A LETTER from a Right Hon. Person, to —— in the City.

DEAR SIR,

FINDING, to my great Surprise, that the Cause and Manner of my resigning the Seals, is grosly misrepresented in the City, as well as that the most gracious and spontaneous Marks of his Majesty's Approbation of my Services, which Marks followed my Resignation, have been infamously traduced as a Bargain for my forsaking the Public, I am under a Necessity of declaring the Truth of both these Facts, in a Manner which I am sure no Gentleman will contradict; a Difference of Opinion with regard to Measures to be taken against Spain, of the highest Importance to the Honour of the Crown and to the most essential national Interests, (and this founded on what Spain had already done, not on what that Court may farther intend to do) was the Cause of my resigning the Seals. Lord TEMPLE and I submitted in Writing, and signed by us, our most humble Sentiments to his Majesty, which being over-ruled by the united Opinion of all the rest of the King's Servants, I resigned the Seals on Monday the 5th of this Month, in Order not to remain responsible for Measures, which I was no longer allowed to guide. Most gracious public Marks of his Majesty's Approbation of my Services followed my Resignation: They are unmerited and unsolicited, and I shall ever be proud to have received them from the best of Sovereigns.

I will now only add, my Dear Sir, that I have explained these Matters only for the Honour of Truth, not in any View to court Return of Confidence from any Man, who with a Credulity, as weak as it is injurious, has thought fit hastily to withdraw his good Opinion, from one who has served his Country with Fidelity and Success, and who justly reveres the upright and candid Judgment of it, little solicitous about the Censure of the capricious and the ungenerous. Accept my sincerest Acknowledgements for all your kind Friendship, and believe me ever, with Truth and Esteem,

My Dear Sir,
Your faithful Friend, &c.

COPY of the THANKS
TO THE
Right Hon. WILLIAM PITT,
FROM THE
Court of COMMON-COUNCIL,
October 22, 1761.

RESOLVED, That the Thanks of this Court be given to the Right Hon. WILLIAM PITT, for the many great and eminent Services rendered this Nation, during the Time he so ably filled the high and important Office of one of his Majesty's Principal Secretaries of State, and to perpetuate their grateful Sense of his Merits, who, by the Vigour of his Mind had not only rouzed the ancient Spirit of this Nation, from the pusillanimous State, to which it had been reduced; but, by his Integrity and Steadiness uniting us at Home, had carried its Reputation in Arms and Commerce to a Height unknown before, by our Trade accompanying our Conquests in every Quarter of the Globe.

Therefore the City of LONDON, ever stedfast in their Loyalty to their King, and attentive to the Honour and Prosperity of their Country, cannot but lament the national Loss of so able, so faithful, a Minister at this critical Conjuncture.

The ANSWER of the Right Hon. WILLIAM PITT, To the COMMON-COUNCIL.

MR. PITT requests of Sir JAMES HODGES, That he will be so good to represent him, in the most respectful Manner, to the Lord Mayor, Aldermen, and Commons of the City of LONDON, in Common Council assembled, and express his high Sense of the signal Honour which they have been pleased to confer on him, by their condescending and favourable Resolution of the 22d of October; an Honour which he receives with true Reverence and Gratitude, not without Confusion at his own small Deservings, while he views with Exultation the universal Public Spirit dispersed through an united People; and the matchless Intrepidity of the British Sailors and Soldiers, conducted by Officers, justly famed through all the Quarters of the World: To this Concurrence of national Virtue, graciously protected by the Throne, all the national Prosperities (under the Favour of Heaven) have been owing; and it will ever be remembered, to the Glory of the City of LONDON, that through the whole Course of this arduous War, that great Seat of Commerce has generously set the illustrious Example of steady Zeal for the Dignity of the Crown, and of unshaken Firmness and Magnanimity.

The REPRESENTATION of the Lord Mayor, Aldermen, and Commons of the City of LONDON, in Common-Council assembled, to Sir ROBERT LADBROKE, Knt. Sir RICHARD GLYN, Knt. and Bart. WILLIAM BECKFORD, Esq; and the Hon. THOMAS HARLEY, this City's Representatives in Parliament.

WE the Lord Mayor, Aldermen, and Commons of the City of LONDON, in Common-Council assembled, think it at this Time our Duty, as it is our natural and undoubted Right, to lay before you, this City's Representatives in the great Council of the Nation, soon to be assembled in Parliament, what we desire and expect from you, in Discharge of the great Trust and Confidence we and our Fellow Citizens have reposed in you.

That you take the earliest Opportunity to use your utmost Endeavours to obtain the Repeal or Amendment of the late Act, entitled, An Act for the Relief of Insolvent Debtors, in Respect of the Inconveniences arising from this Compulsive Clause, by which a Door has been opened to the greatest Frauds and Perjuries; and if continued, must become the Destruction of all private Credit, so essential to the Support of a Trading People.

That you concur in, and promote all necessary Measures for establishing that Œconomy in the Distribution of the national Treasure; and for that Purpose that you endeavour to have a Committee appointed, in Order to enquire into any Abuses, which may have arisen in the Application of it, and to prevent any Frauds or illicit Practices in the Management thereof.

That you entertain just Sentiments of the Importance of the Conquests made this War by the British Arms, at the Expence of so much Blood and Treasure; and that you will, to the utmost of your Power and Abilities, oppose all Attempts for giving up such Places, as may tend to lessen our present Security, or by restoring the naval Power of France, render us subject to fresh Hostilities from that natural Enemy; particularly that the sole and exclusive Right of our Acquisitions in North-America, and the Fisheries, be preserved to us.

As the present happy Extinction of Parties, the Harmony and Unanimity of all his Majesty's Subjects, their Zeal and Affection to their native King, and the great Increase of Commerce, are most convincing Proofs to us of this Nation's Ability, still to carry on, and vigorously prosecute, the present just and necessary War.—It is our Desire, that you concur in giving his Majesty such Supplies, as shall enable him to pursue all those Measures, which may promote the true Interest of his Kingdoms, and place him above the Menaces of any Power, that may pretend to give Laws, or prescribe Limits, to the Policy and Interests of this Nation. But as it is apparent, that our Enemies flatter themselves with the Hopes of exhausting our Treasure by the immense Expences, in which we are at present engaged—we therefore require you, in the further Prosecution of this War, to support such Measures, as may frustrate those Expectations; yet to act with the utmost Vigour, in the Reduction of their remaining Colonies, so as to obtain a safe and honourable Peace.

The resignation of William Pitt the Elder, broadside of 1761, depicting William Hoare's celebrated portrait of Pitt. The text includes Pitt's published letter to Beckford, explaining his reasons for resigning office. (British Museum, Chaloner Smith 93.1, © The Trustees of the British Museum) colonies in a global campaign against the French. Behind the scenes, Beckford had also helped to recast the organization and expectations of the West Indian interest to focus their energies on securing support from both ministers and the public. Perversely, the surest measure of their success lies with the opprobrium with which these campaigns were greeted, and their key challenge ahead was whether they could survive without their ministerial protector. Amid these battles for metropolitan recognition, the West Indians had developed a libertarian language of rights that resonated with the urban audiences Beckford had targeted, and they would continue to do so thanks to the common uncertainties facing the imperial polity in the 1760s. These integrative processes had helped to turn the Alderman into Alderman Sugarcane and to convince him that a common calamity would befall mother country and colonies if their mutual liberties and interests were not protected.

CHAPTER FIVE

The Friend of Liberty

When I talk of the sense of the people, I mean the middling people of England—the manufacturer, the yeoman, the merchant, the country gentleman—they who bear all the heat of the day and who pay all taxes to supply all the expenses of court and government. They have a right, Sir, to interfere in the condition and conduct of the nation . . . the people of England taken in this limitation are a good-natured, well-intentioned and very sensible people, who know better perhaps than other nations under the sun whether they are well-governed or not.

—Beckford's speech on the Address, 1761

Beckford's words are perhaps the most often quoted of any he uttered in his life and encapsulate for historians the importance of the 1760s for establishing his lasting reputation as a radical spokesman, as one of the first and most strident movers for parliamentary reform. In more recent studies, historians have been quick to identify him as a torchbearer for the views of the "people," a vision that encompassed a broad and ambiguous social canvas and excluded only the aristocracy and the poor. Few scholars, however, have sought to investigate how his conception of society was influenced by his Creole roots or Jamaican concerns, perspectives that help to explain why the absentee planter was so keen to align himself with the country gentleman and the industrious citizen among the ranks of the virtuous. In fact, Beckford's 1761 speech was in keeping with his outlook of some years and a reflection of his particular Anglo-Jamaican background. After 1761 his outlook was influenced by the domestic upheavals of the early years of George III, but his thinking and the ways in which it was perceived were still influenced by events overseas. In particular, although his radical ideas were clearly fashioned by his relations with his London constituents, and by such novelties as John Wilkes, his conception of rights and liberties continued to be determined by transatlantic events.[1]

In this chapter I will examine some of the most tempestuous experiences of Beckford's career. Having enjoyed privileged political access via his association with Pitt, he had to relearn the political ropes as an outsider after Pitt's resignation, and his status as a self-proclaimed colonial spokesman was severely tested as the empire reached an unprecedented point of crisis. Controversial legislation, most notably the Sugar Act, the Stamp Act, and the Townshend duties, put him on his political mettle to reconcile metropolitan and domestic interests, and forced major rethinking within the West India interest regarding both principle and strategy. Moreover, beyond these headline policies, renewed battles between the Jamaica assembly and its island governor also focused his energies on key questions of right and liberty. His success in arbitrating between metropolitan and Caribbean authorities was a significant achievement, although he could not persuade North American interests to share his imperial vision. He also found severe disappointment when elevated to a new prominence as a frontline figure in the ill-fated Chatham administration of 1766–68, and as a leading spokesman for London he struggled to contend with the Wilkite agitation. These various challenges had a significant impact on his political outlook, and the near constant interplay of domestic and colonial forces forced him to define his position on key constitutional issues. This was most clearly highlighted by his experience at the 1768 election, during which he was forced to confront the complex connections between liberty and empire.[2]

His spirited speech on the Address on 13 November 1761 demonstrated that Beckford was determined to ensure that the achievements of the war were not squandered by Pitt's successors. If he harbored any misgivings amid the aftershocks of his friend's resignation, they were brushed aside in a tirade that called for an all-out war with the Spanish. The message might have been familiar, but his reasoning suggested alternative avenues of political interest in the absence of the favor of a leading minister. The House would have been little surprised by his vehement denunciation of the proud Spanish, or by his allusion to recent outrages committed by the Spanish to British shipping, which were clearly designed to stir up the same patriotic indignation that had led to war in 1739. Exhibiting a characteristic aversion to temporizing, he saw an expansion of conflict as unavoidable, for "you must speak to them out of the mouths of a cannon, sword in hand . . . pen and ink will never do any good." In contrast, the direct appeal to the middling sort in a Commons speech was unusual and suggested an increasing belligerence toward the noble factions he held responsible for the ouster of Pitt, and who now placed the gains of war in jeopardy. Significantly, the speech echoed warm praise for the new king, who was commended for the recent Civil List Act and who, "if he will trust his people like Queen Elizabeth[,] he may govern like her, and not by a faction." The general appeal to the people resonated with his attempts to gain popularity in the City over the previous decade and anticipated an even closer relationship with the populace in the years ahead. He was careful not to align himself with "the mob," however, and insisted, "I am sure that it is the general sense of the people that we should have a Spanish war."[3]

The appeal to the public was as much an act of political necessity as it was one calculated to accord with Beckford's principles. With Pitt's resignation still generating numerous column inches, Beckford could not go on the political defensive, and his interventions in the 1761–62 session tried to highlight the deficiencies of the Newcastle administration by contrast to Pitt's prior leadership. In a speech of December 1761, he sought to expose the indecisiveness of the ministry by drawing attention to the conflicting character of reports regarding Britain's relations with Spain. Hoping to expose ministerial divisions, he concluded that "he did not know who were the ministers, nor whether we had a single minister, or a minister depute. It was necessary to have one minister." George Grenville, who was destined to become a political foil for the rest of the decade, taunted him back by observing that "Prime Minister was an odious title," hoping thereby to expose the Alderman to charges of tyranny. Rifts within the opposition were all too evident, and Beckford was called into the defense of former minister Pitt after the latter was bitterly attacked by Isaac Barré for resigning. Recalling their common service in the defense of the colonies, and Barré's own service in Canada, Pitt turned to Beckford to ask rhetorically, "How far the scalping Indians cast their tomahawks?" The subsequent declaration of war with Spain in January 1762 might have brought the allies some political satisfaction, but the resultant escalation of warfare only intensified the battle for supremacy in the Caribbean by encompassing all three major powers in the region.[4]

Beckford had been accustomed to political attacks on his status as a colonial politician since his anointment as Alderman Sugarcane in 1757, but nothing could have prepared him for the virulence of the press in the spring and summer of 1762, as critics of Pitt sought to expose the supposed patriotism of Pittite imperial policies. These diatribes were fueled by continuing speculation on the final form of the European peace and also reflected the increasing importance of the Caribbean as a military theater during the final stages of the war. They were also an acknowledgment that the Alderman represented a still-potent political force, even though out of favor, and he was duly used as a punching bag by those who wished to question the longer-term value of the American colonies. In March 1762 the *London Chronicle* led the way with a searing attack on the leading absentee planters of Jamaica, "whose presence and example [there] in this time of great danger might contribute to preserve that island." The usually apolitical *Gentleman's Magazine* also helped to feed these flames the following month by highlighting the weakness of Jamaica. Keen to stem any doubts in the mind of his most important ally, on 24 April Beckford gave Pitt a very full account of the military readiness of Jamaica, stressing that all the news from the island was "agreeable." He also echoed the sentiments he had aired in the Commons by commending Pitt's "firmness and decision, the only means to make a kingdom great. These qualities are amazingly deficient at present."[5]

The continuing instability of the Newcastle administration was fueled by the influence of the king's favorite Lord Bute, but the duke's departure in May did little to quiet Westminster. The opening salvos of the Spanish war had been indecisive, and the duke's resignation removed one of the genuine political heavyweights who might have brought some ballast to a Bute-led ministry. Although Beckford had little sympathy for Newcastle's stance on the payment of Prussian subsidies, he remained concerned by the rudderless direction of government policy. A fortnight before Newcastle's fall, when arguing that Spain should be attacked by land, he proclaimed that the City "suspected the ministry of wavering, and demanded to have their old minister again." While Bute retained the king's favor, it was unlikely that Pitt would seek any accommodation that might bring him back into the ministry, and Beckford found further cause for discomfort from growing attacks on the self-interestedness of the West Indians. Horace Walpole summed up the feelings of many of Beckford's critics at this time in a withering critique of the pervasiveness of imperial greed: "Beckford is a patriot, because he will clamour if Guadeloupe or Martinico is given up, and the price of sugars fall. I am a bad Englishman, because I think the advantages of commerce are dearly bought for some, by the lives of many more." Cracks also appeared in the ranks of the West Indians themselves, with accusations that Beckford's friendship with Pitt should be blamed for "the little regard to the extension of our sugar colonies." As yet another summer of global campaigning opened, these war-weary pronouncements became increasingly common, and they were more pointedly aimed at the Alderman, especially as he was next in line for the mayoralty of London.[6]

The torrent of abuse Beckford faced over the summer of 1762 was sparked by the *Monitor*'s attempts to justify peace proposals so clearly favorable to his interests. These attacks on Beckford steered discussion of the planter interest in new directions, particularly by taking issue with the libertarian rhetoric Beckford and his colonial allies had employed in past battles with metropolitan authorities. The *Monitor* had been wary of openly defending Jamaica for fear of cries of self-interest, but the various peace proposals it advanced, such as the retention of Canada over Guadeloupe, were quickly interpreted as a sop to the sugar interest. A onetime resident of Jamaica, and Bute's hired pen, Tobias Smollett, took delight in satirizing Beckford's pretension to statesmanship in a series of articles in the *Briton*. Smollett sought to undermine Beckford's credentials to patriotism by taking particular issue with his attack on Grenville's proposed additional excise on spirits, sarcastically titling him as "that eminent patriot of the plantations, so much admired for his eloquence, so warmly beloved for his liberality." The *Auditor* went much further, seeking to besmirch Beckford's ancestry and making an explicit connection between the political principles of the planter class and the Alderman's likely stewardship as mayor. It even alluded to the planters' propensity to call their slaves by the names of Roman emperors and asked, "What regard is that person like to have for the ordinances, appointments, and prerogative of a King, who has had in his own country black princes for his menial servants, and princesses for his concubines?" Warming to this theme, the tirade recalled that "so many creoles" had been recently elected to the Westminster Parliament, and envisioned MPs returned for Kingston and Spanish Town too, and "then shall the sugar-cane triumph over the hop-pole, and barbecued hog over the roast-beef of the English." Even the renewed burst of global military success in the summer of 1762, with the seizures of Havana and Manila, could not stop the torrent of invective coming Beckford's way. The Alderman could not escape the public eye, and in September, Smollett's pen transformed Alderman Sugarcane into Alderman Rumford, bent on self-aggrandizement and willing to sell out his allies in the hope of gaining a title from the ministry.[7]

Beckford was clearly wilting under the multiplicity of these onslaughts and the sheer weight of business on his hands. In a significant move, he was prepared to give up his county militia office, confiding to his commanding officer Lord Bruce, "Your lordship is sensible of my present situation and how difficult it is for one man to appear in several different capacities." Although taking great pride in his three years as a Wiltshire militia captain, he confessed that "City affairs hang heavy on my mind" and stepped down from office in preparation for his term as mayor. Although reluctant to undertake militia service, he continued to perform political duties by acting as host to Pitt and Lord Temple at a rebuilt Fonthill. These visits confirmed the Alderman's political loyalties despite the current pressures he faced in opposition and can be seen as fulfilment of the purpose of Beckford's magnificent new home. Ill health and the prospect of a return to the hurly-burly of London politics cannot have raised his spirits as he contemplated the mayoralty, but he also recognized that in the current political situation the City remained a most promising political platform for the defense of his cherished causes.[8]

As his elevation to the mayoralty drew near, Beckford faced further attacks, including one of the most memorable of all, plate 1 of William Hogarth's *The Times*. In this pro-Bute masterpiece, Beckford has been identified as one of the aldermen paying homage to Pitt as the former minister seeks to fan the flames of global war to frustrate the ministry's attempts to bring it under control. Hogarth wonderfully captured the administration's claim that no conquest would be sufficient to satisfy the wild imperial dreams of the likes of Beckford and Pitt, which military success had only bolstered. For all this vilification, however, the ministry could not stop Beckford's election as mayor on Michaelmas Day. Several accounts suggested that Beckford had firmly resolved not to take the chair, but he relented in response to a huge Guildhall ovation and the resounding support of the court of aldermen. He then issued a defiant speech, taking the opportunity to defend the sincerity of his intentions as the City's leading magistrate. Significantly, he was careful not to appear the outsider, and he laid great store on his family's London connections to reassure the citizens that they could trust him as their leader, proudly proclaiming "that he had also the highest veneration for the name of citizen; that his family were citizens; that some of them had borne the highest offices for a century past." As his forebears had done for a nearly a century, he turned to the City in his hour and need, and he expressed gratitude for its vital support and endorsement. His opponents were more prepared to credit the influence of Pitt behind his election, but Beckford knew that the true success of his mayoralty would rest on the accommodation of interests in both the City and the west end of town.[9]

Beckford's subsequent actions demonstrated that he was willing to take the fight to his opponents and to use the mayoralty to maximize his political impact. With an established reputation for magnificence, he would be hard pressed to live up to expectations, and the press eagerly anticipated the lavishness of his inauguration on 8 November. Conscious of the need to perform to traditional expectations, he was inducted to office with all due solemnity and no expense spared, capped by a "magnificent entertainment" at the

William Hogarth, *The Times*, Plate 1. Hogarth's work is a bitter attack of September 1762 on the bellicosity of William Pitt, who is represented on the right as Henry VIII on stilts, using bellows to encourage the flames engulfing the globe. Beckford has been identified as one of the aldermanic figures at his feet, urging Pitt onward. (© National Portrait Gallery, London, NPG, D21366)

Mansion House. The inaugural ball was seized by Beckford as an opportunity to garner political capital at both ends of town, and the guest list included first minister Lord Bute and Lord Chancellor Henley. Pitt was a conspicuous absentee, but Beckford could count on older friends, such as Lords Mansfield and Effingham. The presence of ministers did incur risks, for he had had to defend himself from charges of neglecting magisterial duty in favor of national politics before, but the ball signaled that Beckford felt no irreconcilable tension between the City and his country. His opponents were ready to exploit such conflict of interests, and one report took delight in noting that the presence of so many peers, judges, and "first-rank" gentlemen relegated some aldermen to the swordbearers' table. This represented a stark reversal of the order of precedence Beckford had upheld at the royal entertainment a year before, and his critics were only too happy to drive a wedge between his power bases in the City and Westminster. If he could reconcile them, the prospects for his wider interests would improve significantly, but it would take enormous energy and test even his resources.[10]

If he was in any doubt of this, Smollett's attack in the *Briton* of 13 November would have cured him of complacency. Perhaps mindful of Beckford's fondness for Roman history, Smollett seized the mayor's inauguration as an opportunity to vilify London's pretensions as a commentator on Britain's global preeminence, asking, "Why should not Augusta [London] bear the same pre-eminence in Britain that Rome bore in Italy, and the *London Empire* be substituted in the room of *the kingdom of Great Britain!*" The new mayor was proclaimed as "the first prime minister of the *London empire*," and Smollett went on to caricature Beckford as the would-be despot of both ends of the metropolis, who would rule the City by appeasing the London masses. Taking the critique of Beckford to a new level of personal invective, he also explicitly linked his Jamaican background to his political principles:

> It is well known that he was born to empire, to immense property, acquired without fraud or extortion, and handed down to him from a long line of illustrious progenitors: that he suckled ideas of government from the breast of his nurse, who was a blackamoor Princess, the daughter of an African Caboceiro, and along with these a disposition to benevolence and humanity: that from his tender years he hath been accustomed to the exercise of absolute dominion, over some thousands of his fellow-creatures; and that, by dint of experience, he hath learned that form of rule which is best calculated to restrain the enormities of human nature.

Some of these charges hit very close to home, echoing the laments of his family's debtors or political rivals, and may even have been gleaned by the writer when both men were on the island in the early 1740s. Whatever their accuracy, Smollett broke new ground by making such a clear link between plantation life and Britain's current political predicament, between the imperial experience of slavery and Britain's pretensions to liberty. On the eve of peace, Smollett had thus highlighted how Beckford symbolized the common metropolitan and colonial challenges facing their generation.[11]

The agreement of peace preliminaries in Paris in November 1762 ensured that the ensuing parliamentary session was dominated by the questions of territorial settlement, and all political commentators knew that it would be a critical test of the ministry's strength. With the first draft of the peace earmarking the captured West Indian islands as trading chips to be exchanged for continental American gains, most politicians expected Pitt and Beckford to claim a sellout of British interests. Lord Hardwicke was bullish at this prospect, observing that, apart "from the interested or wild part of the City of London," the nation wanted peace at all costs and that it was "so tired of the leading of Mr. Pitt and the violence of his friend Beckford." When criticism of the preliminaries duly came on the first day of the session, however, Newcastle reported that "Beckford was never so heard in his life," and the mayor continued to contest the longer-term value of the ceded territories. In a bitter, "very personal" exchange with Townshend on 9 December, which saw the first major debate on the preliminaries, Beckford "compared Florida, which was to be ceded to us, for barrenness to Bagshot Heath." As part of a move to refer the preliminaries to a committee of the whole House, he likened the Commons to the Paris Parlement if it could not advise on treaties, and censured the ministry for suggesting that it was the king's prerogative to make peace and war. Nonetheless, in a war-weary Westminster, the best efforts of Pitt and Beckford could do little to halt the peace process. Although the *Monitor* sought to expose the overgenerous and dangerous nature of the terms, the peace was formally signed on 10 February 1763.[12]

The coming of peace inevitably posed questions regarding Beckford's political standing and direction, and the indecisiveness of his ally Pitt at this juncture left him at an uncertain crossroads. The debate on the peace had earned the lord mayor unprecedented political attention, much of it unwanted, and there was much political speculation that he would seek new alliances. Rumors spread of his possible swing toward Bute, perhaps fueled by the first minister's attendance at Beckford's inaugural ball. The *North Briton* of John Wilkes hinted at this rapprochement by suggesting that Beckford might have done more to halt the peace, criticizing him for a lack of leadership in failing to muster an address from the common council.[13]

This speculation was encouraged by Beckford's less conspicuous political profile in the early months of 1763. It is clear that the demanding role of lord mayor consumed much of his energies, but he may also have welcomed civic opportunities to bolster his reputation after the savageness of recent attacks. This personal rehabilitation was achieved by acting as the epitome of magisterial virtue, protecting the weak, and standing up for liberty and justice. His supporters ascribed the moderate price of both bread and sugar to his paternal oversight, and his actions as a magistrate bespoke his humanity and learning. True to previous form, he was also widely celebrated for his City entertainments. A family friend paid tribute to his success as a host, reporting to Hester Pitt that the Beckfords' hospitality "eclipses all other lord mayors and lady mayoresses in the memory of the present generation," singling out their monthly assemblies at the Mansion House as the venue for many west-enders. As a result, their "magnificence and affability has gained universal applause," although this was achieved only through "a constant round of fatigue of feastings and visits." In the wake of bitter denunciations of Beckford as an unprincipled and uncivilized despot, such liberality and attention to duty were necessary to consolidate his City standing in preparation for a time when Pitt might contemplate a return to national politics.[14]

The continued turbulence surrounding the court gave Pitt and Beckford every hope of a sudden turnabout in their political affairs. The resignation of Bute in the face of universal criticism in April 1763 opened the door for the Grenville administration, but suspicions surrounding the continuing influence of Bute at court gave the ministry little confidence. In the late summer, Beckford acted as go-between for Bute and Pitt about setting up a meeting to discuss the terms of a possible accommodation, which would see the latter return as first minister. These overtures came to nothing, although they proved that the Pitt-Beckford alliance still held firm in opposition and also indicated Beckford's willingness to consider new associations. In contrast, he refrained from playing a leading role in the growing controversy over the arrest of John Wilkes for seditious libel, even though the journalist's supporters championed him as an opponent of "every measure that has appeared inconsistent with the liberty of the press and a free people." The mayor's critics were quick to align him with the populist firebrand, and one caricaturist even depicted a black-faced Beckford rushing to embrace Wilkes. His *politique* stance as mayor was confirmed in the autumn by the speech he gave on leaving the chair, however. He used the occasion to call for moderation at critical times, exhorting London to show its "old good humour and good sense" as an example to other subjects, who lived under "the best of Kings." In a heartfelt oration, he also took the occasion to outline a broader political testament, stressing that "the study of my life" had been "to support the honour and dignity of the crown, liberty and constitutional independency of the people, and the rights and privileges of my fellow citizens, always keeping in remembrance that noble declaration of the great Revolution patriots: that under the House of Hanover only they could, and under the House of Hanover they were determined they would be free." Readers of the *Monitor* could not mistake this political credo, but his decision to reaffirm his principles before the London citizenry suggested that he was still smarting from recent attacks. In a still-fluid political environment, few could predict into which camp these principles would lead him.[15]

The accommodating tone of his mayoralty soon altered in the parliamentary session of 1763–64, and he was quick to censure the ministry on its record during its first few months of office. His dissatisfaction with the peace was evident in his response to the Address, for which he was identified as "the most violent of the opposition." In direct opposition to the ministerial line, he saw no longer-term benefit or security in the settlement, claiming that "the French, as they dismantled the fortifications at Dunkirk, were numbering the stones, so that they might be quickly reassembled." Even a colonial visitor to the House was shocked by Beckford's challenge that the peace was "inglorious and inadequate to our successes, words directly contradictory of those made use of in the [royal] speech," and by Beckford's characterization of the ministry as "incapable of governing, ignorant of geography, arbitrary and despotic." These last sentiments also presaged Beckford's sustained attack on the ministry for its treatment of John Wilkes, who had fought a successful campaign to expose the tyranny inherent in the general warrant issued to silence him. Even before the speech on the Address, Beckford had backed a pro-Wilkite motion to hear questions of parliamentary privilege straightaway, and it soon became clear that Beckford regarded the libertine journalist as deserving of his support for the libertarian issues his case raised. In December he contacted Wilkes and appeared to offer genuine sympathy for his suffering "under the oppression of your enemies." Further warmth was suggested by his jest that the House's "humane" treatment might not be a good sign, observing that "the pagans of old made it part of their religion to pamper high so as to render fat and fair all victims doomed to slaughter and sacrifice." Nonetheless, he promised to call Wilkes "amicum meam" when his case was moved in Parliament, and he stayed true to his word, ultimately gaining the thanks of the London common council in February 1764 for his efforts (alongside the other London MPs) in procuring a parliamentary resolution against the legality of general warrants.[16]

Although Beckford had been a victim of Wilkes's caustic pen, such support could have been anticipated. Wilkes had written in support of Pittite causes for some six years, and his critique of ministerial power fitted neatly with the Anglo-Jamaican political principles Beckford had enunciated with increasing force since the later 1750s. His steadfastness to Wilkes, however, imperiled his relationship with Pitt, who launched into a bitter denunciation of Wilkes's principles early in that session. Beckford's actions gave sufficient alarm for Lord Temple to inform Pitt that the Alderman had written "a very kind and very strong letter to Wilkes, which indicates much dissatisfaction on his part." Harsher critics would see such support only as confirmation of Beckford's demagogic tendencies and as proof that the Alderman had gone in search of a populist London hero to replace Pitt, his wartime muse. Beckford's outspoken support certainly threatened to jeopardize his political alliances in the west end of town, even though those in opposition could enjoy the discomfort of the ministry for its mishandling of the crisis. An open rift was averted on this occasion, and their differences over Wilkes were accommodated in a common language of patriotism and liberties. As Beckford confided to Pitt in 1763, "Although I sometimes differ with you in opinion on certain points, that difference never was of long duration." He still perceived "nothing but anarchy and confusion" in another turbulent year and saw Pitt as the politician to supply "the panacea to our sickly constitution."[17]

In the immediate aftermath of the general warrants affair, however, Beckford did not feature as a frontline opposition spokesman, a somewhat surprising political reticence given his earlier denunciations of the Grenville administration. This relative silence might be linked to his differences with Pitt, but a more likely explanation lies with the Alderman's health and the pressing nature of his private affairs. In his letter to Wilkes the preceding

December, Beckford had hinted at continuing infirmities, promising support in Parliament "if I am alive and able." More intriguingly, it also appears that Beckford had definite plans to visit the Caribbean for the first time in fourteen years, with Lord Temple reporting that he "meditates on a voyage to Jamaica in the spring [of 1764]." Newspaper reports also appeared in that vein, suggesting that he planned "to visit his large estates in that island." Ill health may well have put an end to this scheduled trip, but the seriousness of his intent was represented by Beckford himself in late 1764 when he hoped to have "an opportunity of seeing the vessel that is to carry me to Jamaica." As the next chapter will show, at this juncture Beckford was undertaking a major review of his business affairs, and he may well have intended to survey his plantations, including important recent acquisitions. He would also have not missed opportunities to assess the broader political and economic health of the colony in the aftermath of wartime upheaval, slave rebellions, and much internal factionalism. Since the arrival of Governor Lyttelton on the island in December 1761 a political accord had largely held, and there was no immediate crisis to which Beckford might attend. Nonetheless, he had not lost sight of the importance of his colonial powerbase for his transatlantic interest, however much political capital he might have garnered on the island on account of his metropolitan activities over the last decade. His willingness to contemplate an Atlantic crossing in his mid-fifties suggests that he did not regard the ocean as an obstacle to the management of his far-flung personal empire.[18]

This last Jamaican trip was destined never to happen, although colonial preoccupations steered him back to the political limelight and may well have argued for his continued presence in the capital. In the course of 1764, the Grenville administration famously began to roll out a program of major colonial reforms that were to ignite the empire, leading ultimately to the secession of the thirteen continental colonies. Recent research, led by Andrew O'Shaughnessy and Jack Greene, has highlighted how issues of taxation and representation reverberated throughout the continental and Caribbean colonies, where the island assemblies chorused the same resentment that cherished liberties were threatened and that metropolitan innovations would destabilize an empire whose success had been built on a common respect for interests and rights. These battles were to dominate the remaining years of Beckford's life and bring him understandable anguish as he feared the ruin of both colonies and mother country. The ultimate loss of the North American colonies might highlight the dysfunctional nature of imperial relationships, but in the 1760s the London-based West Indians continued to play an active part in healing such rifts, often in a most effective manner. Beckford's role as a recognized spokesman for Britain's richest Atlantic colony has particular interest for understanding the working of imperial networks at this time. Furthermore, his stubborn defense of colonial rights since the 1750s render his interventions particularly significant, especially when they converged with the preoccupations of a nascent metropolitan radicalism. More important, these critical debates were not only fired by metropolitan events and directives but were also vitally influenced by continued turbulence within the islands, placing even more responsibility on London agents to act as efficient brokers of imperial interests.[19]

The Sugar Act passed in spring 1764 has been long regarded as an imperial watershed, representing an increased determination by the metropolitan government to regulate colonial trade and to extract more imperial revenue. The measure did not open a gulf between ministers and the Jamaican interest, however. Metropolitan regulation had always been regarded with caution by Caribbean interests, but Grenville's first major initiative in the field of imperial revenue offered them much encouragement. Some critics rightly argued that it favored the West Indian planters over the North Americans by raising duties on the import of foreign-produced sugars in the American market. Foreign-produced rum imports were also banned, although this was balanced by the halving of import duty on foreign molasses. The West Indians managed to prevent this last duty from falling even further, but with tighter customs controls they could hope to profit from a measure that might more generally undermine the covert trade between their foreign rivals in the Caribbean and the American mainland. Having sought to expose this clandestine commerce for many years, Beckford and his allies could derive much satisfaction from the act.[20]

At this key juncture Beckford's spur to metropolitan action on behalf of Jamaica came from a more familiar direction, in the form of another standoff between the island assembly and the governor. Since his arrival in Jamaica in late 1761, William Henry Lyttelton had shown considerable skill in avoiding open rifts between the islanders and the royal government and had even prevented a clash between the assembly and the council over the choice of the colonial agent in 1764. On this occasion, Stephen Fuller finally prevailed to succeed Lovell Stanhope, having this time secured the support of "all the

principal gentlemen that have property in Jamaica residing here [in Britain]."
By December of that year, however, Lyttelton had been forced to dissolve
the assembly after it had made a constitutional stand on the freedom of its
members from arrest during session. Fuller was left in no doubt of the stakes
in this contest when contacted by the island's committee of correspondence,
who argued that "schemes are forming against us in the mother country,
which if executed will strip us of our birthright as Britons." A newly elected
assembly was just as unrepentant and obdurate when it sat in March 1765 and
made new demands on the governor to expunge offensive decisions from the
records of the Jamaican Chancery. With the Privy Council choosing to back
the governor soon afterward, the battle was fully joined, and politicians on
both sides of the Atlantic geared themselves for a protracted campaign whose
significance ranked alongside that of the Knowles affair.[21]

    This controversy galvanized Beckford as a regular critic of the ministry
in the Commons, where he sought every opportunity to defend colonial
interests or to highlight potential threats to Britain's imperial superiority
from their European rivals. He showed characteristic colonial belligerence in
response to the king's speech on 10 January 1765 by denouncing any attempt
by the Spanish to renege on their pledge to repay Britain's costs for preserving
Manila from pillage in the previous war. Less than a fortnight later he crossed
swords with Charles Townshend in a debate on the standing army by
defending the freedom of the colonies from billeting. "In his boisterous
[West] Indian style," Beckford insisted that the American colonies were
entitled to greater freedoms than Ireland since they had not been conquered
and furiously rejected Townshend's rejoinder as a "diarrhoea of words."
This colonial claim to the status of a free people resonated strongly with the
white Jamaicans, and the Alderman continued to defend the inherent rights
of the colonists. When the notorious Stamp Act was first moved in the House
the following month, Beckford distinguished himself among its opponents
by being the "only" speaker who "seemed to deny the Authority of
Parliament" to pass such a measure. Ireland's colonial status also featured
when Beckford sought to block the bill by proposing that the measure should
be a preliminary to British taxation of Ireland, doubtless hoping that this
would weigh the bill down and spark wider protests. Even Beckford's critics
conceded that this strategy was "not altogether ill-conceived," but the plan
"was so very unably and miserably executed, that instead of creating terror,
it was productive of nothing but a great deal of laughter." Undeterred,

Beckford continued to oppose the direct imperial tax and gained recognition on both sides of the Atlantic as the only spokesman to broach the issue of fundamental rights. The Alderman's singular stand on the measure soon earned him the mantle of the transatlantic friend of liberty, with verses chorusing as early as March 1765:

> In Freedom's cause, around thy banner stand;
> And a few Beckfords save a sinking land.

His isolated stance proved in vain when opposed by a ministry determined to reform the revenue and management of the empire.[22]

In contrast to Beckford, general West Indian resistance to the Stamp Act was half-hearted and incoherent, although there can be no doubt of the animus of the islands against the measure, which fell more heavily on the Caribbean than on the northern colonies. O'Shaughnessy has shown that there were manifold reasons why the West Indians did not protest as strongly as the North Americans at this juncture, even though the islanders were just as sensitive to their rights of taxation as any in the north or in Britain itself. In the immediate postwar period Jamaica and the other islands were keen to appease the metropolitan authorities amid continuing uncertainties over possible foreign reprisals or further slave rebellions. These political realities were not lost on metropolitan spokesmen such as Beckford and even gave heart to a beleaguered Governor Lyttelton, who received assurances from his noble brother in London that the leading absentees, including Beckford and the Fullers, were censorious of the Jamaica assembly for their "late extravagant behaviour." The governor was even given hope that "the receipt of letters from England will bring them to their senses." This optimism proved largely ill founded, but the acquiescence of the Caribbean to the Stamp Act signaled the readiness of planter leaders and absentees to preserve bridges with the government.[23]

Although understandably wary of all metropolitan politicians in a still-fluid political arena, the London West Indians may also have been biding their time, sensing that the increasing travails of the Grenville ministry might soon see a swift change of both administration and policy. Jamaican agents had often complained of the fickleness of metropolitan politics and of how island affairs suffered "alterations as the time and the state of parties might subject us to," but the general turbulence of Westminster could work to their advantage in the short term. The furor caused by the North Americans and their allies might have heaped pressure on the administration, but it was Grenville's loss of the king's support, confirmed by his poor handling of the regency crisis in the spring, which led to his ouster in July. Beckford had again been conspicuous as one of the few to openly oppose Grenville's regency bill, but his spirits would not have been lifted by the subsequent appointment of the Rockingham ministry, which represented the rump of the Newcastle faction. His relations with the duke had always been cool, and his loyalties still remained with Pitt, whose return to office was now blocked by Newcastle. With close connections to several Atlantic interests, however, the young Marquess of Rockingham might prove more open to overtures from colonial representatives.[24]

Battle was rejoined on the Stamp Act in December 1765, and Beckford was immediately to the fore as a proponent of its repeal, "severely" treating the anti-repealer Richard Rigby for moving for the submission of all papers sent to the colonies since the passage of the Stamp Act. The following month saw the Alderman working for immediate repeal alongside a revitalized Pitt in the Commons, perhaps sensing equivocation behind the ministry's expressed sympathy for the colonists. He again crossed swords with Grenville in a "bitter" exchange in February, when the author of the tax moved for the government to enforce the law in America. His efforts were rewarded with the repeal in March, although the passage of the Declaratory Act suggested that the British Parliament still regarded itself as the master of the colonies. Pitt's famed outburst in April, in which he spoke up for colonial rights of self-government while stressing the power of Parliament to regulate its commerce, remained a lone voice among the metropolitan grandees, and subsequent ministerial policy only emphasized that the repeal had done little to change British views on the rights of America.[25]

Just as worryingly for colonial politicians, the subsequent debate on the establishment of free ports in the Caribbean again highlighted the potential gulf between the West Indians and the North Americans. In the spring of 1766 Beckford was active in mustering resources and information for the "managers of the sugar island interest," believing that they had a "right" to be heard on matters so directly pertaining to their future. He was in favor of postponing the matter until the next session, declaiming to Pitt that the proposal to relax the navigation laws had opened up "a vast field . . . of more consequence than our wisest ministers are aware of." This conviction resulted in Beckford flooding MPs with paper, and he was reported to have "treated the House of Commons every day this week, and I may say, until night too" with evidence pertaining to Caribbean commerce. Pitt was initially prepared to back his stance, but the failure of the North Americans to do likewise elicited much comment. Beckford himself was seen to be "prejudiced . . . in favour of his own particular system," which exposed how "there are frequently distinct interests between the Islands and North America." These divisions were critical in ensuring that the West Indians could not stop the bill, and more moderate counsels prevailed to secure a new scheme which was more amenable to interests of the North Americans and the West Indians. On this occasion Pitt proved himself a less dependable ally, but Beckford could take some comfort from the fact Pitt appeared politically engaged and perhaps ready to challenge the Rockingham ministry. Amid these debates Beckford had expressed concern that the removal of the Pitt family home from Hayes to Burton Pynsent was a possible sign of his ailing leader's retirement and lamented, "Is the interest of these kingdoms to be considered in the deeps of Somersetshire?" Horace Walpole thought that there was little chance of this and interpreted Pitt's stance on the free ports as one designed "to humour Beckford's local interests and his own spleen to the ministers." This verdict was ultimately vindicated when Pitt accepted the seals of office in July, and by that time Beckford had gained further encouragement by a successful resolution to the Lyttelton affair.[26]

In contrast to the stormy debates that had raged around the Stamp and Free Port Acts in 1765–66, the standoff between the Jamaican governor and the islanders had been maintained with fewer dramatic incidents. The island assembly had settled into a "sullen defiance" of Lyttelton, and the metropolitan politicians were probably too preoccupied to risk another constitutional battle. Growing impatience with London can be detected in the conciliatory petition of the grand jury of the Jamaican county of Middlesex, which observed to Lyttelton in February 1766, "It is our peculiar infelicity in this colony to be at so great a distance from our mother country that our cries are too long in reaching it and often too feebly heard." Their "faithful and artless" attempt to reach some form of accommodation found Lyttelton in no mood to compromise, and both sides looked to the metropolis to break the deadlock. In a significant move, the absentees formally asked Southern Secretary Henry Seymour Conway not to broach the matter in Parliament and to instead seek arbitration through the Privy Council. This request betrayed their reading of the mood of the Commons, for they clearly expected MPs to be unsympathetic to their fundamental rights. For certain, the Lyttelton affair had encouraged the assemblymen to develop their thinking on the legal basis of their rights, and they now believed their privileges to be inherent and not dependent on royal authority. They did not air those views in public, and it is unclear whether the absentees in London shared their principles, but neither group could doubt their explosive potential in any metropolitan forum at this juncture. Even without this constitutional red rag, the absentees were doubtless grateful when the Crown granted permission for the Lyttleton affair to be heard at the Privy Council in May, where once again Beckford and the Fullers represented the islanders. A satisfactory compromise duly emerged, with the immunities of the assemblymen respected and the island treasury's shortfalls refunded. A weary Lyttelton could leave the island, to be succeeded by a respected Jamaican, Roger Hope Elletson. Both sides retained deep resentments, however, and the London-based absentees continued to work hard to keep transatlantic relations on an even keel.[27]

The prospect of ally Pitt back at the helm of government doubtless boosted Beckford's spirits, and he probably had both colonial and domestic matters in mind when he expressed hopes that the first minister would "settle and establish the constitution of your country on a solid and firm basis." He was even prepared to accept the news that the Great Commoner was to take a peerage, although some reservation might be detected in his caveat, "If you are to be the head statesman, I am content." Recent events at home and in the colonies clearly troubled him, however, and the following month he painted a much bleaker picture of the nation's predicament, warning the newly elevated Lord Chatham "not to be moved at the virulent and rancorous abuse of certain pseudo-patriots: we live in *Faece Romuli*, where self-interest and ingratitude are fashionable." Classical allusions to an era of civil discord would remain a recurrent theme of his correspondence with Chatham for the rest of his life, and Beckford's trepidation can be linked to the prospect of facing major battles without the minister's inspirational presence in the Commons. Even during this summer recess, Beckford was already suffering the renewed scrutiny of London writers, whose personal attacks were angrily dismissed as written "with virulence and rancour." He took special exception to rumors of his own elevation to the peerage, observing, "I should be as much ashamed of a title as of a fool's coat; I can never deserve such honour." Reports of "the sugarcane peerage" even reached the Caribbean, but Beckford remained resolute, insisting to a close ally that "I have during my life walked in one path, which I shall endeavour not to lose sight of." Above all, he was confident that the new first minister would never desert "the cause of liberty."[28]

There can be no doubt that the parliamentary sessions of the Chatham administration were the most tempestuous of his career to date. Not only did the departure of Pitt to the Lords expose him to the barbs of his critics, but the first minister's illness ensured a weak and divided administration, which struggled to resolve complex, intractable matters of high national importance. Although the Alderman held no office of state, Chatham entrusted the management of major issues to Beckford, elevating him to new heights of prominence in the Commons and also subjecting him to new lows of despair as he struggled to defend the ministerial line. In past conflicts, Beckford might have relished the opportunity to take the initiative in formulating governmental policy, especially with regard to colonial affairs. The 1766–68 ministry indeed marked the apogee of his formal political influence, as the closest fulfilment of the interest-led strategies he had pursued since his return to England. Despite his proximity to power, he found himself very much on the defensive on the front benches, where his self-interest was savagely attacked, and where his views brought him into open conflict with his supposed government allies. Coupled with a re-escalation of tensions in the debate on America, it is little wonder that he "did despair of the Republic."[29]

On the eve of the new session, Beckford could already see the danger signs for the ministry. New taxes would have to be raised to service the enormous national debt, and there were already reports that the Bedfordites were plotting the ministry's demise, although Beckford thought that the ministry could survive "provided the countenance and protection of the crown be not withdrawn." With a tricky parliamentary agenda to pursue, the ministry's vulnerability was evident, especially in the case of the settlement of the East India Company, whose recent transformation to quasi-sovereign status in India raised a host of constitutional, financial, and diplomatic issues. For Beckford, it presented a tempting target for a cash-strapped government, and he urged Chatham to recognize that for government funding, "we must look to the East and not to the West." Self-interest clearly guided him here, but he might have thought twice about recommending this swing to the East if he had been half-aware of the difficulties that India would bring him as a spokesman for the ministry.[30]

Even though Beckford's political pennant had long been attached to the mast of the first minister, from the outset of the new session observers appeared genuinely shocked that Pitt was ready to entrust the management of major governmental business to the Alderman. On 25 November, Edmund Burke reported that Beckford, and not Pitt's "nominal ministry," moved for the affairs of the East India Company to be heard by a committee of the whole House. Beckford's motion was carried, but the contentiousness of the matter was signaled when the Commons "gave up all his grounds, amended his motion, and rejected that part of it which required the laying of charters, accounts, etc, etc, before the House." The unforgiving Horace Walpole recorded that "men were amazed to see a machine of such magnitude entrusted to so wild a charioteer," and Beckford's standing as a government spokesman was further damaged by the Alderman's unfortunate outburst on 9 December. The occasion was a debate on the authority of a recent royal proclamation enforcing an embargo of grain exports, which endeavored to bring rapid relief for the poor during the parliamentary recess. Although the emergency had been genuine, sensitivities over the use of the royal prerogative had reached acute levels thanks to the machinations of George III and Bute. Beckford had been no friend to the prerogative in the recent past, but he sought to defend it in the Chathamite interest, stressing that necessity justified its use in this instance. His opponents positively relished this clumsy attempt to uphold emergency royal powers, especially Grenville, who took full advantage to become his chief tormentor. He was even able to move successfully for Beckford's words to be entered in the *Journal* as a warning to future generations and gloated as the Alderman beat a hasty retreat, pleading "ignorance, and that he was not of the docti." Another bitter critic, Robert Nugent, immediately quipped that the members of the House had "often been witness to his ignorance," and in this instance they were happy to exaggerate it in order to excuse him. Beckford escaped formal censure, but the humiliation clearly haunted him for the rest of the session.[31]

The pressing matter of the East India Company's affairs would not permit him to retire from the parliamentary frontline, however, and he soon established himself as one of the ministry's hard-liners on the issue, launching attacks on company members "who were practising all arts to convert into a selfish job a source of riches that ought to be conducted to national advantage." This led him into battles not only with the opposition, led by the Rockinghamites, but also with more moderate ministerialists, such as

Secretary Conway, who sought an accommodation with the company rather than challenge its charter or raise issues of right. Beckford was not unhopeful of some form of robust settlement when reporting matters to an indisposed Chatham in January 1767, although he was clearly concerned by the "kind and comfortable words" of Chancellor of the Exchequer Townshend toward the company. Secretary Conway remained opposed to a parliamentary settlement, and adversaries like Grenville stood out for the company's rights. Beckford's suspicions toward the company were most evident the following month when he regarded their proposals as "insolent" and insisted that "they must look on those they are treating with as knaves or fools." His own discomfort was highlighted by his ever more desperate pleas for Chatham to come to town to steady both the ministry and the stock market. Matters came closer to a head on 6 March when Beckford attempted to force the matter by tabling the company's proposals, only to have Townshend defy his ministerial colleagues by arguing that they would form a sound basis for a settlement. In such chaotic circumstances, Beckford's management was continually called into question, with Burke sneering in late March that the Alderman was still the conductor of the government's East India business, "if it can be called conducting." The mixed ministerial message continued throughout April, with Beckford criticizing the Company "with a violence that will not be supported," only for later reports to suggest that the administration was more amenable to the Company, and were prepared "to decline the question of Right; a language very different from that which Mr. Beckford . . . opened with."[32]

Through all these tribulations, Beckford's industry and loyalty to Chatham cannot be doubted, but the latter's absence brutally exposed the Alderman's poor standing in the House and his vulnerability in the service of a weak and divided ministry. His position was further undermined by a resurgence of agitation in the North American colonies, which left him open to charges of self-interest and even treachery. The touchpaper for renewed exchanges on the liberties of the colonists was the continuing opposition of the New York assembly to the Quartering Act of 1765. Given his previous pro-American stance, Beckford might have been expected to show sympathy for the embattled colony. His role as government spokesman placed Beckford in a difficult position, however, and he attempted a policy of accommodation that resonated with his recent interventions in Jamaican affairs. At first he appeared confident of defeating the hard-liners in the Commons, refuting

Grenville's motion to raise an annual £400,000 in the colonies for troops as "so miserably mistaken in law and policy" and was gratified to see the former premier "little attended to." In private, he was clearly exasperated by the provocative acts and the inflammatory language of the American patriots. Although he had distinguished himself in opposition to the Stamp Act, he regarded the New York petition as "a most insolent and ill-timed composition; the devil seem to have taken possession of the minds of the colony of N. York." He confided to Chatham that he hoped that "a prudent firmness" might allay "the foul fiend" raised by Grenville, but the hardening positions on questions of imperial right brought him growing anxieties. He still hoped that a withdrawal of troops might elicit a positive response from the American assemblies, but he reiterated that "the devil seems to have taken possession of their understandings." The colonial crises of east and west thus served to drive a firm wedge between him and the metropolitan hard-liners, but he could do little that session to prevent the passage of further controversial measures such as the Townshend Revenue Act. By the time of the summer recess, he found himself increasingly disenchanted with a rudderless ministry. As he complained to Chatham, "the manners of a factious age are not favourable for a proper management," and there was little prospect that the ministry's miserable predicament would improve.[33]

The relative tranquillity of Fonthill did little to breed greater optimism, and in September he confessed that "I have been very low in spirits ever since my late disorder, and the foul fiend had, in some measure, got possession [of] my mind." After suffering humiliation and disappointment in the previous session, such desperation was understandable and suggested that the strain of his personal and public affairs was beginning to tell on the fifty-seven-year-old. He longed for the return of Chatham to full health to deflect the political pressures of the day, and he hoped that the great patriot could provide the drive that he felt himself to be losing. At this low point, the first life-size statue of the Alderman was completed, by John Francis Moore, and celebrated Beckford's achievements as mayor. The Alderman's pose is dramatic and decisive, as if caught mid-oration, with the veins on his temple raised in the heat of debate. With the Magna Carta to hand, the statue suggested no compromise and no hint of irresolution in the service of liberty. Following its public exhibition at the Free Society of Artists, his critics could not allow this opportunity for attack to go begging, and they faithfully replicated the image, with slogans that linked him to his defense of the dispensing power some six months before.

Away from the capital, he was still prepared to serve the ministry in the county by-election and continued to style himself as the dutiful militia officer, but even he must have doubted whether he could summon the energy and spirit to face his adversaries in the Commons for a second session.[34]

William Beckford, life-size statue of the Alderman by John Francis Moore, completed in 1767 and thought by contemporaries to be a striking likeness of Beckford. It was donated to the Ironmongers' Company by Beckford's son in 1833. (The Worshipful Company of Ironmongers, London)

A Late Lord Mayor of London. This print of June 1767 depicts Beckford's statue by John Francis
Moore, which was exhibited at the Free Society of Artists in Pall Mall. The scroll and the column
both make reference to his defense of the prerogative in a debate of December 1766. (British
Museum, Satires 4395, © The Trustees of the British Museum)

In a telling bout of inactivity, again suggesting ill health, Beckford contributed little to the ministerial cause in the early stages of the new session. His role in routine Commons business was largely confined to London improvements, and even his adversaries appear to have had little occasion to fix upon his words or actions. Perhaps encouraged by the prospect of a forth-coming general election, in late January Beckford went on the offensive as the instigator of a bill to prevent bribery in parliamentary elections. Although such a measure was not without precedent, it was remarkable to see it proposed by a prominent government supporter, and it signaled a significant shift in the Alderman's political agenda. From the mid-1750s he had taken opportunities to trumpet his contempt for the venal electorates of the smaller boroughs, but the bill represented his first attempt to address structural reform. The ideological basis for this initiative was his long-term concern for the independence of the Commons, but its timing was a measure of the Alderman's exasperation with the aristocratic factions he blamed for the country's current ills, both at home and abroad. On 26 January, Beckford moved the bill, and was the first named to its drafting committee. A week later he presented it to the House, where Horace Walpole described it as "a flaming bill . . . equal to a self-denying ordinance of the last century, and as if Satan himself had drawn it; the only result would have been perjury." Its regulation of candidates and members through an oath against bribery was clearly too strong for MPs to stomach, and was duly rejected by all sides of the House. Beckford then met with equal frustration when he moved for an address to the king to prosecute the Oxford corporation for offering seats to candidates for £7,500 apiece in order to pay off its debts. His animation in the radical cause might have achieved little in the short term, but it served notice of Beckford's re-found libertarian energies, which would serve him well as he faced the challenge of re-election in the City contest of the spring of 1768.[35]

Given the political turmoil of the past seven years, with no less than five administrations since the last election, it was inevitable that there would be bitter contests in 1768. In Beckford's case, his prominence as a spokesman for the ministry ensured that his candidacy in the City would be followed with particular interest. His recent stance on parliamentary reform would also attract the attention of more disenchanted minds, which could look to the Alderman as one of the few politicians of any standing ready to contemplate serious reform. As yet there was no coordinated radical movement or

THE FRIEND OF LIBERTY   133

leadership to channel the discontents raised by a decade of war, economic distress, and imperial dysfunction. At the eleventh hour, John Wilkes would return from his French exile and stand as a candidate at London, but the outspoken opposition of the Alderman to general warrants and the Stamp Act rendered him the most consistent voice of reform in the 1760s. His enemies clearly relished the opportunity to label him as a dangerous demagogue alongside Wilkes, as the darling of the mob, who would undermine the constitution to gain the popular vote. Beckford, however, recognized that the poll offered him the opportunity to clarify his views and to alert the electorate to the dangers the country now faced. Furthermore, thanks in part to Beckford's recent campaigns, the battle developed into a heated debate on the intertwined challenges to liberty faced by Britain and its colonies.[36]

Beckford formally announced his candidacy in the press in mid-March, declaring that he had "served my country and my constituents . . . faithfully and honestly." He faced six rivals, the most significant of whom was undoubtedly Wilkes, whose quest for publicity promoted his candidacy in the City's high-profile parliamentary poll. While Wilkes attracted most of the headlines, the candidacy of the American merchant Barlow Trecothick also elicited much discussion and prompted debate on the colonial sympathies of Beckford too. Although they shared similar political views, and Trecothick held significant Jamaican lands, at no point did either suggest that the two were standing in the same interest. Beckford's supporters appeared careful not to align the two Creole politicians together, suggesting the continuing reticence of the West Indians to establish a common platform with the northern colonists. Early attacks on Trecothick suggested the wisdom of this tactic, with the *Public Advertiser* dismissing him as "a Bostonian . . . [who] has upon all occasions shown himself a true friend to the trade and interests of —— America." By contrast, in the very same issue Beckford was heralded as "an orator, a man of sense, spirit and independency, and one who has always loved to put himself forward in the service of his country." Despite these precautions, in a bitterly fought contest it was impossible to prevent damaging attacks on the Alderman's colonial links. On the eve of the election, the *Political Register* warned electors not to return any colonial figures, rounding on the West Indians as monopolists who limited market supply to keep prices high and endeavored "to buy us out of our native inheritances and votes with our own money." These censures only intensified, with the scurrilous *City Races* satirizing Beckford as Chatham's "brown horse

PREROGATIVE." His ancestry was even linked to "Noll's [Oliver Cromwell's] Old Trumpeter," highlighting Jamaica's status as a Cromwellian conquest to emphasize his radical pretensions. His promiscuity "as a stallion to the African Fillies" was another mark of dishonor, proven by his "very numerous" offspring. As the butt of remarkable anti-colonial attacks in 1762–63, Beckford could not risk the poll being turned into a personal plebiscite on imperial policy, but his allies struggled to protect him.[37]

Beckford's appreciation of the electoral toxicity of the colonies was most powerfully displayed on the hustings on election day itself, 16 March. Beckford gave a defiant performance, insisting that he had been misrepresented "not only in common conversation, but in the public papers, and in hand bills dispersed in coffee-houses and other places." He then confronted more specific charges against him, defending his support for the use of the dispensing power in the grain emergency of 1766 on grounds that it was subject to subsequent parliamentary review. He also sought to justify his actions toward the East India Company in the 1767 session, characterizing monopolies as "against the spirit of the constitution" and as "injurious to the trade and manufacture of this kingdom." His final flourish reminded those present of his core principles: "I prefer the character of an honest, free and independent citizen of London to the greatest title in the power of the Crown to confer." He did not refer directly to American affairs, however, an omission that was pounced upon by his adversaries. His supposed disregard for the East India Company's charter was held forth as a symbol of his self-interested inconsistency, for "had Jamaica been a charter government like the City of London, he probably would have not been such a volunteer" in leading this assault on the Company. His denial of Parliament's right to tax the colonists was also dismissed as "his creolian creed," and another castigated him as "a Negro man, a mere sugar sop and a rum man into the bargain." These attacks helped his enemies to characterize the speech as "wild, desultory, and better calculated to catch a mob than to collect the deliberate suffrages of a thinking independent and free people." Their vehemence only increased as the votes were counted in the following week when Beckford was forced to issue a published form of the speech in order to refute rival claims. Insisting that he had spoken "without taking a single note," he now dutifully collected his thoughts in print, thereby acknowledging the intense scrutiny to which his public performances were subjected at this time.[38]

Amid "prodigious" noise, with the crowds roaring "Wilkes" and "Liberty" and other political slogans, on 23 March, Beckford was returned in third place with 3,402 votes, some 450 votes ahead of the fourth-placed Trecothick. Although their opponents had sought to exploit recent colonial tensions, the pair had managed to preserve their credentials as loyal servants of the City. The most significant loser on this occasion was Wilkes, who finished last of the seven with only 1,247 votes. His belated candidacy clearly contributed to this failure, but the reticence of any candidate to rally to his cause was a significant blow. Unlike Beckford in 1754, who had associated with City heavyweights, such as Barnard, and appealed to a familial London heritage, Wilkes could not play the loyal citizen. In subsequent months he would seek to rectify this by building a stronger base with the liverymen, who, as the election squibs had indicated, prized their independence as a mark of distinction from mobbish elements in the capital. The election result proved that Beckford, for all his recent tribulations, could still count on the support of the liverymen, and that they regarded him as a credible spokesman for their interests. His critics, such as Horace Walpole, still wished to bracket him (and Trecothick) with Wilkes, by suggesting that the two colonials had shown "much civility" to the latter, but the London electorate demonstrated greater discrimination.[39]

If the election had proved a personal triumph, the overall results did little to lighten the Alderman's mood, and there was little prospect of more stable political waters ahead. Chatham's illness presaged political uncertainties, and "all congratulations from Hayes" for Beckford's victory came through Lady Chatham, not from the first minister. This connection was still firm, and Beckford had earned much opprobrium in the press for having defended recent government policy. He had even been accused of profiteering from his close association with the ministry. In a faction-riven era, it was impossible to escape such invective, but the continuing alliance with Chatham promised to reward the Alderman with access to government on key issues both at home and abroad. The ministry's record did not suggest either clarity or conviction of principle, and fundamental internal rifts remained, but Beckford could still hope for some returns from his considerable political investment.[40]

As Beckford contemplated his political future, his anxieties could only have deepened upon opening a letter which arrived at Fonthill a few weeks after the election. It came from Granville Sharp, who was then embarking on a forty-year crusade to challenge the institution of slavery within the British empire. Sharp was prompted to write to the Alderman after noticing that a "Mr. Beckford" had run a newspaper advertisement to secure the return of a runaway Negro servant; the letter implored him to change his stance on slavery. In common with his fellow planters, Beckford could not have failed to register growing metropolitan criticism of their cruel treatment of their slaves, but he had never faced such a direct, personal appeal that exposed the hypocrisy of his stance on freedom. As Sharp wrote: "I have a very great esteem for the name of Beckford on account of your steady and independent behaviour on all public occasions, and because I believe you to be a sincere well-wisher to the true interest, constitution and liberties of this kingdom." Sharp also sent him a draft manuscript of his *Remarks on the Injustices of Slavery* in the hope that Beckford would focus on the "very growing evil" of the possession of slaves within Britain itself. He did not expect the Alderman to agree with him but instead appealed to Beckford to disavow self-interest in favor of "equity and justice." The abolitionist received a terse acknowledgement and a return of the paper within three days, and that was the end of their exchange.[41]

Although the abolitionist movement would not gain real momentum until after the Alderman's death, Sharp's intervention was a painful reminder of the continued gulf between Britain and the West Indies. As much as the Alderman might try to reconcile his transatlantic heritage, circumstances on both sides of the Atlantic would continue to frustrate him. His metropolitan profile had certainly advantaged his interest, but often at high cost. As Sharp's letter indicated, his public prominence can be credited as the catalyst for the widest dissemination of images of Caribbean cruelty within Britain in recent years, prompting his critics to expose the hollow virtue of the self-declared champion of liberty. He had managed to defend his Caribbean interests through astute negotiation, but he knew that simmering imperial discontents lay unresolved, which could be easily manipulated by hotheads at home and abroad. His increasing readiness to countenance fundamental reforms suggested that he thought the current imperial system unsustainable, but the cold reception for his ideas among the metropolitan political elite gave little room for optimism. These bitter transatlantic realities had been brutally exposed in Beckford's political life, but they were just as evident in the social and cultural worlds he endeavored to transcend.

CHAPTER SIX

The Cultural Chameleon

He is justly esteemed one of the best conductors of an entertainment
in Europe. A man truly great when splendour is required, but content
to be unknown when no munificence is expected.

—*A Genuine Narrative of the Life and Actions of John Rice,*
1763, on Beckford

The contrasts between Beckford's public and private personae were often
highlighted by his contemporaries, either to vilify or to vindicate. Critics
liked to align his private vices alongside his claims to civic spirit, while
supporters championed his learning, generosity, and taste as proof of his
public virtue. The efforts made by commentators to disentangle the public
from private individual highlighted the degree of press interest in the "great"
Beckford and also reflected his social and political advancement on many
fronts. Politics so thoroughly coursed through Beckford's veins that any
consideration of the more private man inevitably encompasses the political
sphere. Whether attending the Commons, a ball, or a shooting party, he was
ever building upon the metropolitan progress achieved since his return from
Jamaica, and the *Genuine Narrative* hints at the constant pressures he faced as
a public figure in the mid-eighteenth-century spotlight. Although problematic for him, the elision of his public and private lives is highly revealing for
the historian, for his social and cultural activity presents further opportunities
for understanding the challenges he faced as a transatlantic figure. In particular, his strategies cast important light on the experience and reception of the
absentee planters, who arrived in increasing numbers in the 1750s and 1760s.[1]

Beckford's social and cultural activities have bewitched both contemporaries and historians in his many guises as the great entertainer, the cultural

patron, and especially as the builder of the great mansion of Fonthill Splendens. In recent years he has been accorded increasing recognition as a connoisseur in his own right, independent of his remarkable son. By any standard of the time, his social advancement was equally impressive, achieved with a rapidity that both dazed and alarmed commentators. When coupled with the prodigious spending of other West Indians, it is easy to understand why the stock stereotype of the profligate, comet-like "pepperpot"—a vain and arbitrary character who represented the more unwelcome novelties of imperial Britain—emerged alongside the Indian "nabob" by the 1760s. The perceived ability of the absentees to rise in British society directly attests to the sociocultural impact of the empire at this time, but little research has been undertaken into the ways in which the absentees gained such advancement or on the outlook of the absentees themselves. In this chapter I will seek to illuminate the familial and social contexts that determined Beckford's interests and success, and in turn shaped his views and those of his fellow absentees. As one of the very richest planters, Beckford's experience cannot be regarded as typical, but his prominence placed him in the vanguard of this imperial invasion, and his strategies illustrate both the challenges and the opportunities the absentees encountered when adapting to a land they regarded as home. His social and cultural choices naturally reflect personal tastes, but in common with his political principles, they can illustrate the "circuitry" of metropolitan-imperial experience and the ways in which the mother country itself adapted to an increasingly imperial Britain.[2]

This chapter concentrates on Beckford's social and cultural investments in the 1754–70 period, seeking to outline both their form and context. Working outward through concentric and overlapping circles of association, I will first consider Beckford's family and home, along with the peculiar challenges of establishing and managing his household, before turning attention to the ways in which he ran his estates and businesses and his development of a working entourage, without which he could not have sustained his social or political advancement in Britain. His wider circles of sociability will then be analyzed for how they straddled metropolis, provinces, and colonies through a host of contacts, including absentee planters, City merchants, and aristocrats. His cultural interests, most vividly displayed in the splendid environs of Fonthill, are likewise revealing of the man. Through these networks and activities, it is clear that Beckford's Jamaican background not only opened doors but also continued to have a vital influence on his opportunities and outlook. Moreover, in all these pursuits, he acted as an important facilitator of imperial integration in spite of the increasing opprobrium his public prominence brought him.

Building a Home

Although the purchase of Fonthill in 1745 signaled Beckford's more permanent domicile in England, the most critical stage in determining his social ascent came in 1755–56. For any aspirant gentlemen, marriage and the building of a house suitable to status represented key watersheds, for both provided a platform for social mobility, if not personal happiness. Within the space of a little over a year the Alderman found himself homeless through fire, married to Maria March, and the projector of one of the grandest houses in the country. These years thus represented major changes in his social position, and laid the foundations for the most ambitious of campaigns for advancement.[3]

At the outset of 1755, Beckford had every reason to be content with his perceived rank in metropolitan society, although his most obvious success had been secured in London rather than within the ranks of the landed classes. Although no simple meritocracy itself, the City had always proved more permeable to outsiders than the upper echelons of rural society, and his dynastic credentials, although somewhat uncertain, were much stronger in London. His political affairs had led him to mix with magnates of the stature of the Duke of Bedford in the west end of town, but there is little evidence that these London connections engendered either familiarity or friendship. As his early electioneering in Penryn and Shaftesbury had suggested, money alone would not secure his acceptance in the rural shires, and the national landed elite represented a still more difficult social climb. In particular, the continuing importance of lineage to personal status presented a major obstacle for any newcomers, whatever their wealth and place of origin. More encouragingly, his Fonthill estate enabled him to play the country gentleman, and the improvements he undertook to the house and grounds consolidated his position as a member of the Wiltshire county elite. In tandem with his brother Julines, with his impressive pile at Steepleton, he could socialize with political friends, such as George Bubb Dodington, away from the capital. Dodington reportedly delighted in the Alderman's company and "set the table in a roar" at his Eastbury home by countering the "intrepid talker"

Beckford with "the happiest flow of his raillery and wit." Thus the catastrophic fire of the night of 12–13 February 1755 imperiled much more than
Beckford's fortune and represented the most serious challenge to his social
advancement to date.[4]

The fire began at around one or two in the morning, and it was discovered by an old retainer when the noise of "rattling" woke him. He saw flames
bursting through the windows of the north front and quickly raised the
alarm. No aid came for another hour, by which time the north front of the
house was consumed, including the great hall. Attention then focused on
saving the rich furniture in the south-side apartments, but the conflagration
soon proved too much for the hard-pressed estate workers, and by 4 AM the
roof had collapsed. Within a few hours, Beckford's home had been all but
destroyed, and both recriminations and speculation about his intentions soon
abounded.[5]

Although the fire represented a personal disaster, the attention it drew
highlighted that the Beckfords had already made their mark in British society.
His family's wealth was clearly widely known, judging by the speculation
concerning the likely cost of the damage. The loss of the house was initially
reckoned at £60,000, including its "very grand" furniture, an estimate that
was later modified to £30,000 when it transpired that many goods had been
saved. Furthermore, there was already some acknowledgment of the
Alderman's role as a cultural patron. Even Horace Walpole, the self-elected
arbiter of public taste, referred to the now-destroyed Fonthill as Beckford's
"fine house in the country, with pictures and furniture to a great value." The
Alderman's predilection for "modern paintings" had been noted by a visitor
the preceding summer, and the losses included William Hogarth's *Harlot's
Progress*, which Beckford had purchased alongside the *Rake's Progress* to
adorn his new home back in 1745. Other casualties included the "very large
fine organ" in the hall, which had been installed only eighteenth months
earlier, and Beckford's "handsome library." The profundity of these losses
led initial newspaper reports to predict that the forty-five-year-old Beckford
might never rebuild "at this time of life." In keeping with his putative status
as a country gentlemen, this loss was further magnified by its impact on the
local community. It was feared that along with the house "we lose him also,
who for ten years past has not paid out less than £5,000 p.a. [per annum] in
improvements . . . whereby the poor labourers of the several neighbouring
parishes have been constantly employed and their families happily supported."

From all these perspectives, the fire represented a public loss, thereby high-lighting the very real social progress the Alderman had made during the preceding decade.[6]

Happily for all concerned, only a week later it was reported that he would rebuild Fonthill "in a most elegant manner, and as soon as possible," a prediction that proved largely correct. In fact, within a fortnight, Horace Walpole informed a friend that Beckford had responded to news of the fire with the nonchalant observation: "Oh! I have an odd fifty thousand pounds in a drawer: I will build it up again." Although it is impossible to corroborate this story, the attractiveness of which ensured its constant retelling in the press, there is no doubt that Beckford was resolute in his determination to stake a claim to status in landed society. Moreover, even though considerable doubt can be thrown on Beckford's supposed cavalier attitude toward his finances, it soon transpired that he was resolved to build on a much greater scale than before. Up until this point he had taken great interest in the estate, but his initiatives had sought to improve and refurbish, and there was little evidence that he had designs as a great builder. The fire presented him an opportunity to make a much more definitive statement regarding his arrival in landed society, and the phoenix that emerged from the ashes of the remod-eled Elizabethan country retreat was uncompromisingly fashionable and aristocratic in tone. In short, Fonthill became a residence befitting the first-rank political status to which he aspired, a stage from which he could face the country's noble leaders eye-to-eye. He could have few illusions that a house alone would gain him social acceptance or accord him noble status, but the Palladian palace that replaced the old Fonthill was the clearest statement yet of his ambitions for both himself and his Anglo-Jamaican interests.[7]

On a more personal note, the fire also presented Beckford with the opportunity to shape his first family household in England. Only weeks before the fire, the first reports had begun to circulate that the Alderman was to marry Maria, daughter of George Hamilton, MP and gentleman of Wells, Somerset. Although always a momentous step for any individual, Beckford's decision to marry represented a most significant change in lifestyle. By 1755 he already had at least eight illegitimate children, by at least three different women, and in the eyes of metropolitan observers he conformed to the worst stereotypes of sexual behavior exhibited by the Caribbean planters. Horace Walpole's response to the Fonthill fire had alluded to Beckford's sexual proclivities by suggesting that the rebuilding "won't be above a thousand pounds apiece difference to my thirty children." While Walpole's figure must remain suspect, the youngest of these illegitimate children had been baptized in Soho as recently as June 1752 and was probably the third child born to his mistress Hannah Maxwell, alias Thwaites. Even though Beckford took great pains to care for his illegitimate offspring, Walpole's ridicule demonstrated that his private life presented a direct threat to his social standing. A good match would thus provide a much more stable platform from which to advance his social and political ambitions.[8]

His betrothed represented a happy marriage of Beckford's transatlantic interests. Although his son and later generations would fix most readily on Maria's status as the granddaughter of a leading Scottish peer (the Duke of Abercorn), Beckford first encountered her as the wife of the Jamaican merchant and planter Francis March, who had led just as transatlantic an existence as Beckford himself. He died in March 1752, and Beckford's intimacy with the family is suggested by his signature to a codicil to March's will only weeks before his death. Evidently this acquaintance rapidly developed into a relationship, doubtless aided by Maria's attraction as a good catch for Beckford. When premature news of their marriage circulated in January 1755, Maria was described as "an agreeable lady with a large fortune," a verdict based on her own family's good standing and the wealth supplied by March's successful commercial dealings. Even for a man of Beckford's wealth, such considerations were not inconsequential, and he would benefit from her family's connections in the City and the southwest. The marriage was no mere business contract, however, for it is clear that the pair formed a companionate, loving couple for the rest of the Alderman's life. More particularly, Maria was prepared to accept the "second" family that Beckford brought to the match, having previously learned to live with the illegitimate offspring of her first husband. Only thirty-one and already a mother of one daughter, she was likely to provide Beckford with a lawful heir. Thus, although the wedding was postponed until 8 June 1756, there was every prospect of a settled marriage. The ceremony took place in London, and the happy couple then went to Fonthill "to celebrate their nuptials and spend the remainder of the summer." Although the bride would have been greeted by a building site, the groom could take great confidence that he would soon boast all the accoutrements of the successful gentleman.[9]

The early years of wedded life appeared blissful enough. Work on the new structure proceeded apace, and the Alderman settled into a rhythm of

Portrait of Maria Hamilton Beckford by Benjamin West, 1799, commissioned by her son
William. Although the background here depicts Fonthill and the painting celebrates her
intellectual pursuits, Maria Beckford played a supportive role to advance the Alderman's
political schemes, both at Fonthill and in the City. (The National Gallery of Art,
Washington, D.C.)

spending the summer months there while the construction continued. By his wife's testimony, Beckford loved the Fonthill grounds, and it clearly offered a sanctuary from the intense politicking and hectic social life of the metropolis. Beyond its aesthetic pleasures, the house began to fulfil its sociopolitical role well before completion, and the Beckfords actively used it to advance their social stock. The relationship forged between Maria and Hester, wife of William Pitt, is particularly illuminating, for Maria regarded it as part of her duty to forward the political alliance the Alderman nurtured from 1756. In June 1758 she sent a present of Fonthill fish to the Pitts and took the opportunity to rejoice in the political fortunes of Hester's husband, observing, "These good beginnings will end gloriously for the sake of those that have had the directing of them, as well as for our country's honour and welfare." In September 1759, after the bells of victory has rung continuously, she sent a turtle, knowing Pitt's partiality for it, and enthused that British success abroad "must convince everybody that is not wilfully blind what we may do when we have a wise and good man to direct." Blatant flattery might not win over the Pitts so easily, but the offer of a turtle was a reminder of the support of the West India interest which Maria's husband could secure for the minister.[10]

The happiness of the Beckfords, and the closeness of the two families, were cemented by the birth of William Thomas Beckford on 29 September 1760. The arrival of a legitimate heir brought the Alderman real joy, and contrary to some reports, he proved an attentive and loving father. He was not averse to using the birth as a political opportunity, however, and asked Pitt to stand as godfather. It was a huge coup for Beckford to gain the assent of the national hero, but Pitt could not attend the baptism, and Beckford's brother-in-law Lord Effingham stood in for the minister at the ceremony at the new Fonthill church. In its wake, Beckford vowed to Pitt that he would "instil into his tender mind principles of religion, honour and love of country," a patriotic vow in keeping with Pitt's principles and the national mood. Parenthood would have to compete with the Alderman's increasing political commitments, but his public life would continue to be supported by Maria Beckford, whose fondness for discussing the progress of the children with Hester Pitt helped to establish the Beckfords within the Pittite inner circle.[11]

The birth of William Thomas also coincided with the completion of the outworks of the great palace of Fonthill, and the Alderman was soon ready to present his household to the wider world. The summer of 1762 saw the new home's greatest test, when Fonthill welcomed not only the Pitts but also Lord Temple. The visit of the Pitts was marred by the ill health of both William and Hester and by the recent mishap of the roof having blown off, rendering the house a "thatched habitation." Adversity only worked to cement the relationship between the two families, and Maria subsequently trilled to Hester that "you were so polite to be so pleased with everything." Lady Hester's enthusiasm was genuine, for she subsequently commended "the beauty of the place" to Temple. Only a few weeks later Temple had opportunity to see it for himself and was fulsome in his praise, thinking that a few additions would make it "the finest and best understood palace I know." The approval of the owner of Stowe, one of the greatest country houses in the land, represented high praise indeed. "The Lord and Lady of Fonthill," as Temple affectionately called them, had thus passed a major social test, gaining acceptance for their taste and sociability from families of the very first rank. Political compatibility clearly facilitated this praise for both the house and its owners, but few could doubt that the Beckfords were firmly on the social map within only a few years of their marriage.[12]

This admiration for the lord and lady of Fonthill was a welcome boon for the family interest, but it was not the inevitable and complacent outcome that many contemporaries thought. While Beckford had acquired the means and the connections to play the untitled aristocrat by the early 1760s, his successful social trajectory was built upon a transatlantic business empire which required careful management and engendered continuing uncertainties. Beyond his broad Wiltshire acres he remained fully preoccupied with the development of his Jamaican estates, which demanded both his time and commitment. These concerns in turn ensured that the Alderman would not completely transmogrify into a mere English country gentleman and that he would remain a transatlantic figure.

The Man of Business

For all of Beckford's strategies for cultural immersion within the ranks of the landed classes, he could not ignore his continuing dependence on revenues generated from his Jamaican estates. His English lands generated significant rental income, to the tune of nearly £6,000 annually at the time of his death, but his Jamaican plantations remained the principal source of his

Fonthill Splendens. The dramatic north front of the mansion built by the Alderman in the wake of the Fonthill fire of 1755. (Fonthill estate, courtesy of Lord Margadale)

wealth. He in fact increased his Caribbean holdings during the 1750s and 1760s, and this expansion testified to Beckford's recognition that his success in the mother country was critically linked to his plantations. The challenge of ensuring the mutually supportive development of his Jamaican and British operations was a source of constant concern, and there were times when failures in coordination threatened his plans on both sides of the Atlantic. In order to ensure efficient management, he had to establish a team of trusted associates who would not only provide him with appropriate expertise but would also spare him the time to attend to his demanding political affairs. The stability of his business interests thus remained the backbone of his social and political success, and his methods again underline the important role played by individuals and networks in integrating Britain and the colonies.[13]

The original purchase of Fonthill had already demonstrated that Beckford did not have a blank check for social advancement in the manner suggested by Horace Walpole's post-fire story. That said, his careful management of his Jamaican estates and the consolidation of his holdings there during his trip to the island in 1749–50 had left him in a good position to recover from the Fonthill fire. Despite the sale of plantations to fund the acquisition of Fonthill, and his absence from the island, it appears that his transatlantic business was in good health by the mid-1750s. A general survey of Jamaica of 1754 revealed that he was the greatest landowner on the island, with some 22,000 acres; only eight other planters could boast more than 10,000 acres there. His crop returns for that year record that his lands produced over 900 hogsheads of sugar, besides rum and molasses, virtually all of which was destined for shipment to Britain. According to estimates made by one of the leading London merchant houses in 1752, the value of the sugar alone was over J£18,000 (or £12,900), which would have ranked Beckford as one the thirty greatest landowners in England and Wales in terms of income. Nonetheless, Beckford would fret over the price of sugar for the rest of his life, for plantations returns could fluctuate wildly, and the market in London was unpredictable. Sugar prices held up well from the mid-1750s, but such anxieties never deserted him.[14]

The absence of estate records precludes exactness in tracing Beckford's management strategies as an absentee planter, but there is clear evidence of his continued development of his Jamaican estates and of the overall increase in their productivity (see table 6.1). Although individual plantation returns

Table 6.1 William Beckford's Jamaica lands, 1754–80

Plantation	Sugar hogsheads		1774 stock (J£)	Slaves 1779–80
	1754	1770		
Estates held by Beckford in 1740 (Clarendon, unless stated)				
Retreat	89	53	11,628	129
Kay's	32	208	18,196	228
Malmsey Valley	60	—	—	29
Dank's	12	164	15,529	215
Bodle's Pen (St. Dorothy's)	—	—	23,007	193
Rock River	32	147	26,221	201
Seven Mile Walk (St. Dorothy's)	10	36	—	—
Esher (St. Mary's)	113	171	—	267
Guanaboa (St. Catherine's)	20	—	—	—
Estates acquired by Beckford post-1740				
Moore's	40	51	12,134	145
Harbour Head (St. Thomas-in-the-East)	69	—	—	—
Stanton (St. Thomas-in-the-East)	174	—	—	—
Ackerdown (Westmoreland)	72	24	—	154
Bog (Westmoreland)	80	71	—	225
Retrieve (Westmoreland)	107	72	—	120
Strathbogie [Pen] (Westmoreland)	—	—	—	—
Drax Hall (St. Anne's)	—	233	—	339

Sources: The main source for Beckford's holdings are the crop return series: JA, 1B/11/4. The 1754 returns were compiled by his agents Richard Lewing and John McLeod and signed on 25 March 1755: vol. 3, fol. 2. The stock values of 1774 come from inventories compiled following the Alderman's death: JA, 1B/11/3, fols. 87, 90, 94, 96v, 99, 101v, 103. The figure for Drax Hall production is from D. V. Armstrong, *The Old Village and the Great House* (Chicago, 1990), appendix 2. Figures for slaves in 1779–80 come from NA, C107/143.

could vary enormously from year to year, and accounting practices might inflate the apparent improvement of certain plantations (especially in the case of Rock River, which may have been amalgamated with another estate), it does appear that Beckford was successful in developing both his family's historic holdings and the estates he purchased himself. In the latter category, the acquisition of plantations in the eastern and western parishes of the island represented significant extensions of his interests and reflected his uncompromising attitude toward his father's debtors, especially the Hynes family of Westmoreland.[15] Such hardheadedness was undoubtedly influenced by his growing commitments in Britain, both personal and political, and at times he risked his reputation on the island through his ruthlessness. His acquisition of Drax Hall in 1762, the most productive of his estates at the time of his death, epitomized this expansive drive. Even by island standards, the haste with which Beckford seized the estate from a defaulting debtor was regarded as indecent. Enacted less than two years after the original mortgage arrangement, Beckford's foreclosure "excited the indignation of every honest man who became acquainted with the transaction." The grandeur of Beckford's first estate map of the area suggested that the Alderman was unrepentant, and by confirming his interest on the north side of the island, the new property emphasized his pan-Jamaican eminence.[16]

Although there can be little doubt that Beckford retained overall responsibility for key strategic decisions, such as the acquisition and sale of estates, the day-to-day running of the plantations was inevitably left to his managers and overseers on the island. Although few records survive of Beckford's intervention in routine plantation management, he clearly retained a close interest in such matters and took great care in the appointment of his key deputies. Since leaving the island in 1750, he had entrusted the management of his estates to various agents, although, as he had done from the late 1730s, his first instinct was to rely on his brother Richard until the latter left the island in 1754. Richard was clearly attentive to his elder brother's interests, and we can gain some sense of his views on plantation management from the instructions he left for his own estates when departing to Britain. Notable for their thoroughness and practicality, Richard stressed the need for "a regular plan" to prevent "miscarriages" on plantations, a verdict drawn from his "long experience" of a variety of different managements. More significantly still, Richard revealed a thinly disguised remorse for the use of slaves, observing that "the unhappy situation of the slave is a circumstance that will touch every generous heart with sentiments of compassion." He regarded it both the "duty" and the "interest" of the master to treat slaves "with justice and benevolence." He dismissed any suggestion that their color or condition could be used as justification "for not treating them as rational beings" and warned that punishments should only be used to set an example, for otherwise cruelty could only "dispose them to revenge that may produce fatal consequences." It is unclear whether his overseers heeded these warnings on either his or William's plantations, but his observations reveal the core

Drax Hall. Depiction of the plantation's great house, inserted on an elaborate estate plan. The acquisition of Drax Hall in 1762 marked a significant expansion of the Alderman's Jamaican holdings. (Courtesy of the National Library of Jamaica, Maps St. Ann 1275)

dilemmas facing the planting elite, and these fears would be multiplied by their absence from the island. A good manager could help to minimize the dangers of slave unrest and could act as a check on the indolence or tyranny of the overseers. The courage and loyalty of some of Beckford's slaves amid Tackey's rebellion in 1760 suggests that some of Richard's warnings might have been heeded by William's agents, although there is no evidence to suggest that the Alderman was regarded as a benevolent slave owner. Even if he did share his brother's compassion for their plight, he showed no compunction in enlarging the number of slaves on his estates, and through his agents he continued to buy and sell slaves as human chattels.[17]

Alongside his brother, William had sometimes employed two of his brother's agents, Richard Lewing of Spanish Town and Robert Mason of Clarendon, to oversee his island affairs. His satisfaction with their management is suggested by their more prominent role in his affairs after Richard's death in 1756, and they became trusted and loyal employees for the rest of his life. A power of attorney of March 1761 gave them responsibility for not only the Alderman's plantations but also the dispatch and sale of their produce. Even in the case of new acquisitions, such as Drax Hall, they retained overall control. Although little correspondence survives to clarify their level of autonomy during the Alderman's lifetime, continuity was clearly prized within the family and contributed substantially to the improvement of its estates. Beckford's bank accounts demonstrate that he continued to channel direct payments to his agents for the maintenance of his plantations, and on occasion he intervened to recommend appointments to his white workforce. Nonetheless, with an exchange of letters likely to take some three to four months, the agents had to be delegated wide powers to ensure that these estates functioned efficiently.[18]

While critically important to the family's fortunes, the management of the estates was merely one part of the economic chain, and Beckford was equally fortunate to find loyal and sustained service from those charged with his commercial operations. With direct experience of the Atlantic trade since the 1730s, he continued to monitor the flow and price of his sugar throughout his life and did not hesitate to offer opinions on a host of mercantile matters, ranging across shipping, partnerships, and insurance. Increasing political commitments did not permit close supervision, however, and he relied on metropolitan agents to oversee the shipping of his goods and the management of his financial and personal affairs. His solicitor Arthur Beardmore was a most trusted lieutenant, whose loyalty and political skills accorded him the Alderman's "strictest friendship." Preeminent among his commercial advisers was Captain Thomas Collett, whom Beckford described as "my agent" by March 1756. Collett had considerable experience in the West India trade as a ship captain from the 1720s to the 1740s, and he subsequently set himself up as a London merchant. He had established an independent name for himself in that capacity and served as a director of several City companies, but by the mid-1750s he was prepared to devote his time and expertise to the Alderman's cause. He duly became Beckford's general man-of-business, serving in both a commercial and political capacity. Their intimacy was confirmed by a report of 1756, which suggested that the captain regularly attended the Alderman at breakfast when Beckford was in town, and Collett based himself in King's Street, Covent Garden, within easy reach of Soho Square. The two men became very close, and the Alderman valued Collett's input in the most sensitive of affairs. In return, Collett was prepared to run all sorts of family errands, and his loyalty was to be proven by the fondness with which he was regarded by the family long after the Alderman's death.[19]

Although heavily reliant on Collett, Beckford was still keen to advertise himself as a merchant in the London directories, if only as a political statement rather than as a reflection of his contribution to commercial operations. More certainly, as his business empire developed, he required other agencies to manage his affairs, and by 1761 he had deputies in both Liverpool and Bristol to manage his imports to those provincial ports. By 1763 he had also established a commercial partnership based in Nicholas Lane in the City, which handled his affairs until the time of his death. Thomas Collett was the mainstay of the firm, but it also provided commercial opportunities for his eldest natural son, Richard. According to the testimony of these deputies, the Alderman retained an important influence on these commercial operations, even to the extent of determining the destination of goods to profit from possible market differences between London and the outports. Beckford's orders could run counter to the views of his agents, which again suggests his overall control of this business empire.[20]

In both Jamaica and Britain, Beckford thus established a small coterie of trusted associates, who managed to make the complex and unpredictable business of transatlantic commerce work to his interest. With no recorded investment in the slave trade and little interest in stock speculation, these plantation managers and commercial agents were the key stewards of the

Beckford fortune and were responsible for providing the Alderman with an annual income, averaging some £14,000 in the 1760s. Their returns varied enormously, from £33,600 in 1762 to only £4,294 in 1767. These figures help us to understand why wild speculation surrounded Beckford's wealth, and also why the Alderman himself was so preoccupied with the price of sugar. Clearly, he was a very wealthy man by any standard, but these fluctuations in income highlighted the fact that there could be no complacency in the management of his estates, and that his trusted lieutenants were vital supports of the Beckford business empire. Having taken such pains to defend his inheritance and to build up his Jamaican holdings, Beckford recognized the importance of effective networks of communication across the Atlantic and needed no reminder of the interdependence of his Caribbean and British interests. Although the size of Beckford's estates gave him opportunities beyond the reach of most absentees, those commitments piled considerable pressure on these connections and on his resources. This would become ever more apparent in the course of the 1760s, when he sought to develop his British estates at the same time as he sought to expand operations in Jamaica.[21]

The success of Beckford's personal affairs at the start of the decade would suggest that few ambitions were beyond him. In particular, the triumphal summer of 1762, which saw the entertainment of eminent friends at Fonthill and the seizure of Drax Hall in Jamaica, raised the prospect that young William Thomas might inherit a transatlantic estate to surpass that of Speaker Peter. Behind the scenes, however, the Alderman was struggling to manage his empire. The sheer scale of his expenditure at this time might have impressed contemporaries, but his actions underlined the basic problems faced by the absentees as they attempted to manage their socioeconomic future on both sides of the Atlantic.

Even as Beckford played host to the Pitts and the Temples, he already had his mind on a still grander scheme, the building of a second palatial home at Witham Friary, some fifteen miles northwest of Fonthill. Recent research has shown that the Witham project was no pipe dream and that Beckford did make considerable strides toward completing the structure before his death. The perceived faults of the site of Fonthill have been regarded as the impetus for this new project, in particular its dampness and proximity to a main local road. These are plausible explanations for a reconsideration of a rural retreat, although insufficient on their own to explain why in 1762 the Alderman commissioned the fashionable Robert Adam to design an even bigger mansion at Witham, which offered breathtaking views through the Frome Valley. This commission in fact suggested greater ambition than Fonthill, but even Beckford was to overreach himself and cause reverberations throughout his Atlantic empire.[22]

News of the purchase of the "grand and ancient family seat of Lord Egremont" was aired in the press in September 1762, and the touted sale price of £44,000 doubtless impressed readers as another example of Beckford's spending power. The vendor was in fact another Jamaican, John Pennant, who had recently bought the house and grounds from the Egremonts. The Alderman's bid was thus probably opportunistic, and it originated in his circle of West Indian acquaintances. This impression is confirmed by the financial arrangements required to secure the deal, for, as with Fonthill in 1745, Witham was secured only with a huge mortgage on the property, prob-ably to the tune of £31,000. His bank account at Hoare's suggests that he had been husbanding his resources in 1761–62, having plowed nearly £50,000 into a range of public securities, but this massive war chest was insufficient to meet such a major outlay. Even for Beckford, this new commitment demanded a reordering of finances, and the Witham purchase may have been the cata-lyst for reports in September 1762 that he planned to step down as alderman at the prospect of a costly year as mayor.[23]

Further landed investment by the Alderman the following year suggests that Witham was part of a broader strategy to enlarge his landowning port-folio in England. There could be no mistaking the pressure that Witham and continuing work at Fonthill placed on his finances, but the Alderman pressed on, securing the manor of Eaton Bray in Berkshire in 1763. This new purchase was financed by another five-figure mortgage, and the combined strain of these obligations led to often fraught relations with his creditors and agents for several years. By March 1765 he had taken out yet another mortgage of £25,000 with his Wiltshire neighbour Henry Hoare, and the following summer he was experiencing cash flow problems. He even started to impose on his Bristol agent John Curtis, asking to draw some £1,000 to £1,500 on Curtis in July, only to complain to him the following month, "Thy demands for money are so many and so great." In a more conciliatory move, when writing to Curtis from Witham to give notice that he had drawn £200 on his account, Beckford cravenly assured him, "I will trespass on your indulgence as little as possible." Further financial turbulence was suggested in the summer of 1766 when he transferred the Witham mortgage to Hoare's bank, thereby lumbering himself with the payment of a yearly premium of £2,240 to his Wiltshire neighbor. Given these commitments, it is easy to sense the anxieties behind his remark to Curtis in August that "I shall be glad to hear of the arrival of the expected ships." That he could raise such sums was a testament to his existing credit and connections, but the process of balancing his investments across the ocean clearly caused him great difficulties.[24]

The unsettled state of Beckford's affairs is also suggested by his resolution to make another trip to Jamaica. As we saw in the previous chapter, in December 1763 came the first report from Lord Temple that the Alderman "meditates a voyage to Jamaica in the spring." By August 1764, Beckford had made firm plans for taking the journey across the Atlantic, for he made arrangements to visit friends in Bristol in the expectation of being "obliged to wait for a fair wind" there. Given his age and recent record of ill health, this represented a significant decision and can be compared to the genesis of his last trip in 1749–50, when he visited the island to settle his affairs in the wake of the War of the Austrian Succession. He may have been particularly keen to tour his new Drax Hall estate and to review the state of the island more generally in the wake of the upheavals of the Seven Years' War, especially the slave rebellions of 1760. Visits to friends and relations would also have been a likely draw, including a possible rendezvous with his brother Julines, who had returned to Jamaica. There were also plenty of pressing legal matters to attend to, an almost inevitable consequence of the size of his estate and his family's still-extensive network of debtors. Whatever the true cause of his travel plans, he was still intent on leaving as late as December 1764, when he hoped that a trip to Bristol would permit a view of the vessel expected to take him to the island.[25]

Despite his fixed resolve, Beckford did not make the trip. His growing financial worries in Britain might have argued against his absence, and further bouts of ill health in 1765 may also have counseled his continued residence in the mother country. His political commitments were also substantial, but his readiness to consider a sabbatical from City and national politics bespeaks some disenchantment with metropolitan affairs, which may be linked to the indisposition of his ally Pitt. The return of Pitt to political life in 1766 may have been decisive in ending Beckford's immediate travel plans, but the firmness of his resolution to make the trip highlighted the importance he placed upon a direct familiarity with the island. As his fellow Jamaican absentee Florentine Vassall observed in the late 1760s, "The want of . . . intelligence [of island affairs] has often been very near the ruin of many persons residing here." He may even have had Beckford in mind when he argued that "the want of this information" had "obliged me to go to Jamaica, as it has and will do many others."[26]

In his final years, Beckford's finances appear to have righted themselves to a significant extent, and by the summer of 1769 he felt sufficiently solvent to commence repayments of the capital of his massive loans to the Hoares. Nonetheless, the Hoare mortgage still stood at £48,000 at the time of his death, and his expenditure in the last year of his life amounted to some £20,000. There was no apparent cause for panic, however, and there appeared few signs of retrenchment. While the price of sugar held steady, Beckford could face the future with some confidence, and there is no evidence to suggest that he ever doubted the capacity of his plantations to sustain his social ascent in Britain. He might have increased his landed stake in England, but the expansion of his Caribbean estates demonstrates that his commitment to the island was still as strong as when he rebuffed a gold prospector during his residence on Jamaica: "Whilst we have got so profitable a mine above ground . . . we will not trouble ourselves about hunting for any underground." Out of his earshot, even Beckford's banker questioned "the certainty of Jamaican estates" and thought that "no one can depend upon them," but the Alderman's wealth was never seriously doubted in his lifetime. In truth, Beckford had seen the tug-of-war of transatlantic interests at its most exposed, and the experience had only confirmed the need for close monitoring of his island investments. Even if he declined a last trip to Jamaica, this attentiveness also bespoke the continuing draw of the island itself. This broader attachment can be most directly revealed by study of the social networks Beckford had developed by the end of his life, centered on the remarkable Fonthill Splendens.[27]

Life at Fonthill

For all the difficult personal decisions Beckford faced in the 1760s, he had every reason to feel pleased with his social advancement. At least to contemporaries, there were no signs that he could not maintain his family in the most fashionable splendor. In material terms, the spectacular furnishings of Fonthill rendered it a comfortable home as well as a stage for him to play the part of the virtual aristocrat, lacking the title he so strenuously disavowed but enjoying every cultural and practical accoutrement available to the nation's elite. Just as members of the planter elite in Jamaica increasingly sought to emphasize their British virtues in the later eighteenth century, so Beckford invested heavily in the bricks and mortar of metropolitan respectability. But how far did this stage secure him social acceptance, and how far did his cultural immersion distance him from his colonial roots? Closer inspection will suggest that he did manage to maintain a dynamic, productive dialogue between his European and American worlds, although his Creole background inevitably constrained his access to elite social circles in the mother country. New evidence confirms that his fabled social expenditure was no hyperbole, but the inherent limits to the success of his social progress must also be acknowledged.[28]

Fonthill remained at the forefront of Beckford's social strategy, even though it might have been eclipsed by Witham had he lived longer. For all his socializing in London during the winter and spring months, Fonthill provided him with perfect opportunities to define himself and his family. Cultural historians have also demonstrated how it gave him an outlet for his creative talents, and his accounts confirm that no expense was spared in securing leading artists to contribute to this "magnificent edifice." Although it is impossible to verify that he spent as much as £250,000 on it, it deserved its reputation as one of the most ambitious projects of its age. Even though its subsequent destruction makes it hard to reconstruct its meaning for him, his cultural and social outlook resonated throughout his Wiltshire home.[29]

Visitors to Fonthill Splendens all chorused their admiration for the taste and hospitality of the Alderman. Although its site was generally deemed to be unfortunate, the sheer grandeur of the main front was breathtaking. Beckford clearly enjoyed greeting his visitors by appearing at the head of the majestic external double staircase before ushering them inside through the massive, giant-order portico, its pediment topped with the London-Beckford arms. This entrance led directly to the principal (first) floor, beginning with the grand Egyptian hall, sumptuously paved with black and white marble and adorned with murals by the Alderman's favorite artist, Andrea Casali. The centerpiece here was a richly ornamented "noble" organ, commissioned to replace the instrument that perished in the fire. To the left of the hall lay the "state" apartments, including a dining room, a bedroom dominated by "a magnificent state bed," and another room hung with Gobelin tapestries. To the right lay a tea room, which in turn led into the great gallery, seventy-three feet long and twenty-four feet high, where the Alderman's restocked picture collection hung against a background of blue damask, with more Casali ceilings. Guests were reminded not only of the Alderman's artistic taste but also of his public figure, for from 1767 the Moore statue stood here to recall Beckford in his most political stance. Beyond the principal floor, visitors could view further lavish furnishings in the bedrooms on the attic floor or take the grand staircase down to the basement rooms, which included a library of over 1,500 volumes.[30]

While the opulence of the interiors was such that it could dazzle the most noble of visitors, it also remained a family setting, and the artistic interests of the Alderman should not overshadow the more intimate, personal nature of this spectacular household. Familial touches were most obvious in the dining room on the principal floor, which had paintings of both Beckford and Maria "in the year of his mayoralty," and of Beckford's mother Bathshua and his sister Elizabeth, Countess of Effingham. The room did not overlook his Jamaican roots either, housing portraits of William's father and grandfather, Speaker Peter and Colonel Peter, reportedly completed by William Hoare, the successful society portraitist based in Bath. The Alderman also had his grandfather's bed from Jamaica installed in the house as a further reminder of his dynastic colonial origins. More subtle material reminders included the use of Caribbean mahogany in the forty-plus doors on the principal floor. The most direct Jamaican link, however, remained the African servants who attended him. Unlike many of his West Indian contemporaries, Beckford does not appear to have commissioned a portrait with them, but he followed family tradition by retaining their services in Britain. Thus, although the overwhelming tone of the building was unmistakably fashionable and grand, Beckford was proud to acknowledge his Anglo-Jamaican roots and his London connections, and the house sought to highlight his family's role in the advancement of the metropolis and its empire.[31]

Furthermore, if Fonthill might be magnificent, it also served as a home in keeping with the temperament and interests of Maria and William. According to the house tutor, who had plenty of opportunity to see them in a domestic setting, both had "a very philosophical taste, that is to say they look to essentials and less to ornament than perhaps that of any other in Great Britain." Maria, in particular, was said to prefer "virtue and religion to any other accomplishment," and Beckford himself, although famed as a superlative host, appeared just as keen to feed his mind. He retained his scholarly interests throughout his life, continuing to subscribe to learned works relating to history, the classics, and modern literature. He also celebrated learning and debate in the household, judging by the way he commended the spouse of Anglican cleric Thomas Wilson: "If I could envy you any blessing it would be the conversation of such a wife." In a more outdoor vein, he shared the genteel love of horse racing, and owned several horses, although none appear to have achieved much success. He was also proud of the quality of the game raised on his lands and commissioned Robert Adam to design a hunting lodge so that visiting guests could partake of the sport. His active interest in the development of the Fonthill estates also drew attention, and he won a gold medal from the Society for the Encouragement of Arts, Manufactures, and Commerce for his planting of some 61,800 Scotch pines at Witham and Fonthill. All these pursuits suggest a restless, improving energy matching his public persona in many respects, but it is clear that he also enjoyed Fonthill as a place of calm where he could think and reflect.[32]

Fonthill also gave him the opportunity to enjoy family life. Given the fragile health of his only legitimate son, Fonthill was increasingly favored over London as a family base, and the Alderman took great interest in his son's development there. "Contrary to their own desire and inclination," the parents were blamed for overindulging their preciously talented son, who by the age of eight "begins already to think of being master of a great fortune." In the only letter surviving between father and son, the Alderman mixed both affection and discipline, stressing that "manly behaviour" and the improvement of mind would earn the youngster not only the "love and respect of mankind" but also "the tender regard of your parents." He commended the classical reading his son was already engaged with and was keen to encourage a respect for religion, assuring him that "nothing great or good can be done" without divine assistance. He even urged him to keep an eye on "my works and workmen" at Fonthill, when leisure time permitted, and allowed him to give "necessary directions" as he saw fit. Although the Alderman has often been held to have been a terrifying presence in his own household, there can be little doubt that he felt "the best love and affection" which he conveyed to his family in this letter. These more personal glimpses need to be set alongside the palatial grandeur in order to appreciate the multiple functions of Fonthill for the Beckfords.[33]

Even though Fonthill was regarded by the family as a refuge from the busy-ness of their lives in the metropolis, such opulence cried out for an

William Thomas Beckford, by Sir Joshua Reynolds, 1782. (© National Portrait Gallery, London, NPG, 5340)

audience, and a key criterion for Fonthill's success lay with the Beckfords' ability to draw visitors through their doors. News of the glories of the house spread quickly and established Fonthill on the itinerary of Wiltshire great houses for domestic tourists. The Alderman's political profile doubtless helped to spread its fame. Despite his success in tempting the likes of Pitt and

Temple to stay as early as 1762, he struggled to attract a wider section of the national elite beyond his family, political allies, and his gentle neighbors. As tutor Drysdale reported in 1768, "there comes very little company to this house," listing only Wiltshire dignitaries such as the bishop of Salisbury, Lord and Lady Arundell of Wardour Castle, and Lord Shelburne of Bowood. Other known visitors included fellow absentees, such as Edward Morant. The Jamaicans clearly enjoyed one another's company during the summer months as much as they did while residing in London. These guests suggest a considerable degree of social eminence, but Beckford's social milieu was still largely restricted to his political and colonial connections.[34]

Fortunately, an account of a Fonthill summer party in 1769, which has survived in the papers of the Countess of Shelburne, provides detailed insight into the ways in which the house acted as site of social and political advancement. By this time, the Beckfords and the Shelburnes had been on friendly terms for at least two years, but the hosts were still desperately keen to impress their important guests. The countess was a sharp social critic and was not prepared to overlook the failings of the site of the house, but she could not fault the hospitality she received during a visit of several days. She was very taken by the intimate family pleasures as much as by the grandeur of the surroundings, and she was charmed in the evenings by the talents of the young William Thomas as he sang to the accompaniment of the great organ in the hall. During the day, the Alderman was keen to demonstrate the pleasures of his estate, riding alongside her chaise for over two hours. Other pastimes included tea in "the Banquetting House" and walks or drives through the shrubberies. Beckford was also keen to show off his property at Witham, even though it was as yet "a very beautiful shell of a house." Adding to these material pleasures was the company of political associates and neighbors—the Hoares of Stourhead, Lord Lyttelton, Colonel Barré, and James Townsend. All in all, Lady Shelburne confessed, "I had been very well entertained and [had] received great civilities," a verdict suggesting that Beckford's social investment had gained some real reward. Over the next twelve months he embarked on a series of City entertainments of staggering size and cost, but these family parties constituted an acid test of social acceptance and were critical to both his dynastic plans and his political agenda.[35]

Beckford continued to invest in his social advancement at Fonthill to the very end of his life. Detailed payments survive from May 1769, and they show that the Alderman was keen to advance the prospects of his family on all fronts. His son's education was spared no cost, nor that of his step-daughter. He was even prepared to spend significant sums to give his illegitimate children a solid platform in life through the provision of schooling and training. The palace of Fonthill received further embellishment, with Chippendale, Moore, and Casali continuing their work to render it an ever grander stage for exhibiting Beckford's status and taste. Many other tradesmen were employed to render the finish as exquisite as possible, with remarkable bills from consortiums of paperhangers (£1,309) and from uphol-sterers and cabinetmakers (£1,973). This mammoth outlay came at the same time that Beckford was plowing huge sums into entertainments in London, and the concurrent expenses highlight the importance he placed on the performance of social status. Although these expenditures allowed him to mix with the cream of the aristocracy, they also suggest an urgency for social acceptance that never found true fulfillment.[36]

In his social and cultural choices, Beckford epitomized the predicament of his fellow Caribbean absentees as they adapted to life in the mother country. Although blessed with considerable financial resources, which secured access to elite circles, their path to social acceptance was often prob-lematic. Fonthill and its house parties might represent a remarkable testament to their potential social advancement, but its magnificence could not mask the family's arriviste status, for which Maria March's pedigree could not compen-sate. The profuse expenditure of the Alderman at Fonthill and Witham also bespeaks the uphill battle he faced in attempting to assimilate himself fully into the national hierarchy, and these demands rendered him ever more dependent on his Jamaican plantations. He evidently shared the common identification of the white planter with the English country gentleman, but he would not shed his Creole colors completely and actively sought the company of his fellow absentees. These continuing island ties can be espied in his more mundane expenditures at the end of his life, such as the £8 spent on six jars of Barbadian sweetmeats, ginger, pawpaws, and limes, which were given as a present to a family friend. Thus, although his education, cultural tastes, and raw patriotism helped him to blend into British society, he retained an exotic character, which his controversial political profile did little to diminish.[37]

Nonetheless, given the closed character of the English aristocracy's upper tiers, his social progress constituted an achievement of real substance,

and in both his private and public capacities he assisted the continuing integration of British and colonial society. In common with most eighteenth-
century social commentators, Beckford knew that money alone could never
suffice for true social success, and that his Jamaican roots would not be easily
overlooked, especially by those critical of colonial influences in British
society. Equally, he recognized that any advancement of his metropolitan
interest could only be built on the success of his plantations, and this ensured
that he remained transatlantic in outlook even as he immersed himself in
British society. His firm attachment to Jamaica inevitably limited his social
circles and ensured that his closest friends would share either his colonial or
political affinities. Even if he might smart from the barbs of sneering critics,
he saw no fundamental dichotomy between the elite cultures of America and
Britain. Alarmingly for him, the last two years of his life would test their
common values as never before and place even greater pressure on him to
resolve those tensions to restore a transatlantic understanding.

CHAPTER SEVEN

Apotheosis

Wilkes

Liberty

—Inventory of Beckford's slaves

The last two years of Beckford's life saw his British and imperial interests intertwined as never before. Although the identity of those responsible for naming the slaves Wilkes and Liberty remains obscure, their deliberate juxtaposition symbolizes the continued interplay of colonial and metropolitan life in the Alderman's final months. As his critics had endeavored to do in their name-calling during the 1768 election, Beckford's pretensions to be the spokesman for fundamental liberties could be severely challenged, and ensuing battles would test his Anglo-Jamaican sensibilities to their utmost. The intense divisions revealed by the Middlesex election and the Boston Massacre forced Beckford to take an ever clearer stand on his principles and loyalties, and in turn these crises elevated him to new heights of public prominence. His confrontation with George III in April 1770, only weeks before his own death, cemented his status with the radicals as a martyr to their cause. Although the focus of his energies was largely centered in London circles, he gained wide recognition as a representative of the broader colonial interest. In his final years he wholeheartedly embraced the cause of the North Americans, transcending an Atlantic divide that had previously forestalled a common colonial response to imperial reforms of the postwar era. His sudden death precluded a more permanent alliance and prevented him from acting as a moderating figure in the longer-term Atlantic dialogue of rights and liberties. He never deviated from this mediational role until the last, despite earning growing criticism for his hypocrisy as a slave owner, a charge damningly vindicated by the naming of two of his plantation slaves.[1]

His prominence in these stormy debates produced the most searching examinations of his principles in his whole career, and it is thus fortunate that his contribution to Commons debate has been preserved in extenso by the Cavendish parliamentary diaries of 1768–70. These sources allow us to see Beckford beset by continual pressures, in the course of which he provided his most expansive commentary on the historical and ideological roots of the present discontents of both mother country and colonies. Furthermore, by undertaking a second term as lord mayor, he sought to use his London connections to advance the cause of liberty and intensified his efforts to secure common cause among the various constituencies of interest that he sought to broker. His successes, failures, and frustrations can be read as a personal commentary on the continuing challenges he faced as an outsider to British politics and society and on the limits to imperial integration. These structural flaws lay at the heart of his diagnosis of the causes of the imperial malaise, and well before his death he despaired that a complete cure could be found.[2]

Although Beckford's political position had been bolstered by the results of the 1768 City election, the declining health of Chatham presaged grim political times for the Alderman. The opening skirmishes of the session suggested that the new Parliament was going to be no less difficult to manage, and he found himself swiftly called into action on the Address, which moved to thank the king for suppressing pro-Wilkite demonstrations in St. George's Fields on 10 May 1768. Several protestors had been killed by troops that day, leading to popular calls for the prosecution of those responsible for the "massacre." Mindful of accusations of demagoguery, Beckford walked a fine political line, defending the actions of the civic authorities while also drawing attention to the economic discontents that had helped to fan the violence. He echoed caution about the use of troops to quell the disturbances, warning the hotheads that "they who raise mobs raise the devil; and when they have raised him, they know not how to lay him again." He ended with a heartfelt appeal for unity, for "the kingdom is in danger," and on 16 May argued against a subsequent bill for the calling out of the militia, on the grounds that the main body of rioters had been dispersed. Later debate on the measure saw him again call for calm, and he thought himself "in Berlin, or in Potzdam," such was the zeal for militarization. He was even censorious of the "patriots" in his own City militia regiment and urged its members to "have a regard to the constitution." Beckford clung to his principles, but he recognized that the polarizing influences of recent events might place them in jeopardy. True to his word, the following month he advised Secretary of State Shelburne not to send troops into Wapping after reports of "an insurrection" of coal-heavers at the dockside, and his intervention helped to prevent a full-scale riot.[3]

The summer recess offered little respite for the Alderman, and news from abroad did little to lighten the gloom. Not only was there a resurgence of discontent in North America, but his libertarian instincts were clearly stirred by news of France's seizure of the island of Corsica, against the wishes of many of its inhabitants. He wrote at length on the matter to Shelburne, expounding on the treachery of the French and the need to be prepared for another war. He did concede, however, that the nation's precarious finances counseled caution and advised a continuing alliance with other European powers. He referred obliquely to "former profusion and dissipation" as the cause of the mammoth national debt, but his target here was clearly "every little contractor and jobber" rather than his ally Chatham. Given his concerns, and the still unresolved issue of ministerial leadership, it is unsurprising to learn that even in Fonthill he had "numberless things to attend" in October. At this juncture the ailing Chatham resigned office, thereby ending ceaseless speculation about his political plans. In reality, his passing changed little, with the first Lord of the Treasury, the Duke of Grafton, taking the helm. Beckford comforted himself by interpreting the resignation as a temporary retirement and continued to seek Chatham's advice.[4]

The weightiness of the business of the next session demanded strong political direction, and Beckford was quickly drawn into the heated debates arising from Wilkes and America. On 14 November 1768, Beckford was the third MP to respond to the submission of a petition from Wilkes for redress of grievances, although he appeared keen to keep clear water between himself and the disgraced journalist. He stressed that "I am under as little obligation to Mr. Wilkes as any man," especially after the *North Briton* had made "free with me" and fabricated "speeches for me," but nonetheless argued that the now incarcerated Wilkes "has met with hard usage" and that his case should be examined by the House. He even confessed himself to be "tired of Wilkes and Liberty," and boldly asserted himself to be "as strenuous a supporter of real liberty as any man." He spoke regularly on the Wilkite proceedings in that session, including an intervention on 24 November to urge the House to allow Wilkes to be heard. He adopted a more combative tone on 7 December to put pressure on the Upper House to allow several peers to testify to the substance of Wilkes's petition, observing, "I never knew an instance in which the Lords did not join with the Crown against the people." He again slighted the Lords and defended the privileges of the Commons the next day and continued to vent his anger over the former conviction of Wilkes for seditious libel. By mid-December, his tone appeared to have cooled, for he argued that the proceedings against Wilkes should be heard by a court of justice rather than by the Commons.[5]

The reason for his change of heart probably rested with events unraveling across the Atlantic, which he wished the Commons to make its priority. He had first clashed swords with the ministry over America on 15 November, challenging Lord North's attempt to limit Commons debate to disturbances in Boston rather than embark on a general inquiry led by a committee. Insisting that "America has been misrepresented," the Alderman queried the partiality and ignorance of British views on the colonies and stressed their commercial value. Echoing his stance on the peace of 1763, he even averred that "you ought to be the monopolists of America." His stance elicited positive support from Barlow Trecothick, who, in a more conciliatory tone, argued that "a few factious individuals" had rendered America "deluded."[6]

The debate turned to fundamental rights, however, on 7 December, when the House considered the petition of the Pennsylvania assembly against the Townshend duties, in which the colonists defended their opposition to taxation without representation. Beckford tried to steer a middle course, recognizing the power of Parliament to regulate trade but urging members not to "exercise that power wantonly." Having defended the rights of the Jamaica assembly in very similar terms, he argued that the petition was "drawn up in modest terms" and exhorted the House to recognize the truth of its content. It was of no use, prompting Beckford to move that the Crown lay before the House all government papers relating to the discontents in America. In a wide-ranging speech that embraced the empires East and West, he urged moderation and unity in the face of internal upheaval and a continued French threat. Sensing the "unfriendly spirit" of the House toward America, he vowed never to move the repeal of the Declaratory Act, but only to "explain and amend it," and conceded that, "no doubt, there are faults on both sides." He disowned any intention of delaying the Commons but warned that "the Americans" believed that the British were intent on subjecting them to military rule, and only a clear review of the facts would help to dispel the growing mistrust on both sides. The motion failed, leading a chastened Beckford to make a renewed plea to Chatham, the hero of the empire, begging him for an hour of his time, given that "the times are violent and tend hastily to a crisis." He met a polite rebuff from the Countess of Chatham, but it could not have encouraged him.[7]

Wilkes and America continued to dominate the parliamentary agenda after the Christmas break, and Beckford's impatience with the ministry was signaled by an increasing intransigence. On 23 January 1769 he moved for an address to the king to pardon Wilkes, accusing ministers of evading the core issues raised by the Wilkes case and defiantly asserting, "I trust I shall die an old, real, and not a nominal Whig." Four days later he suggested that "no man has been more persecuted" than Wilkes and subsequently helped to clear him of having been convicted of "blasphemy." He also opposed Blackstone's motion of censure against Wilkes on 1 February, taunting him that "the great lawyers, Coke, etc, were on the side of the people" and insisting that "a thousand precedents will not overset one law, that is, Magna Charta." His support for Wilkes on constitutional grounds continued, with fiery barbs aimed at the ministry for placing revenge ahead of the defense of long-cherished liberties. The ministry proved resolute, however, and finally achieved the expulsion of Wilkes from the House on 3 February.[8]

Beckford's apprehension for the rights of the colonists was no less marked at this time. In late January he moved the House to read a petition from the Massachusetts council requesting the repeal of the Townshend duties and joined with Trecothick and Rose Fuller to argue against North's attempts to block its presentation. Beckford clearly laid the blame for the American discontents at the door of Governor Bernard and in the process showed a characteristic Creole suspicion of gubernatorial authority, observing that "the prerogative has been stretched in the dissolution of almost all the assemblies of America." He succeeded in having the petition read but failed in his subsequent motion to refer it to the committee on American affairs, even though the petition was referenced by papers already submitted to that committee. The next day he failed again when endeavoring to support a Bostonian's petition against a hard-line Lords motion to appoint a special commission to settle the disturbances in Massachusetts. When the Commons proposed a similar address to the king, Beckford expressed his personal fear of coming "under the lash of these resolutions" and made the most direct connection yet between the upheavals throughout the empire: "There seems as if there was a plan of ruling by a military force, both here and in America." He continued his attack on British authoritarianism on 8 February, raising doubts about the executive's power to coerce the colonies. While still prepared to acknowledge the supremacy of the mother country, he asserted in the most uncompromising terms that "in justice, you have no right to tax the colonies." He recommended the urgent recall of Bernard, dismissing the proposed Commons response with the sober reflection that "big words will not hurt the Americans." His seasoned experience in the dangers of mishandling transatlantic disputes fell on deaf ears, and he could not prevent the House from escalating the standoff to new, critical levels.[9]

The sincerity of Beckford's alarm at the present emergency can be detected in his energetic turn to extraparliamentary politics. Probably exasperated by Chatham's continued immobility, and convinced of the hawkish bent of the ministry, he made a key speech "amid the greatest acclamations" to a hastily convened civic meeting on 10 February. With recent defeats on both Wilkes and America, he backed the City's right to instruct its MPs to attend to their grievances, asking how could he "oppose my judgement to that of 6,000 of my fellow citizens?" He then cheerfully supported the drafting of fourteen instructions, which echoed support for the full gamut of libertarian causes raised by the conflicts of the 1760s—habeas corpus, petitioning rights, place bills, standing armies, and the treason and libel laws. There was also strong endorsement for parliamentary reform, and Beckford testified to his growing impatience by declaring support for annually elected Parliaments, although he counseled the livery not to specify the duration of Parliaments in their instruction. A vote of support for the embattled colonists would have encouraged him and sustained his growing conviction that the battle for liberty would have to be fought on many fronts in the months ahead. He still intoned the mantra of "measures and not men," but he clearly had little faith in either the Commons or the ministry. His return to the campaign for structural reform suggested that he felt unable to derail the destructive policies of the self-interested aristocratic factions, and he turned to the respectable livery to challenge them. A new print, *The Conference*, captured Beckford's decisiveness in this encounter, with the Alderman berating the incumbent lord mayor, Thomas Harley, for his timid (and financial) dependence on the ministry. Beckford's figure clearly resembled the one portrayed in Moore's statue and suggested that he was prepared to engage the ministry with vigor.[10]

This strategy inevitably saw him more closely linked with the Wilkite comet than ever before. Despite expulsion from the House on 17 February, Wilkes quickly won the by-election held to fill his place, and his famed series of re-elections ensured that his cause dominated Commons debate for the rest of the session. When it was moved that Wilkes be declared incapable of sitting in the House, Beckford immediately rose to challenge this unusual move, arguing that "by this practice you will choose whom you please, and garble the House of Commons." He stood firm for the rights of the Middlesex electors too, suggesting that they could withhold their taxes if their rights of representation were taken away. He again sought to distance himself from the worst of the actions of the Wilkite mob but was equally resolute in his opposition to aristocratic corruption, insisting, "I will never look for virtue at St. Giles's or St. James's." The locus of this corruption was revealed in the ensuing debate on the civil list in the following weeks. Goaded by the Crown's request for an extra £500,000 to cover government expenses, on 28 February Beckford launched into a scathing attack on the pernicious use of pensions and places by ministers and called for an inquiry into government expenditure from the start of the reign. He praised the present "frugal King" but poured scorn on the practices of ministers: "I am always afraid of a change of administration. Gentlemen get round a table—'you shall go out,' say they to one, 'but you shall have two thousand pounds a year' to another, 'you shall have three thousand a year pension.'" He duly supported Dowdeswell's motion for an inquiry into the causes of the royal shortfall the next day and again stressed that "it is my love and affection for the royal family" that induced him to seek out those embezzling its revenue. Playing to his City status, he also warned that "it is an unmercantile way to pay the money before you look into the account." He took this opportunity to propose that they "cut off the small paltry boroughs," attributing the people's current dissatisfaction to the fact that "there is something rotten in the state of Denmark." He returned to this theme again the next day, speaking out against bribery in elections and affirming the obligation of members to represent the views of their constituents. As in the previous Parliament, few MPs rallied to his standard.[11]

The Wilkite bandwagon continued to dictate the rhythm of metropolitan politics, and his second re-election for Middlesex on 16 March vindicated

Beckford's earlier taunt to the ministry, "Are you to have a holiday at Brentford every fourteen days?" The next day, the Alderman delighted in the success of his prediction but also called for "peace and quietude," pointing out that the people believed themselves to be "oppressed" by self-seeking officials. The ministry again chose not to heed such warnings, only to suffer the ignominy of another Wilkite victory on 13 April, this time over Henry Lawes Luttrell. Beckford attended the poll and acted as one of the guard escorting Luttrell from the contest, again suggesting his concern not to allow violence to discredit the cause of liberty. When the inevitable motion for declaring the election as null and void was tabled the following day, he remained resolute in the Wilkite cause, observing that it would "affect the rights of all the freeholders in England." Dowdeswell again leaped to his defense, supporting the Alderman's view that the motion was "of a very dangerous nature." Undeterred, ministerialists dismissed their fears, and the attorney general, William De Grey, sought to besmirch the Alderman as a rabble-rouser by insisting that Beckford always broached matters with threats, "as if we were coming to an engagement."[12]

Wilkes was duly declared incapacitate, but passions rose even higher the next day when it was moved that Luttrell should take the Middlesex seat without a new election. In effect, this motion threatened to annul the rights of all the Middlesex voters who had backed Wilkes. Beckford could not refrain from declaring the motion to be based on the most "rank Tory doctrines" and felt no compunction to respect any resolution of the House unless it was founded on "reason, justice and the true principles of the constitution." This sparked an angry set of confrontations, with motion-mover Onslow calling for Beckford's words to be recorded if he repeated his disrespect toward a Commons motion passed earlier in the session. Amid this "extraordinary ferment," the Alderman found some support from unexpected quarters, most notably George Grenville and Edmund Burke, the former agreeing with his assertion that the House's resolutions did not constitute the law of the land, and the latter confirming that that the Commons had no right to disqualify its members "at its pleasure." Despite several interruptions, Beckford persisted in his criticism of the ministry and vilified it for inciting the people to violence in order to justify the use of the military, calling for a recent newspaper report to be read out to prove his point. North rose angrily to disown the sentiments of the paper, but Beckford insisted that "every man in the kingdom ought to be alarmed" if the administration continued to wield such arbitrary power. Again, the ministry's strength in the Lower House prevailed to seat Luttrell, but the vendetta against Wilkes gave considerable momentum to the cause of the radicals.[13]

Although the Wilkes affair focused his energies on the battles for the British constitution, Beckford continued to see this campaign in an international light. In April he was listed as one of the fund-raisers for the Corsican freedom fighter Paoli, who had come to London to garner support for his struggle to expel the French. He continued to take the lead in support of America and proudly declared, "I was the first man who said, you ought not to tax her, for the purpose of revenue." He still wanted to steer a "middle course" but urged Britain to withdraw troops and not to be swayed "by the idle tales of that Governor Bernard." True to his thesis on the enervating force of corruption, he warned that the colonists were not likely to become dependent on the ministry through "luxury and dissipation," adding that the Dutch and French would take full advantage of any colonial trade embargoes. Ministerial corruption surfaced in his last recorded speech on the Wilkes affair that session on 8 May, in which he concluded from recent events that "a man speaking his mind, as I do, will be suppressed." There can be little doubt that Grafton regarded him as a nuisance, but the government had managed to preserve control of the Lower House. Beckford may have gained some support from other opposition groups, but he would have to redouble his efforts to capitalize on this if he was to bring about any change in policy.[14]

The summer recess of Parliament saw no letup in Beckford's political campaign, as he sought every avenue to advance the interests of the friends of liberty. The most dramatic opportunity came on 24 June, when radicals James Townsend and John Sawbridge were returned as sheriffs by the London citizenry at the Guildhall. Once they had been elected, the assembled crowd called upon the City MPs to present another petition to the Crown, listing their manifold grievances regarding domestic and colonial affairs. Beckford used the occasion to broadcast his anti-ministerial attacks from the preceding parliamentary session. A Rockinghamite source could not refrain from mockery:

> [Beckford] made his usual speech—short Parliaments—every article of the petition true—some articles true—most articles true—all that he had heard true—heard very little—his duty to obey any commands of his constituents, provided they are wise and reasonable commands, and so forth.

This unsympathetic observer also thought it "bold" of Beckford to attribute all the nation's ills to "a corrupt and venal Parliament." Even this critic, however, was prepared to acknowledge the rousing reception the crowd gave to the Alderman, which surpassed the "very great" applause given to Barlow Trecothick, whose words were drowned out by constant acclaim. He also commended the general good order of the assembly, with "nothing resembling tumult," which would have been equally welcomed by Beckford himself. Further decorum accompanied the delivery of the City petition to the king on 5 July, which Beckford attended.[15]

While these public events helped to sustain the momentum of the true Whig cause, Beckford had sufficient political experience to recognize that he would still need the backing of one or more of the parliamentary factions if he was to defeat the ministry. He was doubtless encouraged by signs that Chatham was beginning to stir from his political exile over the summer of 1769. Barlow Trecothick brought him welcome news that Chatham had made discrete overtures to him (as a fellow resident of Hayes) and asked Beckford for advice on how to respond to this approach. The Marquess of Rockingham also learnt of this exchange and interpreted it as a signal that Chatham was ready to come into office as part of a coalition ministry to resolve the growing crisis in America. These hopes were further bolstered by Chatham's attendance at court on 7 July, only two days after Beckford had been part of the delegation which presented the City petition to the king. Horace Walpole thought the timing of this politicking ill-advised and, in particular, that Beckford's backing for the petition gave Chatham's reappearance "a hostile look." Although it was highly unlikely that the king would readily turn to Chatham after the lackluster ministry of 1766–68, these political maneuvers demonstrated that the nation's travails had reanimated the opposition factions, which were in turn contemplating an alignment with those City forces whose political momentum appeared to be building. Even when subsequently retired to Fonthill, Beckford continued to campaign, and in late July acted as host to the Shelburnes and other political allies. In mid-August, he repaid the visit to Lord Shelburne at Bowood, where they made preparations to widen the metropolitan campaign by securing a petition to the Crown from a county meeting held at Devizes.[16]

Beckford's zealousness in defense of the liberties of the subject duly earned him greater press attention, and speculation mounted in the autumn that he might stand for the mayoralty a second time. The rapturous reception

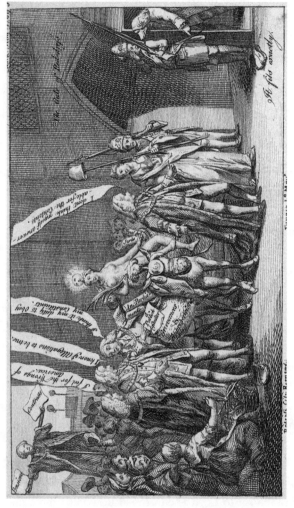

The City Carriers. This print depicts the members of the delegation that accompanied the City's address to the king on 5 July 1769. Beckford has been identified as the figure at center left, asserting the truth of its allegations. (British Museum, Satires 4296, © The Trustees of the British Museum)

he had received at the shrieval election demonstrated his popular support in the City, and as he had shown in 1762–63, the mayoralty could help him garner support at both ends of town. He also supported the publicity campaign for the radical cause, and in late September there appeared a print of the Alderman alongside the two sheriffs, as they plotted the defense of British liberties. Beckford supported this image by paying for thirty-six copies, and it was the talk of the Shelburnes' London home when Beckford visited there to discuss "City business" in early October. By then, speculation over Beckford's candidacy had become more urgent, and the Alderman began to express reservations, being "very determined not to be Lord Mayor." He saw the City corporation as an ordered platform from which to take on his rivals and clearly resented how "the livery in general and myself in particular have been vilely traduced." Yet renewed ill health rendered the prospect of office most daunting, and a mixture of both hope and despair can be detected in his resolve "not . . . to survive the liberty of my country."[17]

His critics suspected him of theatrics, but there is plenty of evidence to suggest that Beckford's health already presented serious problems. When a crowd of some five thousand acclaimed him as mayor at the Guildhall on 10 October, he begged to be allowed to decline the office. This reticence sparked an even greater applause from the liverymen, who "called out for near half an hour, Beckford! Beckford!" The noise was too great for officials to adjourn the meeting, and thus Beckford had to make another plea to be excused on grounds of infirmity before he retired, "great[ly] fatigued with the business of the day." The Shelburnes saw him that evening and described him as "more wore out and fatigued than can be expressed, and as much determined as before not to be Lord Mayor." He relented after further pressure from Townsend, confessing to a friend the next day: "I will serve the office, the consequences be what it may. The feeble efforts of a worn-out man cannot be of much service; such as they are, the public has a right to them." Public notice of his readiness to serve came on the twelfth, leading his critics to suggest that the Alderman demonstrated "all the coyness of a young girl" by again consenting to office after repeated refusals. In a private letter to Chatham the following week, he appeared genuinely distraught at the prospect of the mayoralty, confiding, "I know my old friend will give me credit when I tell him these new honours hang heavy on my mind and repress the spirits: all the reason and philosophy I possess cannot as yet subdue the foul fiend." This depression again led him to conclude that "we live in *Faece*

Romuli, not in *Republica Platonis*," and he urged Chatham to take up the reins of government again, for "then we shall not experience the wild steerage of presumptious young men, which can never bring our political vessel into a safe rest." He again lamented the weight of mayoral honors to Shelburne on 24 October, but he could also excitedly report that a letter from Chatham suggested that the former premier was ready "to enter on business."[18]

Once resolved to serve, Beckford targeted his Lord Mayor's Day celebrations on 9 November as a perfect opportunity for him to demonstrate the strength of the libertarian cause. He earnestly solicited his aristocratic allies to attend to broadcast the solidarity of the ministry's opponents, enthusing to Shelburne that his presence would ensure that "the world may be convinced of my attachment to your lordship." The Shelburnes initially sent their excuses but relented when renewed pleas arrived, insisting that their attendance was "indispensable." In expectation of the publicity, the mayor spent lavishly on preparations for both the procession and the inaugural dinner. He was to be bitterly disappointed by the political turnout, however, and his opponents took delight that so many members of the Westminster elite had snubbed him. The Bedfordite Richard Rigby thought the festivities "miserably attended. Nobody from this end of town but the Chancellor [Camden], who was more huzzaed by the mob even than Beckford, Lords Temple and Shelburne." The City's response was similarly muted, for only six aldermen were present at the Guildhall dinner, and none had bothered to attend the ceremony at Westminster Hall. The wider City elite had also turned their backs, with the bank directors declining the invitation to dine with Beckford, and "no merchants of repute in the City were there." It had been rumored that the Corsican Paoli might attend, but he stayed away, presumably because he did not want to be associated so closely with perceived supporters of the Wilkite bandwagon. Chatham's attendance might have always been a distant hope, but his failure to appear also cast doubt on the recent revivalist noises emanating from Hayes. Even the Shelburnes lamented the lack of "people of fashion" and were relieved to be on their way home by ten o'clock.[19]

This disappointment highlighted the perils of turning to the populace, even in the cautious manner that Beckford had undertaken it in recent months. He could influence peers with whom he had longer-term ties, such as Temple and Shelburne, but there was no sign that he was winning new converts to his cause, even among the opposition factions such as the Rockinghams. The latter were clearly watching his fortunes very closely, but for them Beckford was still seen as a means to an end, the end being Chatham. In a more positive vein, his defense of liberty was clearly gaining him support on the other side of the Atlantic, for in November a parish in Virginia was named after him. Throughout the year, American newspapers had been following his political path, and he had earned approving notices for his defense of Wilkes and his sympathy for the colonial position. The most prominent colonist in London, Benjamin Franklin, took note of his speeches but also reported the growing animus against the new mayor. He even felt compelled to pen an article on the subject of slavery after observing the "many reflections" leveled at the colonists "on account of their keeping slaves in their country" and identified "our worthy lord mayor" as the particular butt of these attacks. As in 1762–63, Beckford's defense of liberty invited accusations of hypocrisy, and his mayoral feast was the cue for further attacks on his family's slave-holding:

> For B---f--d, he was chosen May'r,
> A Wight of high Renown;
> To see a slave he could not bear,
> —Unless it were his own.

Beckford and his fellow planters did not seek to respond to their tormen-tors, or to agitate for West Indian rights at this point, probably mindful of their vulnerability to such charges. The committee of West Indian merchants also stuck close to their commercial remit and refrained from exhibiting any overt support for their northern neighbors. Their reticence was certainly not a reflection of political stability in the West Indies, where several islands experienced continuing constitutional battles between assemblies and Crown officials. The Jamaica assembly itself remained obdurate on the payment of military arrears to the governor, but Beckford studiously avoided reference to this struggle, and none of his fellow absentees sought to coordinate a Caribbean alliance with the champions of liberty in London or North America.[20]

With Parliament out of session, Beckford faced considerable difficulties in sustaining political momentum, and the onerous duties of his office provided further distractions. As the City's first magistrate, however, he continued to find opportunities to protest against the arbitrariness of the ministry, thanks to its heavy-handedness. On 18 December Beckford was alarmed to hear the sound of drums and pipes outside the Mansion House, the source of which proved to be a detachment of troops en route to a disturbance in Spitalfields. Their "warlike appearance" shocked the mayor, and he wrote to the secretary at war, Lord Barrington, to demand an explanation for this unauthorized City march, which had "raised in the minds of peaceable citizens the idea of a town garrisoned with regular troops." Mindful of his recent warnings that military rule might threaten both Britain and the colonies, he seized the opportunity to assert that the civil authorities were more than capable of preserving order, and that there was no pretext for the use of troops in his jurisdiction. Barrington insisted that the troops had been requested by the magistrates of Spitalfields but was forced to concede that the mayor's permission was needed for their admission within the City. Pro-radical journals gleefully reproduced these letters to claim a small victory in their battle with the ministry, and the standoff further confirmed Beckford's importance to their cause. The *Freeholders Magazine* featured a new portrait of Beckford in his mayoral regalia as the third in a series of its heroes, after Wilkes and his lawyer Serjeant Glyn. Despite his continued rejection of mob politics, many radicals looked to him to supply leadership for their cause, particularly in the hope that he might bring respectable popular opinion on their side.[21]

The opposition finally had some good news to cheer in the early weeks of 1770 with the fall of Grafton, whose handling of the Wilkes affair had been mercilessly attacked in the press, most notoriously by the works of Junius. Although Beckford could share their delight, he was probably even more encouraged by the role played in the minister's fall by a resurgent Chatham, whose machinations helped to undermine Grafton. The elevation of Lord North, however, presaged little change in policy, and Beckford and his allies duly renewed their attacks on the ministry to overturn Grafton's policies. Beckford took the opportunity afforded by a bill to regulate the incapacitation of MPs to highlight the servile character of the Lower House and to urge a resolution of the troubles in America, claiming that "all our differences with the colonies might, if we had a good government, be settled in five minutes." He subsequently joined in a series of attacks on the insidious role of the cabinet, thereby displaying a much closer affinity to opposition politicians who had targeted the court for its "secret influence," most obviously the Rockinghamites. In the course of yet another debate on the Middlesex affair on 7 February, he claimed that the first recorded cabinet council had planned the St. Bartholomew's Day massacres of 1572, a charge he repeated five days later when Dowdeswell moved for revenue officials to be disqualified from voting in parliamentary elections. He also continued to hold ministers to account for public expenditure, speaking on the last day of the month to press for a clearer statement of the civil list. He ridiculed the ambiguity of the £218,000 entry for secret service money and questioned whether the minister was "a man of honour" for presenting the accounts in such a way.[22]

His endeavors to marshal the opposition were no less vigorous outside the Commons, and on 9 February his wife, Maria, hosted another lavish entertainment at the Mansion House, which was lauded for its "magnificence and brilliancy." The most significant guest was the Marquess of Rockingham, whose presence confirmed a political accommodation between himself and Chatham. He was joined by more peers "than ever honoured that place at one time before," including six dukes. Lord Temple was also there, as was General Paoli, and the newspapers heralded it a great social success, with the dancing lasting until five in the morning. The entertainment even led to a heated Commons exchange between Beckford and Richard Rigby the following Monday, when Rigby suggested that the opposition's attack on Crown influence was fomented at the ball and sneered that they were now inclined to postpone matters after making "themselves sick with the rich fare they partook of." The lord mayor censured him for making "a ladies' ball a matter of party" and rejected suggestions that he had played host to the "Maccaroni or Dillettanti." The dish he wished to devour was "a fricassee of custom-house officers," whose removal from parliamentary elections would be "well relished by the people of England." Banter aside, Beckford clearly regarded these lavish occasions as important political investments and would only seek further capital at the Mansion House in the weeks ahead.[23]

Perhaps buoyed by the success of the ball, Beckford gave short shrift to North's attempts to defuse tensions over America by repealing the 1767 Townshend duties with the exception of the tax on tea. On 5 March, the mayor argued for a "total repeal" of those duties, taking the opportunity to launch another attack on the ministry for its dishonesty in imposing the tea duty after coming into an agreement with the East India Company. He was mindful, however, to show some moderation and downplayed the significance of the non-importation agreements in the colonies, insisting that "some of the great trading colonies are desirous of coming to you." He also gave unambiguous support for the authority of the mother country and argued that a total repeal would restore the Americans to "their old good-humour," imploring the ministry not to "give with one hand and take away with the other." The new ministry prevailed, again demonstrating that few shared Beckford's urgency or acknowledged the need for generous concessions to achieve a renewed understanding across the Atlantic.[24]

The opposition thus appeared just as powerless as ever, and frustration in City ranks boiled over to produce the most significant radical demands to date. His own patience exhausted by months of fruitless parliamentary debate, on 14 March, Beckford presented an address to the king which called for the dissolution of Parliament and the removal of ministers. Beckford was happy to head a procession of City dignitaries to St. James's, where the address was presented with all due decorum. After the kissing of hands, however, the king and his courtiers broke into laughter, leaving the City delegation much discomfited and fueling popular outrage when news of the audience leaked out. The royal answer also could not have been better designed to inflame matters, for while acknowledging the Crown's willingness to hear grievances, the king censured the address as "disrespectful to me, injurious to my Parliament, and irreconcilable to the principles of the constitution." The following day, when the House nervously debated a motion to consider both the petition and the answer, Beckford rose to defend himself and the City's right to submit its grievances to the Crown. He also insisted that he had intended every respect to the king, and that his only concern was to ensure that those about the king did not alienate him from the affections of his people. The ministerialists did not spare him, and North in particular was keen to slight him as a partisan firebrand, positing whether he deserved the title of "worthy magistrate" after his words to the House. Although widening this attack to query whether the address represented the views of the majority of the alderman or common councillors, North reserved his bitterest attacks for Beckford, recalling other inflammatory figures, such as the Leveller John Lilburne and the firebrand cleric Henry Sacheverell, to remind his opponents of the personal and public costs of raising public disturbances. Beckford hit back, challenging North "as a man of honour" to deny that no member was under undue influence. He even countered North's offer to face charges of impeachment by asserting that "common report is a foundation for impeachment" and challenged, "Am I not an accused man?" This fractious exchange between mayor and minister convulsed the House and resulted in the passage of a motion to address to the king for leave to debate both the petition and his response.[25]

This debate signaled a new intensity of rivalry between North and his critics, and Beckford showed no readiness to back down. On 16 March, a motion was made that a denial of the validity of parliamentary proceedings was tantamount to disturbing the peace of the kingdom, which debate saw a public falling-out between Beckford and fellow London member Thomas Harley. More moderating influences in the ranks of the ministry and the Rockinghams were seen to have "kept the Lord Mayor and sheriffs in bounds," however. The next day, Beckford was again unrepentant when ministerial hardliners sought to keep pressure on the City leaders by moving a loyal address to the Crown in which the punishment of royal critics was left open. In his own defense, and spurred on by another attack from Richard Rigby, Beckford turned on the ministerial supporters in the City, "calling them contractors and remittancers, and scoffing at the courtiers in plain terms for serving for such scanty pay in comparison of contractors who made £5000 and £6000 a year." North sought to defuse tensions by watering down the vindictive tone of the address, and this moderation ensured an easy victory for the court, thereby outmaneuvering the City radicals completely. Horace Walpole attributed the increasing vigor of Beckford's opposition to his disappointment that the Rockinghamites were not prepared to follow him into open defiance of the court, which reticence "alarmed my Lord Mayor, and though he affected to keep up his spirit, it sunk visibly."[26]

If the lord mayor was dispirited by the response of both the court and the Commons to the City petition, it only galvanized his preparations for the next of his great entertainments, a masquerade ball at the Mansion House on 22 March. He had been in consultation with Chatham about this event even before the presentation of the City address, and Chatham had sent assurances that both he and Rockingham thought it would mark "a most important day," urging Beckford to achieve maximum publicity to keep pressure on the court. Its political importance was such that Lord Temple predicted that the ministry would delay the Commons debate "purposedly . . . to interfere with the lord mayor's dinner." There was no doubt that the event would be the first test of the mayor's standing in the wake of the furor of the City petition, and thus it must have been a crushing blow for Beckford to receive word on the eve of the event that Chatham would not be there due to ill health. All political observers thought this a significant absence and a probable sign that Beckford's radicalism had now become distasteful to his longtime ally. The show would go on, but this disappointment may well have fueled Beckford's determination to use the event to secure unambiguous support from his aristocratic allies.[27]

Despite the Chathamite cloud, there is no doubting the sheer splendor of the occasion. Beckford certainly did not scrimp on expenditure, and the richness of the occasion was held "to exceed anything of the kind ever given by a private gentleman in this kingdom." The radical press celebrated the appearance of some fifty peers at the event, and the sheer number of carriages traveling from the west end to the City created an impromptu procession stretching from St. James's Street to the Mansion House, an impression reinforced by the "thousands of people" who lined the route. At the dinner, numerous toasts were made to a variety of opposition leaders, including Beckford. The ball began at 10 PM, attended by another seven hundred guests, including the Countess of Chatham, and the celebrations lasted until the early hours.[28]

Amid these festivities, Beckford took every opportunity to advance his political cause, despite prior warnings from his noble allies that "no new matters should be opened or agitated at or after the convivium." Before the dinner he drew up an engagement for guests to sign in order to signal widespread dissatisfaction with the ministry's response to the City petition. Many refused, however, leading Beckford to resolve angrily that they would "eat none of his broth." He relented and found to his satisfaction that, even without the pledge, the ball had had some success in rallying the opposition cause. Although Rockingham had declined the engagement, he could still report to Chatham that "nothing could be more magnificent or better conducted than everything was there; and indeed the meeting was a very respectable one." Critics who might have hoped to see open divisions within the opposition camp were thus disappointed, and the continuing support of the City spurred Beckford to renew the presentation of their grievances to the Crown.[29]

The campaign to consolidate his public support continued throughout April, and he was even prepared to align himself alongside the controversial figure of Wilkes, whose political value was likely to rise on his imminent release from prison. On 12 April, Beckford appeared at the Guildhall to give the City corporation a formal account of the reception of its petition at St. James's some four weeks before, and he could not refrain from describing the court's response as "very harsh" and unparalleled in English history. Nonetheless, he maintained a distinction between the king and his ministers and stressed that George had honored them by the offer to kiss hands. He also berated three companies for passing resolutions that aped the "opprobrious" language of pro-court parliamentarians and urged them to show "that legal caution and spirit" deserving of "the most respectable citizens in the world." Only forty-eight hours before, he had ordered a double watch over Easter to avoid trouble on the release of Wilkes, and his contribution to the ensuing celebrations suggested a continuing concern that the patriot cause was not harmed by violent disorder. On 16 April, on the eve of Wilkes's release from prison, he hosted another huge dinner at the Mansion House for more than three hundred "of the principal nobility of both sexes." Three days later, his Soho Square home displayed a banner proclaiming "Liberty," spelled out "in white letters three feet high," to rejoice at Wilkes's freedom. The rapid elevation of Wilkes to the aldermanship of Farringdon Without, the ward of Richard Beckford, was welcomed by the mayor, who attended his swearing-in and then hosted him to "a most elegant dinner" at the Mansion House.[30]

The rapprochement with Wilkes was clearly a political gamble, but Beckford's readiness to embrace the radical figurehead was probably influenced by further bad news from America, especially reports of the Boston Massacre, which filtered through to the capital by late April. The killing of five colonists by British soldiers only confounded attempts to improve understanding between the mother country and the colonies, and on 25 April both Beckford and Trecothick appealed to the ministry to give firm assurances that it did not intend to subvert colonial rights. He also seconded Governor Pownall's motion on 8 May for the House to address the Crown to clarify and amend the powers of the military forces in America, observing, "What you want is not more troops, but a steady plan of government." He went on to make dire predictions for the consequences of the government's actions and dismissed any suggestion that America might be reduced in a manner similar to Ireland. His enemies ridiculed him for suggesting that the Bostonians had shown moderation by not inflicting casualties among the troops, leading him to retort, "You may laugh; but I tell you these proceedings are contrary to the laws of God and man." There followed a fateful warning that "men accustomed to the use of arms and animated by the spirit of liberty, are not easily overcome," before a conclusion that encapsulated his constant struggle for the common liberties of the Atlantic: "In all of this I stand upon good British ground. When force subdues me, I must submit; but God forbid it should

ever be used!" These were to be his last recorded words in the House of
Commons.[31]

His impassioned pleas for averting disaster and his general outspoken-
ness in the interest of the radical cause brought increasingly polarized views
of his conduct. He remained resolute, however, and at a civic meeting on
14 May he was reported to have shown a "proper indifference" to a personal
attack by refusing to prosecute its printer. His prominence was signaled by
the radical publications that responded most readily to his vision of the transatlantic crisis. The *Middlesex Journal* was a prominent supporter, and
Beckford indicated his approval of its agenda by becoming a subscriber. In
mid-May, the *Journal* claimed a common brotherhood with the citizens of
Boston and lamented: "Alas! The unhappy town had not a Beckford! He
would have checked the audacious insolence of the army; and dared, as an
Englishman, to make use of his freedom." It was in this spirit of common
calamity that the City agreed to make another address to the king, which
decision was to catapult Beckford to the greatest heights of fame and
notoriety.[32]

After the City's recent cold reception at court, this strategy ran the risk of
further controversy, but few could have predicted the turn of events on 23
May 1770. The address originated in the stormy civic gathering on 14 May,
when those assembled passed a motion to address the king to air their concerns
regarding the royal response to their first address and to the Middlesex election. Altogether 8 aldermen and 57 common councillors wished to focus
solely on the election, but 7 aldermen and 111 councillors insisted on the
inclusion of the king's response. Beckford again openly aligned himself with
Wilkes to rebuff the City recorder's claim that the address constituted a libel
for asserting the high-handedness of the ministry regarding the rights of the
Middlesex electors. Pro-ministerial objections were brushed aside, and the
address boldly reasserted the City's desire for an immediate dissolution of
Parliament and the removal of evil ministers. The radicals also prevailed in
sending a congratulatory civic address to Lord Chatham for his recent
endorsement of parliamentary reform, another sign of Beckford's key role in
helping to turn City grievances into a national platform. The end of the
session on 19 May precluded any legislative movement on these fronts, but
the renewed momentum of the opposition camp was unmistakable.[33]

At this juncture, even the most ardent City patriot could have expected
little change in the court's position. As the civic cavalcade trundled across

town on 23 May, its leaders might have hoped for a more respectful reception, but there was little prospect of the ministry falling. The government had had plenty of opportunities in the preceding session to respond to its critics, but it had stood resolutely firm on its handling of events in Middlesex and Boston. The reception for the delegation at St. James's was thus predictably cool, although the City leaders were permitted to present the address in respectful silence. The king acknowledged the address and gave a gesture of acceptance, but with no indication that his support for the ministry had diminished. If court protocol had been observed, that would have been the end of proceedings. The frustrations of recent times had evidently become too much for Beckford, however, and to the amazement of the assembly he answered the king. In words that were to become venerated by successive generations of radicals, he assured the king of the loyalty of the City and declared that any minister who sought to drive a wedge between the Crown and the City was an enemy of the people. This short outburst clearly astonished the court, and the king himself could not compose himself sufficiently to give a reply. The delegation was permitted to kiss the royal hand, but it was clear that Beckford's breach of etiquette had stunned the court.[34]

Reports of the audience had an immediate and electrifying effect on politicians on all sides. Supporters of the ministry were outraged by Beckford's outburst, his adversary Richard Rigby informing the Duke of Bedford that same day that "the insolence of Beckford has exceeded all his or the City's past exploits." Although he was willing to admit that the speech had aimed to vindicate "the citizens from any impertinent intentions towards the King," he accused the mayor of "violently arraigning those ministers who should endeavour to prejudice his royal mind against the City." It was Beckford's impudence that jarred most, with Rigby declaring, "This is the first attempt ever made to hold a colloquy with the King by any subject, and is indecent to the highest degree." Another long-term critic, Horace Walpole, recorded the next day that the mayor had made "a volunteer speech" and was even prepared to admit that it was "wondrous loyal and respectful" in tone. Nonetheless, as "an innovation," it was said to have "much discomposed the solemnity" of the court and had forced the king into an awkward silence.[35]

Although the speech had been unscripted, the response of the ministry's critics was nothing short of ecstatic. The opposition press immediately circulated fulsome accounts of Beckford's exchange with the king and heralded the mayor's courage for alerting George to the nefarious influence of his own courtiers. Such was the significance of the speech that Beckford was encouraged by his allies to commit the words to paper, and within two days a "text" appeared in the press:

> Most Gracious Sovereign, will your Majesty be pleased so far to condescend as to permit the Mayor of your loyal City of London to declare in your royal presence, on behalf of his fellow citizens, how much the bare apprehension of your Majesty's displeasure would at all times affect their minds. The declaration of that displeasure has already filled them with inexpressible anxiety, and with the deepest affliction. Permit me, Sire, to assure your Majesty that your Majesty has not in all your dominions any subjects more faithful, more dutiful, or more affectionate to your Majesty's person and family, or more ready to sacrifice their lives and fortunes in the maintenance of the true honour and dignity of your crown. We do, therefore, with the greatest humility and submission, most earnestly supplicate your Majesty that you will not dismiss us from your presence, without expressing a more favourable opinion of your faithful citizens, and without some comfort, without some prospect at least, or redress. Permit me, Sir, farther to observe that whoever has already dared, or shall hereafter endeavour, by false insinuations and suggestions, to alienate your Majesty's affections from your loyal subjects in general, and from the City of London in particular, and to withdraw your confidence in and regard for your people, is an enemy to your Majesty's person and family, a violator of the public peace, and a betrayer of our happy constitution, as it was established at the Glorious Revolution.

Radical leaders were quick to capitalize on Beckford's stance, and on 25 May the corporation met to vote thanks to the mayor. There were dissenting voices, most notably from Alderman Thomas Harley, who accused Beckford of slighting the dignity of the Crown by luring the king into an altercation. Wilkes, Townsend, and Sawbridge all rallied to the mayor's cause, and without a division the City agreed to thank Beckford for "his noble conduct on this occasion." At the same time, however, the corporation resolved to present an address to the king to congratulate him on the birth of a daughter to retain a show of loyalty.[36]

That evening Beckford wrote to Chatham and revealed a resolute yet cautious response to the storm which had broken around him. There was clearly some anxiety behind his protestation that his words to the king were "uttered in the language of truth, and with that humility and submission which becomes a subject speaking to his lawful king: at least I endeavoured to behave properly and decently." He knew full well that the courtiers had regarded his actions as "impudent, insolent and unprecedented" but simply lamented: "God forgive them all! Their wickedness and folly will ruin the country." He was heartened by the support of the City corporation for his actions, but he was keen not to burn bridges with the court and expressed hope that the congratulatory address on the birth of the princess would "contain no words that are offensive or reproachable." For his own part, Chatham was overflowing with praise for his friend, commending him for having shown "the spirit of old England," and was proud to address him "by the most honourable of titles, true lord mayor of London; that is first magistrate of the first City of the world!"[37]

As first magistrate, it befell Beckford to present the congratulatory address at court on 30 May. It was another opportunity for all political interests to advance their causes, and it was clear that the mayor's conduct would be subjected to intense scrutiny. Violence threatened even before the civic delegation had left the City precincts, with a crowd trying to block the passage of the coach of Alderman Harley by closing the gates at Temple Bar. Mindful of the need to show no open partiality on this occasion, and of the need to preserve an orderly procession, Beckford gave orders for the gates to be opened. He could not prevent unruly elements from hurling stones and invective at the coaches of the aldermen who had shown less enthusiasm for the cause of liberty, such as Sir Robert Ladbroke, but the general dignity of the cavalcade was preserved. Once at St. James's, Beckford met with a very cool reception, and the lord chamberlain reportedly demanded assurances from him that there would be no repeat of the events of the twenty-third. Once in the Presence Chamber, Beckford entered into a heated exchange with Richard Rigby, who accused him of failing to keep order in the City, sparking a defiant retort from the mayor, who was ready to defend his conduct "at all times, in all places and on every proper occasion." By contrast, the formal presentation was very cordial, with the king responding to the address with the observation that the City could always expect his "protection" while it entertained "these loyal sentiments." In accordance with his moderating tone of recent days, Beckford withdrew without further comment, content that the address had restored the City's reputation as a loyal and orderly corporation.[38]

This occasion had concluded peacefully, but the radical press would not pass up the apparent opportunity to advance its demands. Beckford's every move was followed, and even his routine magisterial duties became the focus for press comment. On 31 May, he laid the first stone for the rebuilding of Newgate Prison and drank the health of the new structure, hoping "that the liberties of the people might be as lasting as the stone, and that the place might want inhabitants." The next day, the thanks of the City corporation were formally presented to Chatham for his stance on parliamentary reform, and Chatham took the opportunity to clarify that he wanted to see more seats for county MPs to preserve the independency of the House. The open support of such a leading politician gave heart to the radical cause and presaged a summer of further agitation. Beckford's connections to Chatham, and his heightened post-audience profile, suggested that he would play a pivotal role in that campaign. It was, however, the bitterest of ironies, that the next event to gain them publicity was the mayor's death on Thursday, 21 June, at five o'clock in the morning.

Although Beckford had suffered infirmities for several years and had offered his health to excuse himself from the onerous duties of the mayoralty, his rapid demise took everyone by surprise. Following the ceremony at Newgate, and the last day of the Old Bailey sessions, he returned to Fonthill, doubtless in an effort to recover his energies and to avoid some of the political limelight after his recent audiences at court. By 15 June, he was reported to have returned to the capital to discharge his mayoral duties and to undertake preparations with Trecothick for the election of new sheriffs on midsummer's day. On that day, Chatham reported that he had heard "a very alarming account" of his friend, and within six days Beckford was dead. The press reported that he had died of "a rheumatic fever," caused by an initial soaking at Fonthill and the subsequent dash to London on business. Others thought that the fever had been caught from his companions, and several reports suggested that one of his servants died soon after him. For certain, he was in "great agonies" through all of this time and suffered "a most violent hiccup and strong convulsions" until his final minutes. According to a pro-radical journal, his last coherent words formed "a warm ejaculation for the dear and sacred rights of his country."[39]

Within hours of his passing, political commentators pondered its immediate consequences and attempted to identify his legacy. Predictably, the radical newspapers claimed a martyr to their cause, and numerous accounts

Beckford tankard. Leeds ware tankard depicting William Beckford as lord mayor, with angels proclaiming his fame, c. 1770. (Museum of London, 82.564)

of his life appeared for the rest of the month. The most generous reviews celebrated him not only as a defender of liberty but also as a benefactor of the arts and a kind and effective magistrate. Others simply speculated on the extent of his wealth and its likely recipients. Sympathetic artists sought to commemorate his life, borrowing heavily from recent images that had proliferated in tandem with his growing prominence in the radical cause. Pro-Beckford verses flooded the press, seemingly seeking to outdo each other in their praise of the deceased mayor. Medals were also struck, adding to the adulatory material culture of spoons and tankards which had already appeared during his mayoralty. The political and mercenary motives behind these eulogies must be acknowledged, exemplified by the young Thomas

Chatterton, whose hopes to publish an essay on Beckford's behalf had foundered with the mayor's death. Thanks to the demand for Beckfordiana, he earned more from elegies and essays and could therefore declare, "I am glad he is dead by £3-13-6." Commercial considerations thus helped to magnify this sense of loss, but the torrent of words and images suggested a genuine and far-reaching fame.[40]

Opinion within the political elite itself was predictably polarized. Horace Walpole, who on occasion had been prepared to acknowledge Beckford's effectiveness as a speaker, was offended by the outpourings of grief at Beckford's death, observing, "The papers make one sick with talking of that noisy vapouring fool as they would of Algernon Sidney." Walpole's correspondents went even further, with one admitting, "I cannot help rejoicing in the extinction of the hero of the City mob, whose vast wealth both made him more audacious and gained him more followers than any other who may succeed him." Even those who knew him better, such as Lord Lyttelton, brother of the embattled Jamaican governor, could not ignore Beckford's extremes: "His spirit was too good humoured to make a devil, and too turbulent for an angel; but he will be a proper companion for the Ghosts that Ossian sings of, who ride in the Whirlwinds and direct the storms."[41]

The loss of such dynamism was certainly felt on the opposition side, and as one observer put it, Beckford's death constituted "a great check to the patriots." Even Wilkes, who had often crossed swords with Beckford, expressed "great grief," admitting that "he had of late behaved with spirit and honour in the cause of liberty, and was of singular service to what we all have the most at heart." Benjamin Franklin also regarded his death as "a loss to the general interest of America, as he had really a considerable weight, particularly with Lord Chatham." The common calamity of British and American patriots was represented most directly by a print that depicted a Native American and a London delegation congregating in common grief. Against a remarkable background juxtaposing the wilds of America with St. Paul's Cathedral, the caption's verses captured Beckford's aspirations superbly:

> When Cato died Rome shed the grateful Tear,
> Like *LIBERTY* and fair *AUGUSTA* here:
> Well may *AMERICA* her Loss deplore!
> Her patriot, Champion, *BECKFORD* is no more!

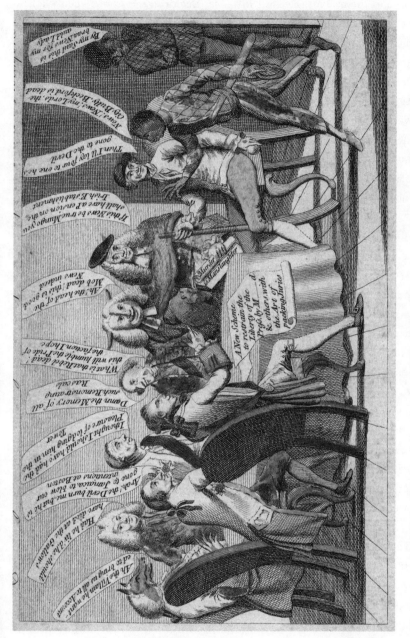

The Courtiers Assembled. The ministers rejoice at the news of the Alderman's death on 21 June 1770. Lord Hillsborough, secretary of state for the colonies, suggests that the Alderman "'is gone to Jamaica, to blow our intentions at Boston." (British Museum, Satires 4393, © The Trustees of the British Museum)

When news filtered across the Atlantic, these sentiments were echoed in the colonies themselves. Even at distance, Beckford's loss was keenly felt, and earnest discussion of its consequences revealed how closely his recent actions had been followed. As one New Yorker mused, his passing "disconcerts the designs of the remonstrants, and Lord Chatham has, in him, lost the mouthpiece of the City."[42]

As in life, so even in death was Beckford's political significance seen to revolve around the figure of Chatham. Supporters of the ministry rejoiced that the Great Commoner's prospects had receded with the loss of his great City ally and took delight in speculation that Chatham might seek to destroy his correspondence with Beckford to save political embarrassment. There were accusations that Beckford's great fortune might ease Chatham's financial worries, which were followed by equally gleeful reports that these reports were false. It was, however, the political cost of the mayor's death that was more eagerly calculated, and, if only to marginalize Chatham, many thought that Beckford's loss was a serious blow, especially in terms of City support. These observations highlight the real substance of the interest Beckford had built within London, which even his critics could not easily dismiss as the product of corruption and mobbish adulation.[43]

The depth and sincerity of his support in the City was represented by the responses from groups of varying character and importance. The common council, which had accorded Beckford such rapturous receptions in recent months, soon moved for a statue of the Alderman to be erected at the Guildhall so that "future lord mayors might be instructed by his aweful figure, and call to mind his zeal and spirit in their service." City politicians paid tribute during the election of replacements for the offices Beckford had vacated by his death, most notably Barlow Trecothick on his elevation to the mayoralty. Even this staunch recent ally risked censure by not providing a eulogy to the satisfaction of the liverymen, and former rivals wisely chose not to criticize the City's hero. The response lower down the civic ladder was even more poignant, especially in his ward of Billingsgate, where the parish vestry of St. Mary at Hill declared three months of mourning and erected banners proclaiming the passing of "amicum populi." Neighboring St. George Botolph Lane sought to commemorate the Beckford family's close association with the parish by hanging up the arms of "our late worthy alderman" in the church, together "with a motto setting forth his many amiable and great qualities to perpetuate the memory of that excellent

Memorial to Alderman William Beckford. In this print of July 1770 mourners from America and London converge at an obelisk commemorating Beckford. The background juxtaposes a colonial wilderness and St. Paul's Cathedral. (British Museum, Satires 4396, © The Trustees of the British Museum)

magistrate." The motto duly confirmed his martyr status, with its dedication to "that real patriot . . . whose incessant spirited efforts to serve his country hastened his dissolution." These moving tributes suggested that Beckford's claims to a City pedigree were neither rhetorical nor in vain and that he had laid the platform for a lasting London fame.[44]

Although Beckford's greatest support and most significant recent triumphs had been gained in the metropolis, his last resting place was destined to be Fonthill. His body lay in state at his Soho Square home for several days, and on 28 June a small cortege of three coaches made the Alderman's last journey back to Wiltshire. His hearse was "decorated with plumes and richly hung with escutcheons" in traditional manner, but in contrast to recent public performances, there was no great theatricality at his funeral on 30 June, when he was interred in the church he had built. The coffin was carried by six "country labourers," each of whom had been left a gray suit by the Alderman, and the congregation included forty-five of his tenants, attending "in deep mourning." Thus, far from the status of City patriot, Beckford was laid to rest as a country gentleman, in the company of his family and rural community. Furthermore, following his death in London and burial in Wiltshire, at least one newspaper reported that his heart had been dispatched to Jamaica.[45]

Reputations

It was inevitable that the first attempts to define Beckford's legacy should have ended in a contest. Amid the outpouring of grief at the death of the City champion, the corporation's decision to erect a monument at the Guildhall promised to give that process its most public form. A committee of sixteen was duly appointed to oversee the project, and their ranks included close Beckford associates, such as Arthur Beardmore, the Alderman's solicitor. This committee advertised for artists to submit designs and received no fewer than seventeen entries over the summer. Only two were chosen for the next round, those of John Francis Moore, Beckford's favored sculptor, and Agostino Carlini, a founder member of the recently established Royal Academy. Their designs concentrated on Beckford's civic status, with Moore, the eventual winner, portraying the Alderman in a speechifying pose between grieving representations of London and Trade. Some of the discarded designs demonstrated very different responses. One entry in particular was much more graphic, with the Alderman depicted as the dynamic conqueror of tyranny, which was portrayed as a prone figure, shackled with chains and submissive beneath Beckford's feet. It is unclear whether the judges were troubled by the possible overt connection between Beckford and slavery, but they were reluctant to take this design to the second round of the competition. Furthermore, when Moore's statue was ready for public unveiling on midsummer's day 1772, the committee thought it wise to publish a description of the work, to remove any possible misinterpretation.[1]

The challenge of capturing Beckford's legacy continued to divide opinion long after his death. The intensification of domestic and imperial crises ensured continuing recollection of Beckford's views and actions, especially from critics of government policy on both sides of the Atlantic. To

Monument to Beckford by Charles Grignion, a print based on Moore's winning design for the Beckford statue at the Guildhall, 1772. Beckford stands between figures representing Trade and London, with the text of his speech to George III inscribed beneath him. (British Museum, 1870, 1008.2447, © The Trustees of the British Museum)

some he was the "immortal" Beckford, whose stock rose as Anglo-American relations deteriorated. In November 1775, the *Pennsylvania Evening Post* resorted to the well-trodden metaphor of the horse race to portray him as "a mare of great spirit belonging to the livery stable of London," who "not long

Failed design for the Beckford Monument. One of sixteen designs rejected for the Guildhall monument, artist unknown, August 1770. In common with other entrants, it references Beckford's speech to George III, but it also provides an allegorical figure of Tyranny. (© National Portrait Gallery, London, NPG, D42240)

since" delivered "an ugly kick" to the inflexible stallion Tyrant. In a more critical vein, Samuel Johnson, who most famously pondered the link between liberty-crying American patriots and their slave holding, contemptuously referenced Beckford's "barbarity" as the essence of the radical movement. Not even the patriots suggested that Beckford could have averted war in America, but the fame of his audience with George III was further magnified as criticism of the Crown reached new heights amid the upheavals of the American and French Revolutions. Memories of his defiance were given illustration by the radical press in 1798 in hopes of reviving the reformist cause. This political legacy was most fondly cultivated within City circles, where his example was advanced to express a stoical London outlook, undaunted by the threats and encroachments of the great. Amid ensuing battles over parliamentary reform and the abolition of slavery he remained a controversial figure, but these struggles secured him a lasting fame. A less partisan character was also promulgated by 1800, and his life was recommended to the young as an inspiration of what might be achieved with fortitude and virtue. By the Victorian era, the colorful life of his son William Thomas Beckford had begun to overshadow him, but commentators still recalled the Alderman's exploits throughout the nineteenth century.[2]

Popular awareness waned in the twentieth century, but historians continued their fascination with Alderman Beckford, although their interest remained piecemeal and episodic, reflecting particular interests and debates. In this book I have attempted to bring the many sides of his experience together to represent the complete man, without fitting him into a preselected mold to suit the needs of another generation or another historiographical vogue. Beckford needs to be viewed as a transatlantic figure, for only in that formulation can we begin to see both the opportunities and obstacles which lay in his path as he endeavored to make his way in a rapidly changing world. Although his most celebrated actions came at the very end of his life and were largely metropolitan in character, they cannot be divorced from influences that stretched across the Atlantic. His life certainly bore witness to transformations in the societies of both Britain and the Americas, and the actions of such individuals as Beckford contributed to the success and failure of the transatlantic empire. The London-based planters were often dismissed as "absentees," fulfilling a parasitic role of self-indulgence and self-interest, but they were in fact critical supports for the integration of an empire of often ad hoc creation. The networks of imperial brokers, such as Beckford,

Portrait of Beckford, including a depiction of his audience with George III. This was the first print to portray the famous exchange between Beckford and the king in 1770, published by J. Wilkes in April 1798. (© National Portrait Gallery, London, NPG, D42241)

were often fluid and highly personalized, but they undoubtedly facilitated imperial development at a critical stage. Even though he never occupied a government office, his impact in political arenas on both sides of the Atlantic was significant, and his public career stands testament to the ways in which the empire's future was determined by structures of varying degrees of formality.

A biographical perspective may run the risk of narrowness and bias, but it enables study of this interplay of personalities, institutions, and more fluid forms of association, especially over time. In an evolving, complex entity such as the early British empire, the fortunes and outlooks of both individuals and the state developed symbiotically. When Beckford was born, the prospects of the West Indian colonies were brightening, even if European competition remained an ever threatening cloud. These distant territories were not yet significant concerns for the vast majority of Britons, and few metropolitans could boast any real familiarity with them. When Beckford's grandfather and father had sought influence in Britain, they could only turn to their mercantile correspondents or make the hazardous trip across the Atlantic themselves. Metropolitan commercial interests were gaining in strength, thanks in part to imperial developments, but by the time Beckford had arrived in Britain for his schooling, there were few signs that the colonies were socially and culturally integrated. Moreover, although an English education might ensure the acculturation of the planter elite to British mores and lifestyle, it also ran the risk of denuding Caribbean society of white leadership, thereby creating a greater chasm between Britain and colonial society.

The emergence of the London-based group of planters from the 1730s onward seemingly confirmed this process, whereby the wealth of the West Indies was steadily drained away from the islands. This book has shown, however, that this desertion was neither as complete nor as unconditional as critics averred. These British residents played a critical role in ensuring that the interests of the islands were served and that imperial communication and understanding was maintained. Although the furor of the war with Spain in 1739 served notice that the West Indians might have to pressure their metropolitan superiors, Beckford and his allies channelled most of their efforts toward building bridges across the Atlantic. Of course, his actions were driven by self-interest, and he did not refrain from clashes with other planters, merchants, and his own family. Nonetheless, the remarkable energy he brought to Jamaican and metropolitan politics, manifested most directly by the six transoceanic voyages he undertook as an adult, was critical in ensuring greater coordination between the whirling cogs of change on both sides of the Atlantic.

These transatlantic processes were critical to Jamaica's success and to Beckford's own continuing advancement. His establishment at Fonthill has often been seen as representing a new start, but his metropolitan progress still rested heavily on the economy and prestige of his Jamaica estates. He was fortunate to inherit the lion's share of his father's vast holdings, but the uncertainties of the sugar economy did not provide him or his fellow absentees with an easy ascent to metropolitan prominence. Closer study of his accounts reveals that his riches were remarkable by any contemporary standard, but he could not be assured of their continued success. The supervision of his plantations necessitated further trips across the Atlantic and counseled caution in his strategies for advancement within Britain. His success in British politics could not be guaranteed by riches alone either, and his efforts in both London and the provinces reveal that he had to work hard to capitalize on likely opportunities. Thus, he respected his family's City roots, networked his fellow imperialists, and beat the drum of commercial patriotism. His great success at the elections of 1754 also highlighted some support among the British landed elite, but he had not deserted his planter friends or forgotten his Creole roots. His parliamentary speeches, in particular, continued to stress the mutual outlooks and interests of Britons and colonists.

Beckford's personal political success spearheaded a wider accretion of influence by the growing number of West Indian planters settling in Britain. Like Beckford, many of them harbored ambitions to remain transatlantic figures, and their direct contacts with the Caribbean helped to build the West India interest into a dynamic force at Westminster. The increasing revenues of sugar and fierce colonial competition among European rivals captured the attention of the metropolitan elite, and the West Indians took every opportunity to broadcast their value to the nation. Their parliamentary presence was closely monitored by ministers, and these planter-MPs served as the tip of a powerful association of complementary associates. Big planters, such as the Beckfords, had the wealth to purchase the metropolitan estates or connections that might secure more immediate status in British society. While they seized the headlines, they relied on key brokers, such as the merchant Stephen Fuller, who served as the men of business to provide wide-ranging services on both sides of the Atlantic. In turn, they were supported by a coterie of professionals, especially lawyers and bankers, who often acted as go-betweens inside absentee circles. Relations within the West India interest could be fraught, as islands argued, and merchants and planters pitched their interests against one another. Yet the overall strength of the association was readily acknowledged by their critics, who saw the absentees as a potential force for social and political change.

In the vanguard of this interest, Beckford epitomized both its potency and the limits to its advancement. As the mayor of London, the builder of Fonthill, and the friend of Pitt, he enjoyed the most dizzying of the sociopolitical heights, but he also felt the most stinging criticism. Feted by the London crowds, he also had to face the derision and contempt of his parliamentary adversaries. Undaunted, he was a dynamic leader of his imperial causes, even if at times he risked the jealousies of both his allies and his enemies. In a factious age, his political strategies often entailed huge risks, both for himself and his interests, but he never shirked his responsibilities and worked tirelessly to use his position to enhance relations between mother country and colonies. His relationship with Pitt contributed to both the highs and lows of his metropolitan political experience, but it undoubtedly served to place imperial concerns firmly on the national agenda. Quite rightly, Beckford's critics accused him of protecting the sugar planter, but such short-sightedness ignores his wide-ranging role as a sponsor of national and imperial improvement. Although contemporaries guffawed at the idea of direct colonial representation at Westminster, Beckford showed that it was possible to act as a truly imperial politician, even as the structural and principled foundations of the empire were brought into doubt.

The Alderman's political principles and outlook represented the inherent problems of imperial development most directly, revealing a fertile exchange between colonial and British experiences. Although usually seen through the lens of his metropolitan associations, his views were heavily influenced by colonial battles, most obviously the enduring tensions between the Jamaican assembly and the royal governors. These contests confirmed him as an independent politician of broadly Whiggish opinion throughout his life, and by 1754 he was already convinced that aristocratic corruption was the chief threat to the cherished British constitution and that only the middling sorts could halt its demise. Again, this conception of the middling was unconventional, encompassing as it did the country gentry, but his prominence as a

London leader bolstered his conviction that the nation's liberties rested with the sober citizen, reflecting his family's attachment to metropolitan traditions of urban independence. His search for political allies led him into some strange alliances in a fluid political world, but these Anglo-Jamaican principles remained unshaken, and he clearly regarded Pitt as the patriotic hero who would eliminate the noble-based corruption threatening the constitution. The combination of domestic and imperial crises after 1765 predictably shook him to the core and pushed him to espouse political interests he had only cautiously embraced in the early sixties, such as Wilkes and the North American colonies. The dramatic audience of 1770 was in many ways inimical to many of his core political beliefs, running counter to his support of the Crown and his aversion to popular violence. His despondency in his final months highlighted the deep personal investment he had made as an imperial broker over many years, and there is no cause to doubt his genuine despair at these crises. As relations between Britain and its colonies unraveled, so too did their common values, which in turn could only presage the destruction of Beckford's own transatlantic empire.

Amid these crises, Beckford continued to act as a bridge between colonial and metropolitan societies, working alongside his fellow planters to avoid an open breach between Britain and its Caribbean possessions. Given the vulnerabilities of the islands to foreign incursion or slave revolt, it was always more likely that the West Indians would remain loyal, but he helped to focus the attention of Westminster on the challenges of empire as never before. As one of the few planter-MPs to speak regularly on non-imperial issues, he endeavored to highlight the common calamities facing Britain and its empire, although this invited increasing criticism of both him and the interests he represented. Most controversially, from the early 1760s his critics attacked him as a hypocrite for standing in the name of liberty, pointing to the hundreds of slaves who suffered to support his station in life. For the Creole planter, liberty was a privileged, overwhelmingly white preserve, and Beckford did not hesitate to sprinkle his speeches with references to slavery, for his fundamental fear was that despotism might return to undermine the rights of white Jamaicans and London citizens alike. Although an appalling distinction to make, it is clear that he garnered widespread support for this racialized conception of freedom. He was celebrated, without any caveat, as a champion of liberty on both sides of the Atlantic. With plantation slavery a distant phenomenon, known intimately only to those who benefited from it, it would take decades of campaigning before Britons could be convinced that it was an inherent evil that could be eradicated without harming their global standing. Beckford's terse exchange with abolitionist Granville Sharp suggested that he recognized his inconsistency of principle. Furthermore, his silence can be read as recognition that his public prominence bore some responsibility for giving sustenance to the embryonic anti-slaving campaign. His death saved him from facing the full force of the abolition movement or from attaining the status of hate figure, which Warren Hastings became for critics of British rule in India after 1780. There can be little doubt that he would have followed the example of his son and other planters who rejected accusations of tyranny and oppression, but it is hard to see how he could have halted the growing tide of moral outrage.[3]

While slavery became an increasingly uncomfortable stigma for Britons and colonists alike, it would be wrong to overlook the more positive signs of imperial integration that Beckford personified. Only a year after his death appeared Richard Cumberland's *The West Indian*, a sentimental comedy that played to "uncommon applause" at Drury Lane from January 1771. The playwright had socialized with Beckford, and some of the Alderman's traits may well have found their way into the portrayal of Belcour, a young heir from the Caribbean, whose escapades in the City were central to this comedy of manners. In common with other critiques of West Indians, Belcour risked censure for his profligacy, for his hot temper, and for his amorousness. He even sparked trouble by the vigor with which he used his rattan stick to part the milling London crowds, being "accustomed to a land of slaves." He respected the Londoners who confronted him, however, and regarded himself as their "fellow subject and a sharer in their freedom." His acquaintances were also prepared to acknowledge that the nature of Caribbean society was the source of his faults, with his indiscipline attributed to his missing parents, his exposure to slavery, and the effects of the tropical climate. Such understanding was epitomized by his long-lost father, who, amid a predictable happy ending, made an impassioned plea on behalf of the white West Indian: "His manners, passions and opinions are not as yet assimilated to this climate; he comes among you a new character, an inhabitant of a new world, and both hospitality, as well as pity, recommend him to our indulgence." Cumberland's sympathetic portrait did not silence critics of Caribbean excess, even if they might be forced to concede that "for sure that country has no feeble claim, which swells your commerce, and supports your fame." Nonetheless, the success of the play highlighted the impact of Beckford and his fellow planters and their efforts to accommodate themselves to British society. As Beckford could testify, they had not always met with indulgence, but their eagerness to be seen as fellow free Britons offered hope that metropolitan society would come to recognize their value and common virtues.[4]

Such open-mindedness was in short supply in the early 1770s, and for all his connections and efforts, Beckford could not have altered the course of the American Revolution. As one of the staunchest critics of Lord North's American policies, he would doubtlessly have exerted greater energies as the crisis deepened after 1774 and would have continued to work for the unification of the Chathamites and Rockinghamites in opposition. His personal connections with Chatham, however, would have been insufficient to overcome these divisions, and, as he recognized during his lifetime, violence in the colonies could only stiffen British opinion against imperial interests. Even Wilkes struggled to rally support in the metropolis for America and could not encourage his erstwhile supporters to seek common cause with the Sons of Liberty. As they had done since the Stamp Act, the West Indians refused to break ranks and join with the northern colonies to protest against metropolitan incursions, however much they resembled their own political experience. Beckford himself would have lashed ministers for their incompetence and censured their misunderstanding of the empire. In this vein, he might well have seconded the call of Rose Fuller that Britain's grandees should send their sons on a grand tour of the colonies for the acquisition of "American knowledge" rather than to Europe's cultural capitals. More certainly, he would have felt the despair of his political impotence even more keenly in 1783 than he had in 1770.[5]

The travails of the late-eighteenth-century empire should not obscure Beckford's importance as a transatlantic figure. Although on occasion he himself felt compelled to play down his imperial roots for the benefit of metropolitan audiences, in thought and action he remained truly Janus-faced. His life reveals that Britain was a major site of imperial exchange, which transcended the worlds of politics, society, and culture. This full-length study will, I hope, encourage others to engage further with the colonial influences which coursed through eighteenth-century Britain, often through the agency of enterprising individuals. Beckford's career suggests that he regarded Britain as the chief locus of power in the empire, but that should not lead us to diminish the wider metropolitan impact of the Creoles as they passed through its schools, clubs, country retreats, and the doors of Parliament itself. Ridiculed for his elocution and censured for his arriviste expenditure, Beckford faced many obstacles to his advancement, but there can be no doubting his real and symbolic importance as an imperial politician. To this day, his Guildhall statue invokes traditions of liberty as well as uncomfortable reminders of the raw injustices of empire and thus faithfully reflects the inner dialectics of Britain's seminal transformation as a global power. A generation of exciting work has opened our eyes to these key dialogues, and the life of William Beckford should inspire further study of the empire within.

Appendixes

Appendix 1 : The Alderman's Immediate Family

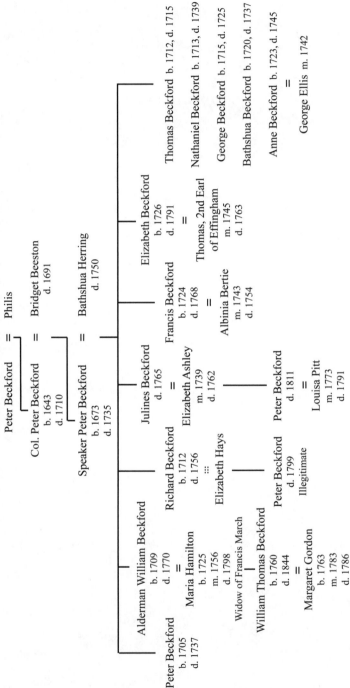

The most reliable source for the Alderman's lineage can be found at the College of Arms (Norfolk Pedigrees, vol. 1, pp. 105-8). For the sake of clarity, not all family connections have been included here. For the Alderman's illegitimate children see M. Fraser, D. Beckford Stanton, and J. Fox, "William Beckford's Paternal Half-Siblings and Their Descendants," *Beckford Journal*, vol. 10 (2004), pp. 14-29.

Appendix 2 : The London Beckfords

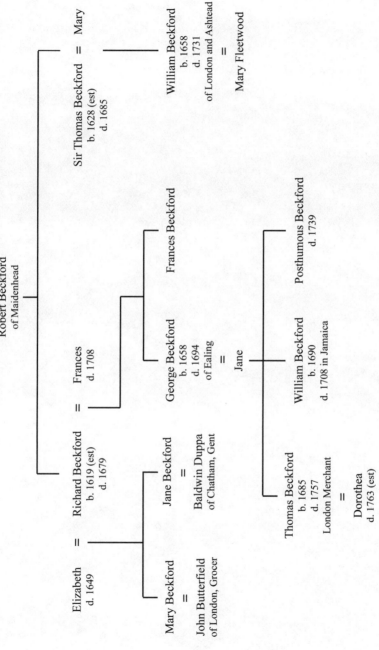

Robert Beckford
of Maidenhead

Elizabeth
d. 1649
=
Richard Beckford
b. 1619 (est)
d. 1679
=
Frances
d. 1708

Sir Thomas Beckford
b. 1628 (est)
d. 1685
=
Mary

William Beckford
b. 1658
d. 1731
of London and Ashtead
=
Mary Fleetwood

Mary Beckford
=
John Butterfield
of London, Grocer

Jane Beckford
=
Baldwin Duppa
of Chatham, Gent

George Beckford
b. 1658
d. 1694
of Ealing
=
Jane

Frances Beckford

Thomas Beckford
b. 1685
d. 1757
London Merchant
=
Dorothea
d. 1763 (est)

William Beckford
b. 1690
d. 1708 in Jamaica

Posthumous Beckford
d. 1739

Notes

Add. Mss	Additional Manuscripts, British Library
BL	British Library, London
Bodl.	Bodleian Library, Oxford
CJ	*Journals of the House of Commons*
Cobbett	W. Cobbett, ed., *Parliamentary History of England* (London, 1806–20)
CSP, Col.	*Calendar of State Papers, Colonial*
CSP, Dom.	*Calendar of State Papers, Domestic*
CTB	*Calendar of Treasury Books*
HMC	*Historical Manuscripts Commission*
JA	Jamaica Archives, Spanish Town
JAJ	*Journals of the Assembly of Jamaica* (Jamaica, 1811–29)
LJ	*Journals of the House of Lords*
LMA	London Metropolitan Archives
NLJ	National Library of Jamaica, Kingston
Pitt Correspondence	W. S. Taylor and J. H. Pringle, eds., *Correspondence of William Pitt, Earl of Chatham* (London, 1840)
TNA	The National Archives, London
Walpole Correspondence	W. S. Lewis, ed., *Yale Edition of Horace Walpole's Correspondence* (London and New Haven, 1937–83)
Walpole Memoirs, George II	J. Brooke, ed., *Horace Walpole: Memoirs of King George II* (New Haven, 1985)

Walpole Memoirs, George III   D. Le Marchant and G. F. R. Barker, eds.,
Horace Walpole: Memoirs of the Reign of King George III (London, 1894)

INTRODUCTION

Epigraph: *City Biography* (London, 1800), pp. 68–69.

1. For a most helpful guide to writing on the Beckfords, see J. Millington, *William Beckford: A Bibliography* (Warminster, 2008). Major studies of William Thomas Beckford, the author of *Vathek*, have included short biographies of the Alderman and his ancestors, most notably, W. Oliver, *The Life of William Beckford* (London, 1932); G. Chapman, *Beckford* (London, 1937); B. Alexander, *England's Wealthiest Son* (London, 1962); B. Fothergill, *Beckford of Fonthill* (London, 1979); T. Mowl, *William Beckford: Composing for Mozart* (London, 1998); D. Ostergard, ed., *William Beckford, 1760–1844: An Eye for the Magnificent* (New Haven, 2001). Also of great interest is Cyrus Reading's *Memoirs of William Beckford of Fonthill, Author of Vathek* (London, 1859), published following the death of William Thomas Beckford. For a recent survey of the absentee planters, in which the Beckfords feature prominently, see M. Parker, *The Sugar Barons* (London, 2011). Modern academic accounts have been brief and largely political, but the following are invaluable: L. Sutherland, "William Beckford," in L. Namier and J. Brooke, eds., *The History of Parliament: The House of Commons, 1754–90* (London, 1964), vol. 2, pp. 75–78; L. Sutherland, "The City of London and the Opposition to Government, 1768–1774," in A. Newman, ed., *Politics and Finance in the Eighteenth Century: Lucy Sutherland* (London, 1984), pp. 115–47; M. Peters, *Pitt and Popularity* (Oxford, 1980), pp. 6–16; Richard Sheridan, "Beckford, William," *Oxford Dictionary of National Biography* (Oxford, 2004), vol. 4, pp. 728–30.

2. The historiography of the Atlantic world is already substantial; for key works, see D. Armitage and M. Braddick, eds., *The British Atlantic World, 1500–1800* (Basingstoke, 2002), and its second edition (Basingstoke, 2009); B. Bailyn, *Atlantic History: Concepts and Contours* (Cambridge, Mass., 2005); E. Mancke and C. Shammas, eds., *The Creation of the British Atlantic World* (Baltimore, 2005); J. P. Greene and P. Morgan, eds., *Atlantic History: A Critical Appraisal* (Oxford, 2009). For a firm rebuttal of its possible shortcomings, see A. Games, "Atlantic History: Definitions, Challenges and Opportunities," *American Historical Review*, vol. 111 (2006), pp. 741–57. For a still broader agenda of reconceptualizing Britain's global exchanges in the period, see, K. Wilson, ed., *A New Imperial History: Culture, Identity and Modernity in Britain and the Empire, 1660–1840*

(Cambridge, 2005). Wilson also notes the vibrancy of recent work on the Caribbean, led by studies of slavery and black experience—*The Island Race: Englishness, Empire and Gender in the Eighteenth Century* (London, 2003), pp. 130–31; also see the historiographical review by C. Petley, "New Perspectives on Slavery and Emancipation in the British Caribbean," *Historical Journal*, 54 (2011), pp. 855–80. An encouraging trend here is increasing study of pre-1760 developments, which helps to right the balance of the historiography, which remains stronger for post-1760 processes (especially the abolitionist era).

3. Games, "Atlantic History," p. 743. For key studies of the impact of individuals and families in the eighteenth-century empire and on a still more global scale, see L. Colley, *The Ordeal of Elizabeth Marsh: A Woman in World History* (London, 2007); V. Carretta, *Equiano the African Miles: The Biography of a Self-Made Man* (Athens, Ga., 2005); M. Ogborn, *Global Lives: Britain and the World, 1550–1800* (Cambridge, 2008); S. Pearsall, *Atlantic Families: Lives and Letters in the Later Eighteenth Century* (Oxford, 2008); E. Rothschild, *The Inner Life of Empires: An Eighteenth-Century History* (Princeton, 2011); S. D. Smith, *Slavery, Family and Gentry Capitalism in the British Atlantic* (Cambridge, 2006); D. Hancock, *Citizens of the World: London Merchants and the British Atlantic Community, 1735–85* (Cambridge, 1995); D. Hancock, *Oceans of Wine: Madeira and the Emergence of American Trade and Taste* (New Haven, 2009). For the crucial role of individuals and networks in the early English empire, see A. Games, *The Web of Empire: English Cosmopolitanism in an Age of Expansion, 1560–1660* (Oxford, 2008).

4. T. Burnard, "Passengers Only: The Extent and Significance of Absenteeism in Eighteenth-Century Jamaica," *Atlantic Studies*, vol. 1 (2004), pp. 178–95; M. Craton, "Reluctant Creoles: The Planters' World in the British West Indies," in B. Bailyn and P. D. Morgan, eds., *Strangers within the Realm: The Cultural Margins of the First British Empire* (Chapel Hill, 1991), esp. pp. 346–49; C. Brown, "The Politics of Slavery," in Armitage and Braddick, *British Atlantic World*, pp. 214–32. Burnard also provides a review of the historiography of the absentees, most notably, F. Pitman, "The West Indian Absentee Planter as a British Colonial Type," *American Historical Association, Pacific Coast Branch*, vol. 2 (1927), pp. 113–27; L. Ragatz, *The Fall of the Planter Class in the British Caribbean, 1763–1833* (New York, 1928); D. Hall, "Absentee-Proprietorship in the British West Indies to about 1850," *Jamaica Historical Review*, vol. 4 (1964), pp. 15–35. The importance of the absentees as an imperial political force has been most directly highlighted by A. O'Shaughnessy, *An Empire Divided: The American Revolution and the British Caribbean* (Philadelphia, 2000). For the

economic mechanics of absenteeism, see B. W. Higman, *Plantation Jamaica, 1750–1850: Capital and Control in a Colonial Economy* (Kingston, 2005). For recent sociocultural studies of the interaction between colonial and metropolitan identities on both sides of the Atlantic, see C. Petley, "'Home' and 'This Country': Britishness and Creole Identity in the Letters of a Transatlantic Slaveholder," *Atlantic Studies*, vol. 6 (2009), pp. 43–61; J. Flavell, *When London Was Capital of America* (New Haven, 2010).

5. Although many historians would remain cautious on the extent of metropolitan interest and understanding of the colonies, there have been a proliferation of studies of the impact of empire on Britain, ranging from the sociopolitical to the economic and cultural—K. Wilson, *The Sense of the People: Politics, Culture and Imperialism, 1715–85* (Cambridge, 1995); E. Gould, *The Persistence of Empire* (Chapel Hill, 2000); D. Armitage, *The Ideological Origins of the British Empire* (Cambridge, 2000); B. Harris, *Politics and the Nation* (Oxford, 2002); J. Walvin, *Fruits of Empire: Exotic Produce and British Taste, 1660–1800* (New York, 1997); N. Zahedieh, *The Capital and the Colonies: London and the Atlantic Economy, 1660–1700* (Cambridge, 2010). For a recent assessment of the ways in which impressions of the West Indies were formulated in the mother country through cultural media, see Kay Dian Kriz, *Slavery, Sugar and the Culture of Refinement: Picturing the British West Indies, 1700–1840* (New Haven, 2008).

6. T. Devine, *Scotland's Empire, 1600–1815* (London, 2003); T. Devine, *To the Ends of the Earth: Scotland's Global Diaspora, 1750–2010* (London, 2011); K. Kenny, ed., *Ireland and the British Empire* (Oxford, 2004); S. Amussen, *Caribbean Exchanges: Slavery and the Transformation of English society, 1640–1700* (Chapel Hill, 2007), p. 227. For an important question mark against the impact of empire, largely focusing on eighteenth-century England, see J. Price, "Who Cared about the Colonies? The Impact of the Thirteen Colonies on British Politics and Society, c. 1714–1775," in B. Bailyn and P. Morgan, eds., *Strangers in the Realm: Cultural Margins of the First British Empire* (Chapel Hill, 1991), pp. 395–436. In a notable call to arms in 2002, Armitage observed that "a cis-Atlantic history [that is, a study of a particular place within a web of wider connections] of early modern England remains the least developed of all those that might apply to the three kingdoms"—Armitage and Braddick, *British Atlantic World*, pp. 21–25.

7. Although I conceive of Beckford as a transatlantic figure, my approach does not strictly conform to the "trans-Atlantic" approach outlined by David Armitage, for I will not provide systematic comparative study of the societies of Jamaica and Britain. Beckford's life also does not fall neatly into categories of

either "cis-Atlantic" or "circum-Atlantic" (embracing the Atlantic as a whole), although Armitage rightly acknowledged that such prescriptions were neither exclusive nor monolithic.

8. Biography of such pivotal figures may also help to bridge the perceived gap between "traditionalists" and proponents of new methodologies and to collapse distinction between micro- and macro-histories—Wilson, *New Imperial History*, p. 22; Rothschild, *Inner Life of Empires*, pp. 6–8.

9. Further studies of the Caribbean absentees are still needed, although note C. Taylor, "The Journal of an Absentee Proprietor, Nathaniel Phillips of Slebech," *Journal of Caribbean History*, vol. 18 (1983), pp. 67–82; C. Taylor, "The Perils of a West Indian Heiress: Case Studies of the Heiresses of Nathaniel Phillips of Slebech," *Welsh History Review*, vol. 12 (1985), pp. 495–513. The most promising candidates remain those with significant surviving archives, such as Beckford's Jamaican associates Stephen Fuller (papers at the Somerset Heritage Centre), Rose Fuller (East Sussex Record Office), James Knight (BL); and the Barhams and Vassalls (Bodl.). Another promising collection is that of the Martins of Antigua (BL), and Simon Smith has exploited the potential of the published letters of the Lascelles-Maxwells of Barbados—S. D. Smith, ed., *The Lascelles and Maxwell Letterbook, 1736–69* (Microform Academic Publishers, 2002); S. D. Smith, *Slavery, Family and Gentry Capitalism*. For a Nevis absentee, see K. Mason, "The World an Absentee Planter and His Slaves Made: Sir William Stapleton and His Nevis Sugar Estate, 1722–1740," *Bulletin of the John Rylands University Library of Manchester*, vol. 75 (1993), pp. 103–31.

10. Particular encouragement for study of the "empire within" comes from scholarship on the Indian "Nabobs," or servants of the East Indian Company, whose metropolitan impact was often compared to that of the West Indians from the mid-eighteenth century—P. Lawson and J. Phillips, "Our Execrable Banditti: Perceptions of Nabobs in Mid-Eighteenth Century Britain," in *Albion*, vol. 16 (1984), pp. 225–41; H. Bowen, M. Lincoln, and N. Rigby, eds., *The Worlds of the East India Company* (Woodbridge, 2002); T. Nechtman, *Nabobs: Empire and Identity in Eighteenth-Century Britain* (Cambridge, 2010).

CHAPTER 1: THE TORRID ZONE

1. *CSP, Col.* 1706–8, p. 340; *CSP, Col.* 1710–11, pp. 70–71.

2. Add. Mss 12422, pp. 251–52. Some accounts are even more dramatic, suggesting that the Colonel's demise was precipitated by a fall down a flight of stairs, but Barham's eyewitness account appears more reliable. It also accords with a report to the Royal Africa Company that the Colonel "running to the

governor, made a false step and fell to the ground and died soon after"—TNA, T70/8, p. 102.

3. College of Arms Mss, Norfolk Pedigrees, vol. 1, pp. 105–8; *Publications of the Harleian Society: Registers*, vol. 9 (London, 1884), p. 156. Significantly, when William Thomas Beckford attempted to reconstruct his family tree at the end of the eighteenth century, the College of Arms could trace the direct line back only to Peter and Philis and to the baptism of Peter in Clerkenwell in 1643. The heralds also could not establish their direct connection to the Beckfords of London, who were granted arms in 1686—College of Arms Mss, Grants of Arms, vol. 3, p. 282.

4. Guildhall Library Mss 6647/1, fols. 16, 28, Butchers' Company apprenticeship bindings. Peter Beckford senior also apprenticed another son, Nicholas, in 1663 to John Wood, a locksmith of St. Sepulchre, another parish on the City's northwestern boundaries. It is possible that this Peter might be the innkeeper who struck trade tokens at the "Guy of Warwick" (tavern), in Field Lane, Holborn Bridge in the mid-seventeenth century—W. Boyne, *Trade Tokens in the Seventeenth Century*, rev. by G. Williamson (London, 1889–91), vol. 1, p. 598. Citizen Peter Beckford also took on an apprentice from Maidenhead in 1658, suggesting a link to the most successful branch of the family in late Stuart London.

5. The parish of St. Sepulchre had been the residence of Richard Beckford, son of Robert of Maidenhead, until at least early 1641—Society of Genealogists (London), *The Poll Tax for London in 1641*, transcribed by T. Dale (1934), p. 31. This might help to explain the later preference of Richard Beckford for the aldermanship of Farringdon Without in 1754.

6. R. Latham and W. Matthews, eds., *The Diary of Samuel Pepys* (London, 1983), vol. 2, p. 6; M. Craton and J. Walvin, *A Jamaican Plantation: A History of Worthy Park* (London, 1970), p. 38. Many accounts have relied upon the famous diary of Samuel Pepys, which records in January 1661 that Pepys was told by the Rev. Thomas Fuller that a parishioner of his "hath a mind to go to Jamaica." This parishioner has been assumed to be Peter Beckford, without any other corroborating evidence. Entries for the Beckford family in the parish records of St. Catherine's, Jamaica, do not commence until 1669. A report of August 1689 also suggested that Peter had "lived about 20 years" on the island—TNA, SP/32, fol. 235, Gilbert Heathcote to Mr. Vernon, 3 Aug. 1689. Boyd Alexander exposed the romance of the lone adventurer model many years ago, although he could only speculate that "there must be some connection" between the London and Jamaican Beckfords—*England's Wealthiest Son* (London, 1962), pp. 29–30.

7. JA, 1B/11/1, vol. 3, fols. 124, 133; Add. Mss 12419, fols. 20v–21; Richard Dunn, *Sugar and Slaves: The Rise of the Planter Class in the English West Indies, 1624–1713* (Chapel Hill, 1972), pp. 154–55. The estates of both Peter and Richard Beckford are marked on the earliest printed maps of Jamaica—TNA, CO700/Jamaica 3; *The Laws of Jamaica* (London, 1684), which includes "A New and Exact Mapp of the Island of Jamaica." Richard Sheridan has shown that only forty-seven landowners possessed Jamaican estates of over 1,000 acres in 1670. They faced similar challenges to landowners on Barbados, where (at an earlier date) planters also took time to prepare their estates for sugar production—R. Menard, *Sweet Negotiations: Sugar, Slavery, and Plantation Agriculture in Early Barbados* (Charlottesville, 2006); R. Menard, "Law, Credit, the Supply of Labour, and the Organization of Sugar Production in the Colonial Greater Caribbean: A Comparison of Brazil and Barbados in the Seventeenth Century" in J. McCusker and K. Morgan, eds., *The Early Modern Atlantic Economy* (Cambridge, 2000), pp. 154–62. By 1681 it was estimated that a 1,000-acre sugar plantation might have necessitated a £5,000 investment to produce an annual yield of £1,000—*Sugar and Slavery: An Economic History of the British West Indies, 1623–1775* (Caribbean Universities Press, 1974), pp. 216, 219.

8. Bodl., Ms Eng. Misc. c. 690, fol. 36. The will of Edward Beckford was written in September 1668. A Captain Beckford, as Richard was titled in Edward Backwell's accounts in 1663–66, was recorded as selling chocolate, cocoa nuts, and "Jamaicia-pepper" at Customs-House Key in London in 1662—Henry Stubbe, *The Indian Nectar, or a Discourse concerning Chocolata* (London, 1662), preface.

9. *CSP, Col.* 1675–76, pp. 131–32. Richard Beckford can be more securely identified as son of Robert of Maidenhead. He was born c. 1619 and, alongside brother Thomas (born c. 1628), became a member of the Clothworkers' Company. He was settled in St. Dunstan's-in-the East from the 1640s. Richard Pares noted the presence of a Richard Beckford in Barbados in the late 1640s but doubted whether he ever set foot in Jamaica—"Merchants and Planters," *Economic History Review*, supplement no. 4 (1960), esp. pp. 6, 60.

10. JA, 1B/11/1/2, fols. 29–30; *CSP, Dom.* 1658–59, pp. 431, 489, 542; National Monuments Record, report on 34 Great Tower Street. Richard's business with the navy may well have led to his interest in Jamaica, for by 1655 he was undertaking important commissions (to the tune of £3,000) for supplying the ships of Vice Admiral Goodson, one of the commanders for the Jamaica conquest—*CSP, Dom.* 1655–56, p. 431. His bank accounts with Edward Backwell reveal brisk business in 1663–66, a co-partnership with Francis Chaplin, and

dealings with the firms of Houblon, Letheuiller, Lordell, and Godfrey—Royal Bank of Scotland Archives, EB/1/1, fols. 63, 67; EB/1/2, fol. 48, 194; EB/1/3, fols. 43, 68; EB/1/4, fol. 369.

11.   Sheridan, *Sugar and Slaves*, pp. 262–63. Powers of Attorney granted by Richard Beckford suggest that his principal agents on the island in the 1670s were Nicholas Hicks, sometime merchant of Port Royal, William Bragge, and Daniel Jordaine—M. Pawson and D. Buisseret, *Port Royal, Jamaica* (Oxford, 1975), pp. 158, 162. Richard Beckford later sold 1,000 acres to Peter Beckford in October 1676, shortly before his death, when the latter was described as "of Port Royal"— Bodl., Beckford Mss b. 8, fols. 8–9. For a striking illustration of the importance of kin ties in forging Atlantic success over several generations, see J. M. Price, *Perry of London: A Family and a Firm on the Seaborne Frontier, 1615–1753* (Cambridge, Mass., 1992), esp. pp. 7–18, 114–19.

12.   *CSP, Col.* 1669–74, p. 107; 1681–85, p. 590; *Caribbeana* (London, 1914), vol. 3, p. 6; TNA, SP/32, fol. 235; Pawson and Buisseret, *Port Royal*, p. 85. On Richard's death in 1679, no mention of Peter was made in either his will or inventory, and thus it cannot be assumed that the Londoner relied upon his less established relations to take the risks inherent with life on the island—TNA, PCC, will of Richard Beckford, proved 1679; LMA, CLA/002/02/01/1646, Orphans Inventory of Richard Beckford, 1680. Richard's estate was valued at £7,960, with a further £8,451 in debts outstanding to him. Richard's interest in the island also led to his investment in the slaving Royal African Company, founded in 1672.

13.   Jamaica Archives, 1B/11/1, vol. 4, fol. 90; vol. 5, fol. 173. A survey of island holdings in 1670 ranked Peter Beckford as the second largest landholder in the parish of Clarendon, with 2,238 acres. Richard Beckford had only 578 acres in St. Catherine's, where sixteen landowners possessed 1,000 acres or more—*CSP, Col.* 1669–74, pp. 101–3. Pawson and Buisseret cite records which refer to Peter as a merchant as late as 1681, and he also held property in Port Royal, including a wharf, which Sir Thomas Lynch thought another argument for his commanding the forts there in 1683—TNA, CO1/53, no. 32.

14.   An account of 1684 suggested that Peter Beckford was Lynch's nephew, but it has not been possible to corroborate this familial connection—*CSP, Col.* 1681–85, p. 590. Both Peter and Richard Beckford had backed Lynch's rival, Sir Thomas Modyford, in petitions of November 1670, and the land patents to both parties in 1671–75 may have been political sweeteners—TNA, CO1/25, no. 91. The date of Peter's marriage to Bridget Beeston is unrecorded, but the birth of his eldest son, the Speaker, occurred in 1673. Colonel Peter later acted as one of the attorneys for William Beeston, a leading spokesman for planter rights in the

island assembly, and later governor 1692–1702—JA, 1B/11/24, vol. 10, fol. 19. For the planter-buccaneer split, see Dunn, *Sugar and Slaves*, pp. 155–63.

15.   Latham and Matthews, *Diary of Samuel Pepys*, vol. 9, pp. 81–82, 405; *CSP, Dom.* 1675–76, p. 168. By 1665, Sir Thomas and his partner were handling naval contracts totaling £24,800—*CSP, Dom.* 1664–65, p. 353.

16.   *CSP, Col.* 1669–74, p. 631; information from the Clothworkers' Company, London. Sir Thomas Beckford's will reveals that he was godfather to Thomas (1682–1731), youngest son of the Colonel, whom Sir Thomas called his "cosen"—NA, PCC, will of Sir Thomas Beckford, proved 1685. Further evidence of the strengthening of this connection comes with the burial of Richard Beckford's grandson in the Beckford family vault at St. Catherine's Church in 1708. The office of island secretary also enhanced Peter Beckford's status on the island, and his responsibility for the public records included the registration of land grants—see J. H. Parry, "The Patent Officers in the British West Indies," *English Historical Review*, vol. 69 (1954), pp. 200–225.

17.   Jamaica Archives, 1B/11/24, fol. 164v. The first evidence of business dealings between Gracedieu and Beckford came in 1686, when it was reported that Peter Beckford had sent 3,000 pounds of bark to Gracedieu for sale in London and/or Flanders—*CTB*, vol. 8, pp. 644–45, 672. In the same year, Gracedieu acted as agent for Peter's purchase of a 62-acre copyhold estate in Kentish Town for £2,200—Bodl., Beckford Mss c. 84, fol. 1. Among Gracedieu's contacts, that with the Collett family might have been of the most enduring importance, presaging the Alderman's close relationship with Thomas. For the developing role of the colonial agents at this time, see L. Penson, *The Colonial Agents of the British West Indies: A Study in Colonial Administration* (London, 1924), chapter 3.

18.   *CSP, Dom.* 1677–78, p. 297; *CSP, Dom. Addenda*, 1660–85, pp. 457–59; *CSP, Col.* 1689–92, p. 22; NA, CO138/6, pp. 166–71. For the problems inherent in slops contracts, see J. Ehrman, *The Navy in the War of William III, 1689–97* (Cambridge, 1953), pp. 122–24. Gracedieu was knighted as sheriff of London in 1697, when he conveyed the City's address to the king to acknowledge the Peace of Ryswick. He acted as the island's agent 1693–1704 but went bankrupt in 1710. Significantly, Heathcote and Gracedieu were both members of the Vintners' Company, which would later offer notable support to the Alderman.

19.   *CSP, Col.* 1681–85, p. 590; *CSP, Dom.* 1689–90, pp. 92, 208; *CSP, Col.* 1693–96, p. 623; Josiah Burchett, *Mr. Burchett's Justification of his Naval-memoirs* (London, 1704), p. 125. Details of the two companies he commanded can be found in TNA, CO137/1, no. 178.

20. The date of the painting (now housed at Devon House, Kingston) and the identity of the artist remain obscure. The inscription of the painting alludes to his appointment as lieutenant governor of Jamaica but suggests this happened in 1692, rather than in 1697 or 1702. In later life William Thomas ("Vathek") Beckford suggested that the Colonel had been painted by a visiting French artist on the island on the occasion of his appointment as lieutenant governor—H. V. Lansdown, *Recollections of the Late William Beckford* (private circulation, 1893), p. 10. However, the style of painting is very much in keeping with the London studio portraits of colonial luminaries, such as Thomas "Diamond" Pitt, and may have been painted during one of the Colonel's visits to London.

21. CO137/1, no. 192, address of Jamaica council and assembly, 1694. An interesting sign of Peter Beckford's limited acquaintance in the capital comes with a letter dated 1684, in which he implored his "cousin" Duppa to take care of his wife's relatives on their forthcoming trip to London. Beckford revealed that his wife's family were strangers to his friends and relatives in the capital, and that he and Duppa had never exchanged any correspondence. The Duppa in question can be identified as Baldwin Duppa of Chatham, who married Jane, daughter of Alderman Richard—Add. Mss 27968, fol. 102. For the "shrinking" of the Atlantic in terms of communications, see I. K. Steele, *The English Atlantic, 1675– 1740: An Exploration of Communication and Community* (Oxford, 1988).

22. W. A. Feurtado, *Officials and Other Personages of Jamaica from 1655 to 1790* (Jamaica, 1896), p. 9. This stance also parallels his dealings with the Royal Africa Company, for whom he acted as agent 1707–9. He supported the company in its battles with those wishing to break the company's slaving monopoly, but he advised the London directors that the best way to win over the islanders was by assuring planters of an adequate supply of slaves—TNA, T70/8, p. 76. Other relatives were less diplomatic, especially the separate trader Captain [Thomas] Beckford, who was accused of stealing £5,000 of company effects—C. Davenant, *Reflections upon the constitution and management of the trade to Africa* (London, 1709), p. 1. For important new insights into these transatlantic battles, see W. Pettigrew, "Free to Enslave: Politics and the Escalation of Britain's Transatlantic Slave Trade, 1688–1714," *William and Mary Quarterly*, vol. 64 (2007), pp. 3–38.

23. Dunn, *Sugar and Slaves*, pp. 163–65; A. Boyer, *The History of the Reign of Queen Anne, digested into annals* (London, 1703), p. 68; *CSP, Col.* 1706–8, p. 340. I am grateful to James Robertson for pointing out that Henry Barham's account of the incident may have been an attempt to heal differences arising from the feud between Governor Handasyd and the Beckfords.

24. For the development of Spanish Town as the island capital, see J. Robertson, *Gone Is the Ancient Glory: Spanish Town, 1534–2000* (Kingston, 2005), esp. chapter 3. Colonel Peter's first investment in Spanish Town may have come as early as the mid-1670s, when his co-partner Francis Price built a storehouse there to serve their plantation at Guanaboa—*A Jamaica Plantation*, p. 38. No detailed survey of the Colonel's lands survives to ascertain their layout, but "great houses" were listed at a much later date at the Retreat plantation (in Clarendon) and Bodle's Pen (in St. Dorothy's)—JA, 1B/11/3, vol. 55, fols. 87, 101v.

25. Speaker Peter spent some time in London as a child, attending the Merchant Taylors' school in 1681–83 (between the ages of eight and ten). He attended New College, Oxford 1688–89. He was evidently known to London merchants, such as Robert Hewytt of Fenchurch Street, who in 1688 left bequests for both Peter and his younger brother Thomas—Add. Mss 34181, fol. 200.

26. *Vindication of the late Governor and Council of Jamaica* (London, 1716), p. 5. For vivid illustrations of the clashes between the assembly and governors at this time, see F. Cundall, *The Governors of Jamaica in the First Half of the Eighteenth Century* (London, 1937), pp. 51–103.

27. The battle saw the most intense coverage of Jamaican affairs since the conquest and was linked to major contests over the future of the Africa trade and the award of the Asiento by the Spanish to the South Sea Company. For the pro-Beckford position, see *The Groans of Jamaica, express'd in a letter from a Gentleman residing there, to his Friend in London* (London, 1714), esp. pp. 42–44; for bitter responses, see *A True Account of the late piracies of Jamaica* (London, 1716); [William Wood], *A View of the Proceedings of the Assemblies of Jamaica for some years past* (London, 1716). A victorious thankful address (for removing Hamilton) to the king signed by the Speaker was presented by Sir Gilbert Heathcote in December 1716, and subsequently appeared in the London press—*Daily Courant*, 29 Dec. 1716.

28. TNA, SP34/20, fol. 100, William Beckford to Lord Dartmouth, 13 Feb. 1713. This is the first evidence of a formal political campaign involving both the London and Jamaican Beckfords, and here William refers to Speaker Beckford as his "cozin." This William (died 1731) would later become a gentleman of the privy chamber under George I—*The Present State of the British Court* (London, 1720), p. 23. He did not seek to emulate the civic success of his father and uncle, but he was clearly prominent, gaining appointment to the City lieutenancy in 1707 (and 1710) and serving as a commissioner for a new Bank of England subscription in 1710—*Daily Courant*, 23 May 1707, 22 Feb. 1710; *Evening Post*, 7 Oct. 1710.

29. Bodl., Rawlinson A312, fol. 105, Peter Beckford to [?], 25 Oct. 1713. Significantly, even Beckford's rivals questioned the applicability of Whig and Tory to the Jamaican political world, seeing them as "too narrow and too dangerous to go upon" on an island with "so few inhabitants"—*Vindication of the late Governor and Council of Jamaica* (London, 1716), pp. 23–24. English observers had no compunction, labeling the Beckford ally and agent Sam Page a Tory and Jacobite—*Vindication*, pp. 3–4.

30. TNA, T70/8, p. 109; *Vindication*, p. 5; *CSP Col.* 1720–21, p. 362; JA, 1B/11/3, vol. 18, fols. 200–202. Land patent records show that the Speaker added 2,600 acres in a burst of patents in 1712–19, including an important first stake in St. Thomas's in the East—JA, 1B/11/1, vol. 15, fols. 251, 256; vol. 16, fols. 102, 140, 167, 224.

31. JA, 1B/11/13/18, fols. 200–202, for the first inventory taken after Beckford's death in 1735; also 1B/11/3/21, fols. 74–75, for the second inventory (with debts totaling J£123,000) after the death of executor George Ellis, 1740; *Post Boy*, 10 Mar. 1719; Bodl., Ms North c. 9, fols. 188–89, Peter Beckford to Lord North, 6 January 1722; *Caribbeana*, vol. 3 (London, 1914), p. 7. The combined value of the 2,116 slaves and "other stock" amounted to J£83,643. At least 374 (17.7 percent) of the slave population were children, and at least 741 (35 percent) were women. These figures do not include Dank's plantation in Clarendon, a major estate which later sustained a slave population of some 200 slaves—JA, 1B/11/3, vol. 55, fol. 94.

32. Add. 12422, p. 254. Sheridan points out that although Jamaican exports doubled in the period 1703–39, the pace of growth was adversely affected by supplies of slaves and planter failures to develop larger estates—*Sugar and Slavery*, pp. 214–21. For the importance of island influences on Jamaican churches, see L. Nelson, "Anglican Church Building and Local Context in Early Jamaica," *Perspectives in Vernacular Architecture*, vol. 10 (2005), pp. 63–79.

33. For Jamaican society and culture at this time, see, Dunn, *Sugar and Slaves*, pp. 262–99. It is possible that the Speaker's education might have been even more extensive, for a pamphlet of 1716 alluded to "the various passages of his life, whether in Jamaica, or other parts of America, or in France or Holland," although this might include his exile after killing a judge—*Vindication*, p. 26. In Barbados, Codrington College gained some renown as an educational establishment, but the white elite still sent their sons to Britain for their education—O'Shaughnessy, *Empire Divided*, pp. 6, 19–20.

34. Somerset Heritage Centre, DD/DN 501, William Lewis to Thomas and Stephen Fuller, 2 Jan., 20 July 1758. By that date, Lewis estimated that the annual

costs of maintaining a pupil at Westminster amounted to £150. Andrew O'Shaughnessy provides an excellent overview of the impact of an English education on eighteenth-century West Indians—*Empire Divided*, pp. 19–27. For the appalling death rates on the island, see T. Burnard, "A Failed Settler Society: Marriage and Demographic Failure in Early Jamaica," in *Journal of Social History*, vol. 28 (1994), pp. 63–82.

35. G. F. Russell Barker and A. H. Stennings, *The Record of Old Westminsters* (London, 1928), vol. 1, pp. 66–67. *London Evening Post*, 27–29 June 1770. For the growth of the metropolis, see George Rudé, *Hanoverian London, 1714–1808* (London, 1971); J. Summerson, *Georgian London* (New Haven, 2006); M. Ogborn, *Spaces of Modernity: London's Geographies, 1680–1780* (New York, 1998). Even by 1750, Spanish Town was probably a settlement of fewer than 2,000 white inhabitants—Robertson, *Gone Is the Ancient Glory*, p. 91.

36. Somerset Heritage Centre, DD/DN 501, W. Lewis to T. and S. Fuller, 2 Jan., 20 July 1758; John Gregory to S. Fuller, 15 Apr. 1758; TNA, C11/1552/12, testimony of Thomas Beckford, 22 June 1739. The warm welcome extended by Beckford's relations contradicts Edward Long's later account of "the imperious domination of strangers," which, according to him, planter offspring experienced in London—*History of Jamaica*, vol. 1, p. 3. Thomas Beckford was a significant City figure, gaining election to the court of assistants of the Royal African Company in January 1721 and serving as director of the Royal Exchange Assurance office for twenty years from 1732—*Evening Post*, 19–21 Jan. 1721; *London Evening Post*, 29 June–1 July 1732. On these boards he mixed with important figures in Caribbean commerce, including Collett, March, Phillips, Tryon, and Drake. Henry Neate, the future partner of Julines Beckford, was also a Royal African director.

37. O'Shaughnessy, *Empire Divided*, pp. 9–10; Edward Long, *A History of Jamaica* (London, 1970), vol. 2, p. 274. A good example of the cultural value of an English education comes through in the remark of a London correspondent to a Barbadian parent that his son's speech "is almost quite changed and he will soon lose the little that he has left of the Barbadian accent and dialect"—S. Smith, ed., *The Lascelles and Maxwell Letterbook, 1739–1769* (Microform Academic Publishers, 2002), H690, fol. 168, Lascelles and Maxwell to Thomas Finlay, 17 May 1744. Planter families could strengthen ties through English schooling. William Lewis wanted his children to board in the same house as the Beckfords' children, "as there is, and always has been, an intimacy between us and our families"—Somerset Heritage Centre, DD/DN 501, Lewis to T. and S. Fuller, 2 Jan. 1758.

38. *Pietas Universitatis Oxoniensis in obitum serenissmi Regis Georgii I et grat-*
ulatio in augustissimi Regis Geogii II inaugurationem (Oxford, 1727), p. 146. The
verse might read as follows: "At last a golden peace smiles across sea and land/
and remains forever undisturbed in the citadel of the gods./You provided her,
Majesty, through your wisdom and your fleet/and now, prince, you seek her on
your own behalf, through your piety." The reference to the fleet may well reflect
Beckford's delight in the relief of Gibraltar from Spanish attack, although the
fleet of Sir Charles Wager had already sailed before George II's succession. Less
plausibly, it may also refer to Francis Hosier's force which sought to blockade the
Spanish treasure fleets in the Caribbean in 1726–28, although its success was
much more doubtful, with the loss of some 4,000 men through disease.

39. Balliol College archives, Clark list of members, fols. 53, 60–61, 66, 69,
76, 81, 84, 90, 92, 98, 100, 106–7, 113; John Jones, *Balliol College: A History*
(2nd ed., Oxford, 2005), pp. 68, 130, 137–63; L. S. Sutherland and L. G. Mitchell,
The History of the University of Oxford (Oxford, 1986), pp. 295–98, 368–71. Balliol
and Christ Church were the most popular colleges for medical students in the
1720s—Sutherland and Mitchell, *History of the University of Oxford*, p. 699. Balliol
was not a common destination for sons of West Indians, with only two others
listed in the 1720s (both from Antigua). It is thus likely that the college's metropolitan links, including its visitor (the bishop of London) and its property in
Clerkenwell and St. Margaret Pattens (adjoining St. Mary at Hill), may have influenced his final choice of college. Few gentleman- or fellow-commoners focused
on their studies long enough to attain an M.A., with only about 1 percent doing so
in the period 1690–1719. By the late 1750s, there were specific complaints of "that
flighty turn" of the West Indians at the universities, although in part this reputation may lie with their readiness to mix with their school friends—Somerset
Heritage Centre, DD/DN 505, S. Whitson to Stephen Fuller, 22 Oct. 1759.

40. R. W. Innes Smith, *English-Speaking Students of Medicine at the*
University of Leiden (Edinburgh, 1932), p. 18. For the early links between the
Fullers and Beckford, see D. Crossley and R. Saville, eds., "The Fuller Letters,
1728–55: Guns, Slaves, and Finance," *Sussex Record Society*, vol. 76 (1991), esp.
pp. 14–15, 25. In 1730 Speaker Beckford advised the Fullers on the plantation
earmarked for Rose Fuller once his medical studies had ended. The education of
Rose Fuller at Cambridge, Leiden, and Paris in 1728–32 came to a hefty £547—
East Sussex Record Office, SAS/RF/15/27, Fuller account book, fol. 390v.

41. BL, Sloane Mss 4050, fols. 140, 160, 220, 272, Rose Fuller to Sir Hans
Sloane, 12 June, 19 July, 15 Oct., 1729, 7 Feb. 1730; T. Gelfand, *Professionalizing*
Modern Medicine: Paris Surgeons and Medical Science and Institutions in the

Eighteenth Century (Westport, Conn., 1980), esp. chapter 6. Rose Fuller acknowledged Sloane's direct intervention as crucial to gaining access to Boerhaave, and argued that for private study "there cannot be a more convenient place than Leyden." Beckford's time at Paris would have been a very informal arrangement with an army physician or surgeon, and its duration remains unclear. The surviving Balliol battels books for the early 1730s only record payments by him for a four-week period in the summer of 1733, but the college lists retained his name until the academic year of 1734–35 (although he paid no battels for that year). His critics still recalled his medical training in 1769, suggesting that his father had him trained as a doctor to cure the "honourable sores" of his slaves—*Public Advertiser*, 18 Nov. 1769.

42. TNA, PCC will of Peter Beckford, 1736; JA, 1A/3, liber 75, fol. 86. The Clarendon estates settled on Peter junior in 1727 would have yielded a sizable revenue, judging by the 105 slaves which accompanied this grant.

43. M. Tinling, ed., *The Correspondence of Three William Byrds of Westover, Virginia 1684–1776* (Charlottesville, 1977), p. 473; *Virginia Magazine of History and Biography*, 9, no. 3 (1902), pp. 234–35.

44. JA, 1B/11/3, vol. 18, fol. 187. For Virginian responses to eighteenth-century slavery, see E. Morgan's classic *American Slavery, American Freedom* (New York, 1975). For the pressures working on Jamaican whites, see T. Burnard, *Mastery, Tyranny and Desire: Thomas Thistlewood and His Slaves in the Anglo-Jamaican World* (Chapel Hill, 2004), esp. chapter 1. The Maroon revolt led to the arrival of an extra six companies of troops in 1734, with official recognition that "the fate of the island may in some measure depend upon their success"—Library of Congress, Vernon-Wager Mss, series 8D/181.6, Some Considerations on the Present State of Jamaica, 25 Oct. 1734. For an account of the anti-Maroon campaign, see M. Lustig, *Robert Hunter, 1666–1734: New York's Augustan Statesman* (Syracuse, 1983), pp. 177–215.

CHAPTER 2: TRANSATLANTIC MAN

Epigraph: Charles Leslie, *A New History of Jamaica* (Edinburgh, 1739), p. 15.

1. Leslie, *New History of Jamaica*, p. 15.

2. T. Burnard, "Passengers Only: The Extent and Significance of Absenteeism in Eighteenth-Century Jamaica," *Atlantic Studies*, vol. 1 (2004), pp. 178–95; B. Higman, *Plantation Jamaica, 1750–1850: Capital and Control in a Colonial Economy* (Kingston, 2005).

3. For the multifarious roles played by transatlantic family networks, see Sarah Pearsall, *Atlantic Families: Lives and Letters in the Later Eighteenth Century*

(Oxford, 2008). For a still wider perspective, see E. Rothschild, *The Inner Life of Empires* (Princeton, 2011).

4. TNA, PCC, will of Peter Beckford, proved 1736.

5. Two inventories of debts survive for Speaker Beckford—JA, 1B/11/13/18, fols. 200–202 (c. 1736); 1B/11/3/21, fols. 74–75 (1740); *Gentleman's Magazine* (London, 1735), p. 737. Charles Leslie recorded that "his money in the banks and on mortgages is reckoned at a million and a half"—*New and Exact Account of Jamaica*, p. 298. The median inventory estate for the period 1741–45 has been recorded as £3,819 sterling, although this would rise to £9,361 sterling in 1771–75—Sheridan, *Sugar and Slavery*, pp. 229–31. For clarification of the superior wealth of the Jamaicans in the British Atlantic world, see T. Burnard, "'Prodigious Riches': The Wealth of Jamaica before the American Revolution," *Economic History Review*, n.s., vol. 54 (2001), pp. 506–24. In England and Wales, only ten landowners drew rental incomes of over £20,000 in 1760—J. V. Beckett, "Landownership and Estate Management," in G. Mingay, ed., *The Agrarian History of England and Wales*, vol. 6 (Cambridge, 1989), pp. 590–640. Richard Pares used Peter Beckford's list of debtors to argue that planters were not dependant on longer-term metropolitan mortgages for capital until the later eighteenth century, although this has been contested—"Merchants and Planters," *Economic History Review*, supplement no. 4 (1960); S. D. Smith, "Merchants and Planters Revisited," *Economic History Review*, vol. 55 (2002), pp. 434–65.

6. JA, 1B/11/24, vol. 28, fols. 59–60, 96v, 175v, 176v, 177.

7. JA, IB/11/3, vol. 18, fol. 187, inventory taken in October 1735. For the growing Creole character of Spanish Town at this time, see James Robertson, *Gone Is the Ancient Glory: Spanish Town, Jamaica, 1534–2000* (Kingston, 2005), pp. 84–89; James Robertson, "Late Seventeenth-Century Spanish Town, Jamaica: Building an English City on Spanish Foundations," *Early American Studies*, vol. 6 (2008), pp. 346–90. For planter estate houses, see Barry Higman, *Jamaica Surveyed* (Kingston, 1988); Edward Brathwaite, *The Development of Creole Society in Jamaica, 1770–1820* (Oxford, 1971), pp. 122–26.

8. Robertson, *Gone Is the Ancient Glory*, pp. 68–79; Add. Mss 12422, p. 278; Bodl., Clarendon dep. c. 389/1, Henry Long to Henry Barham, 10 June 1738; TNA, CO137/23, fols. 2–3, Edward Trelawny to the Board of Trade, 21 Nov. 1738; *JAJ*, vol. 3, pp. 426–39. Long noted that Trelawny had been feted with a ball at the Kingston courthouse and would host his own entertainment at Spanish Town.

9. T. Barnardiston, *Reports of Cases in the High Court of Chancery* (London, 1742), pp. 268–70. Peter Beckford had made a trip to Dieppe during his travels in

1736–37, perhaps at the start of an intended European tour cut short due to illness.

10. Dorset History Centre, D/PIT/T859, abstract of title of Peter Beckford, c. 1815–16. This document provides the fullest account of the settlement reached by the Beckfords after these contests.

11. JA, 1B/11/24, vol. 28, fols. 215v–216; vol. 29, fol. 6; *JAJ*, vol. 3, p. 446; Bodl., Mss Clarendon dep. c. 376, bundle 3. Jannet Hynes to Henry Barham, 27 June 1738. One of William's attorneys was Alex McKenzie, a Clarendon planter with whom the family co-owned the Croft's plantation.

12. JA, 1B/11/24, vol. 29, f. 174; TNA, C12/1107/23; C24/1541, Chancery depositions, Trinity 1739, testimony of Francis Nicholls, 9 October 1739. For a recent study of slave culture and belief, see V. Brown, *The Reaper's Garden* (Cambridge, Mass., 2008).

13. For the importance of the 1730s in determining West Indian relations with both the North Americans and British, see D. Armitage, *The Ideological Origins of the British Empire* (Cambridge, 2000); I. K. Steele, "The British Parliament and the Atlantic Colonies to 1760," in P. Lawson, ed., *Parliament and the Atlantic Empire* (Edinburgh, 1995), pp. 29–46; J. Price, "The Excise Affair Revisited" in S. Baxter, ed., *Britain's Rise to Greatness, 1660–1763* (Berkeley, 1983), pp. 257–321. Walpole's aversion to a war with Spain reflected his more general fear that British commitments abroad might encourage Jacobite plots and other domestic upheavals. By the later 1730s, the prospect of a war over the Austrian succession also gave him further reason for caution in his relations with other key European powers.

14. Bodl. microfilms, Shelburne Mss, vol. 102, fol. 12; *LJ*, vol. 25, pp. 305–6; *The History and Proceedings of the House of Commons from the Restoration to the Present Time* (London, 1742), vol. 11, p. 1. For the background to the war, see R. Pares, *War and Trade in the West Indies, 1739–1763* (Oxford, 1936), esp. chapters 1 and 2. For the importance of the popular campaign against the Spanish depredations, see K. Wilson, *The Sense of the People* (Cambridge, 1995), pp. 140–65. For the centrality of anti-Spanishness to the ways in which the history of the island was imagined, see James Robertson, "Re-writing the English Conquest of Jamaica in the late Seventeenth Century," *English Historical Review*, vol. 117 (2002), pp. 813–37. Richard and Thomas Beckford had both signed an anti-Spanish petition in October 1737—*CSP, Col.* 1737, pp. 259–60.

15. *LJ*, vol. 25, pp. 405–6. After returning to Jamaica, Beckford numbered Yeamans and Sharp among the friends he wished to be remembered to—Add. Mss 12431, fol. 116, Beckford to Knight, 11 Oct. 1740. As agent for both Jamaica

and Barbados, Sharp had led the failed pan-island campaign for the direct import of sugars to Europe in 1735—*The Miserable Case of the British Sugar Planters* (London, 1738), p. vii. For the early West Indian lobby, see L. Penson, "The London West India Interest in the Eighteenth Century," *English Historical Review*, vol. 36 (1921), pp. 373–92; P. Gauci, "Learning the Ropes of Sand: The West India Lobby, 1714–60," in P. Gauci, ed., *Regulating the British Economy, 1660–1850* (Farnham, 2011), pp. 107–21.

16. Dorset History Centre, D/PIT/L73, marriage settlement of Julines Beckford, 16 Jan. 1738[–9]; *Daily Gazetteer*, 27 Jan. 1739; TNA, C12/1123/22, depositions of 26 May 1739; C11/1552/12, Beckford testimony of 2 Oct. 1739.

17. *Lloyd's Evening Post*, 22–25 June 1770. Early attacks on the immorality of Creoles include *Memories of the Life and Travels of James Houston, M.D.* (London, 1747), esp. pp. 292–94. For Beckford's alternative family, see M. Fraser, D. Beckford Stanton, and J. Fox, "William Beckford's Half-Siblings and Their Descendants," in *Beckford Journal*, vol. 10 (2004), pp. 14–29. For Jamaican patriarchy among whites and blacks, see T. Burnard, "Evaluating Gender in Early Jamaica, 1674–84," *History of the Family*, vol. 12 (2007), pp. 81–91. For Creole sensitivity over these negatives images, see C. Petley, "'Home' and 'this Country': Britishness and Creole Identity in the Letters of a Transatlantic Slaveholder," *Atlantic Studies*, vol. 6 (2009), pp. 43–61.

18. *JAJ*, vol. 3, pp. 504–36; Bodl., Mss Clarendon dep. c. 376, bundle 3, Hynes to Barham, 4 Feb. 1740, which reports that Beckford had just arrived from England.

19. Bodl., Mss Clarendon dep. c. 376, bundle 3, Hynes to Barham, 15 May, 10 July, 17 Aug. 1740. John Hynes had served as an assemblyman for Westmoreland, and his estate was not the first to be targeted after Speaker Beckford's death. For instance, in 1736 they had seized the plantation of the Stoakes family in St. Thomas-in-the-East, to secure payment for a debt of J£7,200 contracted with Speaker Beckford in 1729—JA, 1A/3, liber 35, fols. 1–9. The Beckford family did not take over full control of the Hynes estates until the 1750s.

20. Add. Mss 12431, fols. 116, 118, Beckford to Knight, 11 Oct. 1740, 20 Feb. 1741. In the 1740s James Knight was writing a "natural, moral and political" history of Jamaica in the hope of improving British views towards the island, but it was never published—Add. Mss 12418–9. Beckford regarded it as "so useful an undertaking"—Add. Mss 12431, fol. 118, Beckford to Knight, 20 Feb. 1742.

21. Add. Mss 12431, fol. 116, Beckford to Knight, 11 Oct. 1740; Alan Karras, *Sojourners in the Sun: Scottish Migrants in Jamaica and the Chesapeake, 1740–1800*

(Ithaca, 1992); Douglas Hamilton, *Scotland, the Caribbean and the Atlantic World, 1750–1820* (Manchester, 2005). Hamilton argues against Karras that the Scots were not always seen as outsiders in Jamaica, and cites Edward Long's view that they may have accounted for a third of the white population by the 1770s—"Transatlantic Ties: Scottish Migration Networks in the Caribbean, 1750–1800" in A. McCarthy, ed., *A Global Clan: Scottish Migrant Networks and Identities since the Eighteenth Century* (London, 2006), pp. 48–66.

22. Add. Mss 12431, fol. 118, Beckford to Knight, 20 Feb. 1742. Significantly, Beckford had reported that African recruits were keen not to desert or re-enlist, "all declaring that they hoped I would suffer them to remain with their wives and children in the plantations." This remains the most direct evidence of his dealings with slaves, but he clearly did not heed their pleas, for his slaves subsequently featured among the 1,000 Africans sent to support the expedition to Cuba—Add. Mss 12431, fol. 120, Beckford to Knight, 19 Aug. 1741. For discussion of the use of slaves in the military, see C. Brown and P. Morgan, eds., *Arming Slaves: From Classical Times to the Modern Age* (New Haven, 2006).

23. Add. Mss 12431, fol. 116, Beckford to Knight, 11 Oct. 1740.

24. Ibid.

25. Add. Mss 12431, fols. 120, 122, Beckford to Knight, 19 Aug., 21 Nov. 1741. For an account of the use of some 600 Jamaican slaves at Cartagena to erect a battery, see Library of Congress, Vernon-Wager Mss, series 8D/181. 16. For the debate on their use, see Pares, *War and Trade*, pp. 252–57. The appalling casualties at Cartagena are discussed in J. McNeill, *Mosquito Empires* (Cambridge, 2010), pp. 153–64.

26. Dorset History Centre, D/PIT/T859, abstract of the title of Peter Beckford, c. 1815–16; *London Daily Post and General Advertiser*, 18 Sept. 1741. It appears that Bathshua and Julines Beckford both traveled from England to Jamaica to settle the deal—Bodl., Mss Clarendon dep. c. 376, bundle 3, Hynes to Barham, 28 Apr. 1741. For the commodification of transatlantic reputations in Jamaica and England, see the article on the notorious Teresia Constantia Phillips by K. Wilson, *The Island Race: Englishness, Empire and Gender in the Eighteenth Century* (London, 2003), pp. 129–68.

27. His father's lands in total were said to have yielded £41,696 in 1740, £24,000 of which came from William's estates (before subtractions for payments to co-owners)—JA, 1B/11/4, vol. 1, fol. 75. For a fine example of the success of planters in western Jamaica in the wake of the Maroon Treaty, see B. Higman, *Montpelier Jamaica: A Plantation Community in Slavery and Freedom 1739–1912* (Kingston, 1998), esp. pp. 7–28.

28. Add. Mss 12431, fols. 118, 124, Beckford to Knight, 20 Feb., 30 Apr. 1742. For Trelawny's own exasperation with Vernon, see Library of Congress, Vernon-Wager Mss, series 8D/181.15, Trelawny to Vernon, 5 Oct. 1742.

29. Bodl., Mss Clarendon dep. c. 376, bundle 3, Hynes to Barham, 7 Apr. 1742. Beckford asked Knight to obtain a clause to allow foreign-based owners to deal directly with England. By June 1743, he was ready to send 40 hogsheads and 30 tierces of sugar to Hamburg but found little enthusiasm for the venture amongst the Jamaicans. His European ambitions might also explain his increasingly close relationship with Roffey and Chamberlain, a London firm dealing primarily in Mediterranean trade—Add. Mss 12431, fols. 122, 124, 125, Beckford to Knight, 21 Nov. 1741, 30 Apr. 1742, 18 June 1743. The option of a direct export to Europe may have been a lever to keep pressure on metropolitan sugar-refiners and grocers—Sheridan, *Sugar and Slavery*, pp. 69–70.

30. *JAJ*, vol. 3, pp. 616–46; Add. Mss 22676, fol. 145, Vestry of St. Catherine's parish to Bathshua Beckford, 9 Feb. 1743; Robertson, *Gone Is the Ancient Glory*, pp. 81–82.

31. *JAJ*, vol. 3, pp. 641, 649, 667, 672; G. J. Gollin, "The Beckford Family and Ashtead," *Proceedings of the Leatherhead and District Local History Society*, vol. 4 (1981), pp. 135–40. Julines had been elected an assemblymen in May 1742, having returned to the island to inspect his properties in the wake of the family settlement. The timing of William's return to England was probably influenced by the negotiations over the purchase of his Wiltshire estate at Fonthill. The tortuous financial arrangements over its sale can be followed in Wiltshire and Swindon Archives, 1990/2/3, abstract of William Beckford's title, esp. pp. 10–16.

32. *Cobbett*, vol. 14, pp. 190–91, speech in the House of Commons, 8 Feb. 1748. Although lacking definitive lists of absentees, Trevor Burnard has identified the 1740s as a period which saw an influx of significant planter families— "Passengers Only," pp. 181–82. The decision to cross the Atlantic could never be taken lightly, even by the Beckfords. William's sister Anne had recently been "terribly cut in the leg and several parts of the body" after being thrown out of bed into a consignment of bottles. Other passengers had lost use of their limbs "by being so often wet"—*London Evening Post*, 28 Dec. 1742.

33. Add. Mss 12431, fols. 120, 124, Beckford to Knight, 19 Aug. 1741, 30 Apr. 1742. James Knight had himself been expelled by the assembly in June 1737 for leaving the island, but that had not led to any serious breach with the Jamaican elite—*JAJ*, vol. 3, p. 411. For the significance of the defeat of the sugar duty of 1744, see Penson, "London West India Interest," pp. 379–81.

CHAPTER 3: FITTING IN

Epigraph: Thomas Harrison, Jamaica, to Rose Fuller, London, 5 February 1775, East Sussex Record Office, SAS-RF/21, uncatalogued papers.

1. For the most complete survey of absentee immersion in the mid-eighteenth century, see A. O'Shaughnessy, *An Empire Divided: The American Revolution and the British Caribbean* (Philadelphia, 2000), chapter 1. For London's colonial population, especially its North Americans, see J. Flavell, *When London Was Capital of America* (New Haven, 2010).

2. T. Burnard, "Passengers Only: The Extent and Significance of Absenteeism in Eighteenth-Century Jamaica," *Atlantic Studies*, vol. 1 (2004), pp. 178–95. For the best account of Beckford's political rise, see M. Peters, *Pitt and Popularity* (Oxford, 1980), pp. 6–16. For the importance of London as an oppositional center, see N. Rogers, *Whigs and Cities: Popular Politics in the Age of Walpole and Pitt* (Oxford, 1989), esp. chapters 4–6. A survey of members in the 1715–54 period listed only twenty-seven MPs with significant West Indian connections, two-thirds of whom were either born in the Caribbean or had spent a significant time there—R. Sedgwick, ed., *The History of Parliament: The House of Commons, 1715–54* (London, 1971), vol. 1, p. 153.

3. Wiltshire and Swindon Archives, 413/277, Fonthill schedule; 1990/2/3, abstract of Beckford title; *London Evening Post*, 22 Mar. 1729. In 1746 Beckford sold the Spring plantation in St. Thomas-in-the-East for J£11,000 (having improved its value from £6,300 in less than a decade). The 1749 sales included part shares of Lime Hall (for J£10,500) and Croft's (for J£17,500). The former was remortgaged to Beckford the same year (at 8 percent), and, following further legal action, was subject to a public sale in 1758 and sold to Beckford for J£12,300 (although in consideration of the prior mortgage of J£7,500, interest and other charges, Beckford only paid J£62 for the 700-acre estate)—JA, 1A/3, liber 135, fols. 77–79, liber 136, fol. 86; liber 170, fol. 175; *St. Iago Intelligencer*, 14 May 1757. The De Bouverie link with the Beckfords can be pushed back to the late seventeenth century, for Sir Edward De Bouverie (d. 1694) had been a fellow parishioner of Sir Thomas Beckford and signed the latter's will in August 1685—TNA, PCC, will of Sir Thomas Beckford, proved 1685.

4. In 1747, John Fuller, brother of Dr. Rose, was scathing about Francis, noting he "will get money when and how he can"—*Sussex Record Society*, vol. 76 (1991), p. 229. Julines became sheriff of Dorset, and one of his successors was informed that, at £80, the cost of their clothing was £45 cheaper than that of Julines—University of Bristol, Pinney Collection DM58, letters vol. 3, no. 163, Robert Willis to Azariah Penny, 28 Jan. 1750.

5. For a survey of Caribbean purchasers, see John Habakkuk, *Marriage, Debt and the Estates System: English Landownership, 1650–1850* (Oxford, 1994), pp. 453–59. For Steepleton, see *An Inventory of Historical Monuments in the County of Dorset*, vol. 3, *Central Dorset* (London, 1970), pp. 132–35. Julines may well have been drawn to the property as the birthplace of his maternal grandfather, Colonel Julines Herring. A useful indicator of the geographical spread of the Caribbean interest in Britain comes with the agitation in favor Admiral Vernon in 1740–42, as outlined by Kathleen Wilson. Significant clusters of support could be found in the southwest and on the south coast around Southampton, as well as the north-west, Midlands, and in Scotland. London was another evident hot spot—see K. Wilson, *The Sense of the People?* (Cambridge, 1995), p. 144. In time, key Beckford associates could be found in Hampshire (Morant, Dawkins) and Sussex (the Fullers). By the 1760s, William Beckford had employed a Bristol merchant as his local agent.

6. *Survey of London*, vol. 32 (London, 1963), pp. 546–65; vol. 40 (London, 1980), pp. 200–210, 291–303. Francis Beckford was also a resident of St. George's Hanover Square by 1744—Westminster City Archives, C202, poor rate assessment for Grosvenor Street ward, 1744.

7. Marie Peters has provided an excellent portrait of Beckford as a public figure. However, she vaguely refers to an uncle being an alderman for Aldgate and suggests that "more than anything else" the success of outsiders like Beckford was linked to City Toryism, which was "of a strident independent popular variety"—*Pitt and Popularity*, pp. 6–16.

8. TNA, C11/1552/12, testimony of Thomas Beckford, 22 June 1739. A "Captain" Thomas Beckford acted on behalf of the Jamaica Assembly to gain approval for an assembly act in December 1713—*JAJ*, vol. 2, p. 107.

9. Beinecke Library, General Mss 102, box 4, bond of William to Thomas Beckford, 10 Oct. 1739; College of Arms, Book of Grants, vol. 3, p. 282. William Jr. (the writer) obtained a certificate of the use of the arms on the tomb of Colonel Peter Beckford at St. Catherine's in September 1790—College of Arms, Norfolk Pedigrees, vol. 1, pp. 105–10.

10. *Gentleman's Magazine* (1746), p. 106; (1752), p. 286.

11. Add. Mss 12431, fol. 116, Beckford to James Knight, 11 Oct. 1740; Linda Colley, *Britons: Forging the Nation* (New Haven, 1992); T. Devine, *Scotland's Empire, 1600–1815* (Penguin, 2003), esp. chapter 10; D. Hancock, *Citizens of the World: London Merchants and the British Atlantic Community, 1735–85* (Cambridge, 1995). For a consciously British approach to political developments in the 1740s and 1750s, see Bob Harris, *Politics and the Nation* (Oxford University

Press, 2002). For analysis of the success of the Lascelles family with their Scottish partners in the Barbadian trade, see S. D. Smith, *Slavery, Family and Gentry Capitalism in the British Atlantic* (Cambridge University Press, 2006), pp. 79–86.

12. L. Penson, "The London West India Interest in the Eighteenth Century," *English Historical Review*, vol. 36 (1921), pp. 379–81; *Report from the Committee to whom the petition of the merchants and others of Great Britain and Ireland, dealers in and manufacturers of linens, threads and tapes* [1745], esp. p. 19. Further proof of a longer-term alliance of interests here is suggested by the call in January 1748 for a meeting of sugar dealers and British and Irish linen traders in London—*London Evening Post*, 14–16 Jan. 1748.

13. A. Campbell, *State of the Process of Proving the Tenor, Archibald Campbell of Budgate . . . against Sir William Dalrymple of Cousland, baronet* [London? 1768?], pp. 14–33; *Charter of the British Linen Company* (Edinburgh, 1773), pp. 4–5. Beckford invested £500 in the Linen Company. For Dupplin's Jamaica connections, see Metcalf, *Royal Government*, p. 101.

14. TNA, PRO 30/24/28, fols. 343, 345, 347, 349, 351, Lord Shaftesbury to William Beckford, 1 and 2 July 1747; the same to Peter Walter, 6 July 1747; the same to John Benne[t?], 6 July 1747; the same to Mr. Stanly, 13 July 1747. The fourth Earl of Shaftesbury (1711–71) had followed family tradition by his earlier interest in Georgia, although he had no evident connection to the West Indies—J. Spurr, ed., *Anthony Ashley Cooper, First Earl of Shaftesbury, 1621–1683* (Farnham, 2011), pp. 101–26. Beckford's allies later faced similar rebuffs in their electioneering, most notably his fellow Jamaican Henry Dawkins when he attempted to take a seat at Salisbury in 1768, even after purchasing an estate nearby—L. Namier and J. Brooke, eds., *The History of Parliament: House of Commons, 1754–90* (London, 1964), vol. 1, pp. 419–20.

15. TNA, PRO 30/24/28, fols. 354, 357–58, 362–63, Lord Shaftesbury to William Beckford, 6 Aug. 1747; the same to Lord Ilchester, 22 Dec. 1747; Lord Ilchester to Lord Shaftesbury, 26 Dec. 1747; William Beckford to Lord Shaftesbury, 30 Dec. 1747; list of Shaftesbury club members, 30 Dec. 1747; Sedgwick, *History of Parliament, 1715–54*, vol. 1, pp. 236–37. Note Beckford's bold, partial claim in March 1769 that "I never gave a shilling for being a representative: I mean for the City of London"—J. Wright, ed., *Sir Henry Cavendish's Debates of the House of Commons* (London, 1840–43), vol. 1, p. 304. Honeywood himself had few ties to Shaftesbury, and another local patron, Lord Ilchester, confessed to having "never heard of Honeywood" before his candidacy. Shaftesbury did fear that the Treasury might interfere in the contest, but Ilchester later confirmed that the ministry had tried to dissuade Honeywood from

petitioning after Beckford's return. Undeterred, Honeywood petitioned the Commons in January 1748, alleging "open and excessive bribery" and pro-Beckford bias by the mayor/returning officer, but to no effect—*CJ*, vol. 25, pp. 474–75.

16. See in particular, Sedgwick, *History of Parliament, 1715–54*, vol. 1, pp. 651–52.

17. National Archives of Scotland, GD110/529/2, 5, William Beckford to Sir Hew Dalrymple, 15 Dec. 1748, 22 May 1749.

18. K. Morgan, ed., *The Bright-Meyler Papers: A Bristol-West India Connection, 1732–1837* (Oxford, 2007), pp. 217–18; NLJ, Ms 306, Edward Trelawny to Henry Pelham, 13 Apr. 1749; National Records of Scotland, GD110/529/5, Beckford to Dalrymple, 22 May 1749; Bodl., Mss Clarendon dep. c. 357, bundle 1, William Smalling to J. F. Barham, 30 Mar. 1771. In August 1749 Kingston merchant Henry Bright reported that Beckford had bought fifty-five "fine men" at £37 each, and would probably buy more. A great deal of estate business is recorded in the Jamaican Chancery in 1749–50, with his island residence confirmed on 10 April 1749 (JA, 1A/3, liber 135, fol. 77) and as late as 5 May 1750 (1A/3, liber 138, fol. 111). This included further ratification of the settlement between William and brothers Richard and Francis regarding their father's estate—1A/3, liber 174, fols. 134–38. The two brothers had been recently cited as among the "great men" of the island—University of San Diego, Hall Mss B1/28, William Hall to Thomas Hall, 21 June 1748. For the Fuller-Trelawny split, precipitated by removal of Fuller as judge in early 1746, see Metcalf, *Royal Government*, pp. 91–98.

19. Wiltshire and Swindon Archives, D1/60/1/1, D1/61/4/15, D1/61/16/3, papers relating to Fonthill Gifford church; 413/277, schedule of Fonthill deeds, 15 and 16 Aug. 1750; Bodl., Ms photogr. c. 5, fol. 132, picture of Fonthill Gifford, undated. The foundation stone at Fonthill Gifford alone survives of the original church, which was demolished and rebuilt in the 1860s. Few eighteenth-century visitors took any note of the church, although in 1754 Richard Pococke thought it "a good termination of the prospect" from the house—*Camden Society*, n.s. 44 (1889), p. 47.

20. *CJ*, vol. 26, pp. 5–287 passim; NLJ, Ms 1792, John Gray to Jack Sharp, 9 Dec. 1750, 5 and 6 Mar. 1751; William Beckford to Jack Sharp, 5 and 6 Mar. 1751. Significantly, Julines Beckford was censured for having threatened the unity of the lobby by a heated exchange with Jack Sharp.

21. NLJ, Edward Trelawny to Henry Pelham, 13, 29 Apr. 1749; Library of Congress, Vernon-Wager Mss, series 8D/181.15, Trelawny to Charles

Knowles, 23, 25, 26 Oct., 2 Nov. 1751. Trelawny's answer to the threat of the London West Indians was for the executive to send a chief justice to Jamaica and to appoint two itinerant members of the Board of Trade (one of them based on Jamaica) to lead the council as a counterbalance to the assembly. Another key mediating figure in the Association of 1751 was Henry Moore, a friend of Beckford's from his Leiden days—R. M. Howard, *Records and Letters of the Family of the Longs of Longville, Jamaica and Hampton Lodge, Surrey* (London, 1925), p. 109.

22. NLJ, Ms 1792, John Gray to Jack Sharp, 5 and 6 Mar. 1751; William Beckford to Jack Sharp, 5 and 6 Mar. 1751; *Survey of London: Volume 33, the Parish of St. Anne Soho* (London, 1966), pp. 45, 81. Soho (or King's) Square still retained some eminence as the residence of several peers and foreign envoys— Westminster City Archives, A1439–40, St. Anne Soho watch rates, 1751. Julie Flavell notes that Soho Square also brought Beckford into close proximity with absentees from South Carolina, replicating the close ties between the southern continental colonies and the West Indian islands—Flavell, *When London Was Capital of America* (New Haven, 2010), pp. 21–23. For the role of coffeehouses as meeting places for London's West Indians, see L. Penson, *The Colonial Agents of the British West Indies* (London, 1924), pp. 180–82.

23. I. Doolittle, *City of London Politics from Shaftesbury to Wilkes: Another Viewpoint* (Haslemere, 2010); LMA, COL/CHD/FR/07/1767; Guildhall Library Mss 16967/10, pp. 418, 451; E. Glover, *A History of the Ironmongers' Company* (London, 1991), pp. 93–94. Thomas Beckford was still in residence in Mincing Lane as late as 1754–55, and was sufficiently forceful to dissuade William Beckford from placing brother Francis as a candidate at the 1754 election— Guildhall Library Mss 11316, assessments for 1754–55; *Correspondence of John, Fourth Duke of Bedford* (London, 1846), vol. 2, p. 145. Nicholas Rogers has read his decision to join the Ironmongers in June 1752 as a reaction to the strong Whiggism of the Clothworkers, while the Ironmongers were characterized as divided in their political allegiance—N. Rogers, *Whigs and Cities* (Clarendon Press, Oxford, 1989), pp. 150–53. For certain, Beckford was not an active member of the company, but he served as master in 1753–54 and used the newly built hall for several celebrations. For evidence of the Beckford's sociability with the Pennants, see Sussex Record Office, SAS-RF 19/78, John Pennant to Rose Fuller, 29 June 1757. The travails of the colonial merchant Micaiah Perry as a London MP in 1727–41 highlighted the potential perils of active politicking—J. M. Price, *Perry of London: A Family and a Firm on the Seaborne Frontier* (Cambridge, Mass., 1992), chapter 6.

24. Add. Mss 15154, fols. 146, 168v; 15155, fols. 53v–54; *General Advertiser*, 8 Feb. 1752; *London Magazine*, vol. 21 (1752), pp. 90–91. Beckford's speeches were also reported by colonial newspapers—*New York Gazette*, 6 Jan. 1752. For the impact of these societies, see Harris, *Politics and the Nation*, esp. chapter 6.

25. *London Evening Post*, 1–3 Feb., 12 Apr., 26 Apr. 1753; *General Advertiser*, 8 Feb. 1752; *London Daily Advertiser*, 25 July 1752. The enhanced dignity of Beckford as a City figure was well represented when he was sworn in as alderman on 6 July 1752; accompanied by MP George Cooke, he was taken in the state coach from the Guildhall to be dined by the mayor at the elegant new Ironmongers' Hall—*London Evening Post*, 7–9 July 1752. The Mansion House (1739–52) and Ironmongers' Hall (1748–50) have been identified as two of the handful of classical buildings of note to have been built in the mid-eighteenth-century City—J. Summerson, *Georgian London* (New Haven, 2003), pp. 46–48. The gift of a turtle suggested, however, that he was not afraid to broadcast his Caribbean connections either.

26. J. Carswell and L. A. Dralle, eds., *The Political Journal of George Bubb Dodington* (Oxford, 1965), pp. 106–7; *Walpole Memoirs George II*, vol. 1, pp. 143, 146, 167, 174, 176, 202–3, 209, 230–31; *Correspondence of John, Fourth Duke of Bedford*, vol. 2, p. 128. The Dodington journal also provides details of his social connections in Wiltshire—pp. 10, 80, 117, 129, 131, 167–68, 233, 247, 249, 289. As southern secretary, the Duke of Bedford had defended Governor Trelawny against his rivals, but the duke's resignation (and the dominance of the Duke of Newcastle, who favored Fuller) may have encouraged the governor's allies to come to terms—Metcalf, *Royal Government*, pp. 98–104. Before 1768, the secretary of state for the Southern Department was responsible for the American colonies, as well as for Britain's diplomatic relations with several European states.

27. For brief reviews of his parliamentary interventions, see Sedgwick, *History of Parliament, 1715–54*, vol. 1, pp. 651–52. The most cutting critic of Beckford's performances remains Horace Walpole, whose first notice of Beckford on 20 May 1751 is of "a long bad speech" on the regency bill. His reports, if anything, get worse thereafter—*Walpole Memoirs, George II*, vol. 1, p. 101.

28. Add. Mss 12431, fol. 125; *Walpole Memoirs, George II*, vol. 1, p. 210; S. Smith, ed. *The Lascelles and Maxwell Letterbook, 1739–69* (microform Academic Publishers, 2002), p. 104. Most West Indian MPs contributed little to debate in the Commons, except on imperial issues. For contemporary concern about this, note Samuel Martin's admonition to his son that "you must speak often and be not overnice to avoid the declamatory"—Add. Mss 41346, fol. 18.

29. *Walpole Memoirs, George II*, vol. 1, p. 209.

30. *Cobbett*, vol. 14, pp. 188–202.

31. Ibid., pp. 1098–1108, 1156–61.

32. Ibid., pp. 1212–21; vol. 15, p. 175.

33. *An Enquiry into the Causes of the Present High Price of Muscovada Sugars* (London, 1753), esp. p. 21; *An Account of the Late Application to Parliament from the Sugar Refiners, Grocers, etc of the Cities of London and Westminster* (London, 1753), esp. pp. 45–46. Andrew O'Shaughnessy has stressed the bipartisan tactics of the West India interest later in the century, and they could be equally applied to the earlier part of the century—"The Formation of a Commercial Lobby: The West India Interest, British Colonial Policy and the American Revolution," *Historical Journal*, vol. 40 (1997), pp. 71–95. In November 1750, Samuel Martin advised his son to consult both ministry and opposition when pursuing Antiguan interests— Add. 41346, fol. 16, S. Martin Sr. to S. Martin Jr., 25 Nov. 1750.

34. L. Namier and J. Brooke, eds., *The History of Parliament: The House of Commons, 1754–90* (London, 1964), vol. 1, pp. 156–57. Beckford was clearly planning a multiple assault in the summer of 1753 and continued to discuss electoral matters with the Duke of Bedford from that time—*Correspondence of John, Fourth Duke of Bedford*, vol. 2, pp. 128, 145–46, 150. Their connection can explain the erroneous report in the press in September 1753 that Beckford had been elected a freeman of the town of Bedford after treating the corporation to another large turtle—*London Evening Post*, 6 Sept. 1753. Beckford later sought a seat for Francis Beckford from the Duke, at which time he intimated that his only non-fraternal campaign (for Dawkins) had resulted in the return of "a good friend and patriot"—*Bedford Correspondence*, vol. 2, p. 145.

35. Doolittle, *City of London Politics*, esp. pp. 5–6; F. G. Stephens and E. Hawkins, eds., *Catalogue of the Prints and Drawings in the British Museum* (London, 1877), vol. 3, pp. 909–10, 913, 915; all newspaper references are from the *Public Advertiser*, 14 Feb.–25 May 1754.

36. For contemporary perceptions of Beckford's alliance with City High Tories, see Harris, *Politics and the Nation*, p. 53.

37. *A Short Account of the Interest and Conduct of the Jamaica Planters* (London, 1754), esp. pp. 3, 12, 15, for charges against Beckford personally.

38. East Sussex Record Office, SAS-RF 20/5, case of Edward Wilson [c. 1757]. The previous year Beckford had argued strongly against Jewish naturalization—Sedgwick, *History of Parliament, 1715–54*, vol. 1, pp. 651–52. He also became strongly identified as a supporter of Blackfriars Bridge, and it would later appear in one of his civic portraits of 1769–70 (now at Parham House,

Sussex)—S. O'Connell, *London 1753* (London, 2003), p. 125. The first reference to him as Alderman Sugarcane, the despotic and mercenary slave owner, came in 1757—*The City Farce*, a modern edition of which can be found in *The New Foundling Hospital for Wit*, ed. D. W. Nichol (London, 2006), vol. 1, pp. 231–38. Andrew O'Shaughnessy notes growing metropolitan familiarity with West Indian stereotypes by the 1760s—*Empire Divided*, pp. 12–14.

39. For Bristol's role within the Atlantic and resultant influences on its society, see K. Morgan, *Bristol and the Atlantic World* (Cambridge, 1993); M. Dresser, *Slavery Obscured: The Social History of the Slave Trade in an English Port* (London, 2001). For a survey of its eighteenth-century politics, see Rogers, *Whigs and Cities*, esp. chapter 8.

40. Bristol Record Office, SMV/8/2/2/1, pp. 67–70; *Felix Farley's Bristol Journal*, 6–13 Apr. 1754; *The Bristol contest: Being a collection of all the papers published by both parties on the election of 1754* (Bristol, 1754), pp. 37–39, 64–66. The proposal for the removal of the island's government from Spanish Town to Kingston had been mooted for some time but gained momentum with the arrival of the controversial governor Admiral Knowles. Richard Beckford had arranged an anti-Kingston petition before he sailed for Britain—Metcalf, *Royal Government*, pp. 118–26; Roberston, *Gone Is the Ancient Glory*, chapter 3.

41. *Felix Farley's Bristol Journal*, 15–22, 22–29 June 1754; Add. Mss 32735, fols. 48–50, 228, Duke of Newcastle to the King, 6 Apr. 1754, J. Gordon to the Duke of Newcastle, 24 May 1754. Gordon also reported that Beckford had bought the seat at Petersfield for £2,200.

CHAPTER 4: EMPIRE AND PATRIOTISM

Epigraph: William Beckford to John Kirke, 25 May 1754, Beinecke Library, General Mss 102, b. 4, folder 81.

1. K. Wilson, *The Sense of the People: Politics, Culture and Imperialism, 1715–85* (Cambridge, 1995), esp. chapter 3; M. Peters, *Pitt and Popularity: The Patriot Minister and London Opinion during the Seven Years War* (Oxford, 1980); E. Gould, *The Persistence of Empire* (Chapel Hill, 2000); Bob Harris, *Politics and the Nation: Britain in the Mid-Eighteenth Century* (Oxford, 2002); M. Peters, "Early Hanoverian Consciousness: Empire or Europe," *English Historical Review*, vol. 122 (2007), pp. 632–68. For a question mark against the coherence of "middling" views on the empire, see Harris, "American Idols: Empire, War and the Middling Ranks in Mid-Eighteenth Century Britain," *Past and Present* 150 (1996), pp. 111–41. For the broader impact of the war on society, see S. Conway, *War, State and Society in Mid-Eighteenth Century Britain and Ireland* (Oxford,

2006). Brendan Simms also offers an important reminder of the centrality of European affairs during this age of imperial expansion—*Three Victories and a Defeat: The Rise and Fall of the British Empire, 1714–83* (London, 2007).

2. For the fullest account of the interaction of metropolitan and colonial authorities during the stormy tenure of Admiral Knowles, see G. Metcalf, *Royal Government and Political Conflict in Jamaica, 1729–83* (London, 1965), chapter 5. J. P. Greene, "'Of Liberty and the Colonies': A Case Study of Constitutional Conflict in the Mid-Eighteenth-Century British American Empire" in David Womersley, ed., *Liberty and American Experience in the Eighteenth Century* (Indianapolis, 2006), pp. 21–102. Jack Greene has highlighted the sensitivity of the Caribbean assemblies to metropolitan interference with their rights but regards the disputes of the 1760s as much more important than those of the 1750s—"Liberty, Slavery, and the Transformation of British Identity in the Eighteenth-Century West Indies," *Slavery and Abolition*, vol. 21 (2000), pp. 1–31. See also his edited collection, *Exclusionary Empire: English Liberty Overseas, 1600–1900* (Cambridge, 2010), although it does not engage directly with the "backwash" of colonial influences in the mother country.

3. Add. Mss 32737, fols. 272–75, James Ralph to [Duke of Newcastle], 4 Nov. 1754; Warwickshire Record Office, L6/1336, John Dobson to George Lucy, 16 [Nov.] 1754. His first speech, on the Address on 14 November, was regarded as "very bad" and aligned him alongside Pitt and Vernon in opposition—*Walpole Correspondence*, vol. 37, pp. 414–15.

4. *London Evening Post*, 12–15 Oct. 1754. Peters and Rogers highlight the oppositional traditions of Richard's ward, Farringdon Without, and he certainly took an anti-court line in his thankful speech, recognizing the ward as "one of the most principal and independent wards of this City." However, the historic connection of the London Beckfords with the ward should be noted, and his choice of livery company—the Goldsmiths' in Foster Lane—may have been recommended by its convenient location (for the ward) rather than by its Tory associations—Peters, *Pitt and Popularity*, p. 10; Rogers, *Whigs and Cities* (Oxford, 1989), chapter 4; *London Evening Post*, 24–26 Oct. 1754.

5. Somerset Heritage Centre, DD/DN/493, Rose Fuller to Stephen Fuller, 15 June 1754; Metcalf, *Royal Government*, pp. 120–27. Fuller's appointment as chief justice of the island had been approved by Knowles in the spring of 1753, in accordance with the Jamaica Association agreement signed in 1751 to secure Knowles's succession to Trelawny as governor. However, the dismissal of one of Fuller's co-judges sparked all-out war, and Rose Fuller resigned office. In July 1754, Rose Fuller, acting on behalf of the Spanish Town group, authorized

Richard Beckford and his own brother John Fuller to amend a petition to the crown if they thought it "not well drawn"—Somerset Heritage Centre, DD/DN/487, Rose Fuller to John Fuller, July 1754.

6. *Cobbett*, vol. 15, pp. 349–60, 388–94; *Walpole Memoirs, George II*, vol. 2, pp. 22. Although a great distance away, an Antiguan planter echoed rumors that Beckford had "enlisted" under the opposition of Fox—Add. Mss 41346, fol. 126, Samuel Martin Sr. to Samuel Martin Jr., 20 Dec. 1754. Walpole thought Beckford more amenable to Fox in March 1755—*Walpole Memoirs, George II*, vol. 2, pp. 42–3.

7. *Cobbett*, vol. 15, 493–500, William Beckford's speech on Bristol night-watch bill, 15 Jan. 1755; Rogers, *Whigs and Cities* pp. 294–99. The argument against popular election thus distinguished Beckford from the more "herrenvolk" view espoused by Thomas Thistlewood—T. Burnard, *Mastery, Tyranny and Desire: Thomas Thistlewood and His Slaves in the Anglo-Jamaican World* (Chapel Hill, 2004), pp. 84–88. For discussion of the enduring impact of classical republican thought, see J. G. A. Pocock, *The Machiavellian Moment: Florentine Political Thought and the Atlantic Republican Tradition* (Princeton, 1975); Q. Skinner, *Liberty before Liberalism* (Cambridge, 1998).

8. *Cobbett*, vol. 15, pp. 449–58, 479–88. Richard Beckford's speech on the Bristol night-watch bill, 15 Jan. 1755; on the Oxfordshire election, 23 Jan. 1755. Earlier (27 Nov. 1754), Richard had clashed with Lord Barrington over the level of standing forces, with Richard arguing for a reduced figure, and Barrington castigating him for his lack of knowledge of British politics. For a survey of the interaction of discourses regarding English urban and North American colonial rights, see Wilson, *Sense of the People*, chapter 3; for domestic urban rights, see P. Halliday, *Dismembering the Body Politic: Partisan Politics in English Towns, 1650–1730* (Cambridge, 1998). Evidence of William's active support for the slaving interest at this time comes with his attacks on the newly established Company of Merchants trading to Africa in 1753–58—C. Brown, "The British Government and the Slave Trade: Early Parliamentary Enquiries, 1713–83," in S. Farrell, M. Unwin, and J. Walvin, eds., *The British Slave Trade: Abolition, Parliament and the People* (Edinburgh, 2007), pp. 27–41.

9. Metcalf, *Royal Government*, pp. 128–29; *Journal of the Commissioners of Trade and Plantations*, 1754–58, p. 125, minutes of 25 Mar., 30 May, and 5 June 1755; Jamaicanus, *The Jamaica Association Develop'd* (Jamaica, 1755; reprint London, 1757); Harris, *Politics and the Nation*, p. 57; L. Namier, *England in the Age of the American Revolution*, 2nd ed. (London, 1966), p. 197. In January, the board had backed the release of the pro-association provost marshall Francis

Delap, who had been imprisoned by Knowles for hiding the assembly election writs, but this could not prevent Knowles from orchestrating a successful election campaign in the spring of 1755.

10. Historians have long assumed William's involvement in the *Monitor*, especially due to the key role taken by his solicitor Arthur Beardmore in the publication—Peters, *Pitt and Popularity*, p. 14. His direct contribution is confirmed by Stephen Fuller's papers, which include a draft piece for issue 3, on the back of which is the endorsement "for Captain Collet," William's general man-of-business. A letter of August 1755 also saw Richard Beckford in discussion with Fuller about a paper on "the origins of government," which was subsequently sent to William—Somerset Heritage Centre, DD/DN/487, draft papers; DD/DN/490, Richard Beckford to Stephen Fuller, 10 Aug. 1755. These papers also include printed copies of issues 2–4 of the *Monitor*.

11. Metcalf, *Royal Government*, p. 128; East Sussex Recored Office, SAS-RF 21/25, Rose Fuller to ?, 3 Sept. 1755; 21/28, Edward Clarke to Rose Fuller, 4 Sept. 1755; Add. Mss 32860, fol. 89, Newcastle to Lord Chancellor, 18 Oct. 1755; fols. 471–72, account of debate, 13 Nov. 1755; Add. Mss 32861, fols. 55–56, John West to Duke of Newcastle, 21 Nov. 1755.

12. *Cobbett*, vol. 15, pp. 584–86; Add. Mss 3286, fols. 271, 290–91; *Walpole Memoirs, George II*, vol. 2, p. 90. Walpole suggested that Beckford's speech on 5 December preempted a more organized attack by Charles Townshend. Beckford's professed interest in shipping and the Admiralty in the speech of 2 December helps to substantiate a report in November 1755 that he had some interest with Lord Anson, the First Lord of the Admiralty—East Sussex Record Office, SAS-RF 19/16, D. Pryce to Rose Fuller, 4 Nov. 1755. For evidence of the continuing suspicion of the Jamaicans toward the North Americans, see the letter of Governor Moore of 29 Mar. 1759 (sent either directly to Beckford or intended for him via an intermediary), where doubts are cast on the readiness of the northerners to prosecute smugglers and little "redress . . . from those quarters" is expected—TNA, PRO30/8, vol. 78, fol. 147.

13. *Walpole Memoirs, George II*, vol. 2, p. 122; *CJ*, vol. 27, pp. 399–400; Metcalf, *Royal Government*, pp. 134–35; Somerset Heritage Centre, DD/DN/496, Henry Moore to William Beckford, 18 May 1756. Although a planter, Moore had been Knowles's lieutenant governor, and his appointment did raise some resentment among the Spanish Town group, which the London agents sought to dissipate. Stephen Fuller wrote to Charles Price the following July, imploring "let patriotism stifle animosity, your community, you country depends upon it"— Somerset Heritage Centre, DD/DN/496, Fuller to Price, 23 July 1756.

14. *The Monitor, or British Freeholder* (London, 1756), vol. 1, dedication. The body of Richard was drawn through Salisbury en route for burial at Fonthill on 7 March—*Public Advertiser*, 11 Mar. 1756. Richard's designs on the City seat are mentioned by Thomas Fuller in a letter to brother Stephen on 26 June 1755—Somerset Heritage Centre, DD/DN 491. In February 1757 William also had cause to mourn the passing of Thomas Beckford of Ashtead, who had remained a resident at Mincing Lane until 1754–55.

15. *Walpole Memoirs, George II*, vol. 2, p. 144; East Sussex Record Office, SAS/-RF 21/45, John Gordon to Rose Fuller, 15 June 1756; 21/54, William Nedham to same, 24 July 1756; 21/49, John Gregory to Stephen Fuller, 7 July 1756; Somerset Heritage Centre, Fullers Mss DD/DN/496, Stephen Fuller to Lord Halifax, 28 July 1756 (which includes extract of the letter from Price to Beckford, 26 Apr. 1756).

16. C. N. Dalton, *The Life of Thomas Pitt* (Cambridge, 1915); A. Olson, *Making the Empire Work: London and American Interest Groups, 1690–1790* (Cambridge, Mass., 1992); P. Gauci, "Learning the Ropes of Sand: The West India Lobby, 1714–60," in *Regulating the British Economy, 1660–1850*, ed. P. Gauci (Farnham, 2011), pp. 107–21. Diamond Pitt had accepted the governorship of Jamaica in 1716, but following discussions over terms he never took up the post.

17. East Sussex Record Office, SAS-RF 21/67, Stephen Fuller to William Beckford, 30 Oct. 1756; 21/73, Stephen Fuller draft letter to Duke of Halifax, c. 1 Nov. 1756; 21/81, Rose Fuller to Duke of Halifax, 4 Nov. 1756; 21/84, William Beckford to Stephen Fuller, 6 Nov. 1756; 21/86, 88, Ferdinand John Paris to same, 9, 16 Nov. 1756. Lovell Stanhope had no familiarity with the Caribbean but had acted as a legal clerk for the secretaries of state—Namier and Brooke, *House of Commons, 1754–90*, vol. 3, pp. 463–64.

18. *Pitt Correspondence*, vol. 1, pp. 185–86. For the contentious debate on the militia, sparked by the 1757 act, see Gould, *Persistence of Empire*, chapter 3.

19. TNA, PRO30/8/19, fol. 40, William Beckford to Dr. Cole, 13 Dec. 1756; R. Phillimore, ed., *Memoirs and Correspondence of George, Lord Lyttelton from 1734 to 1773* (London, 1845), vol. 2, pp. 585–86. It was also reported by Lyttelton that Beckford had assured Pitt and Fox of the support of all Tories "without any authority."

20. East Sussex Record Office, SAS-RF, 21/93, 94, Stephen Fuller to Jamaican planters, 9 Feb. 1757, Metcalf, *Royal Government*, pp. 141–42; Robertson, *Gone Is the Ancient Glory*, 92–95. The planters still had to wait until September 1758 for the arrival of an unequivocal directive from London to return the government to Spanish Town.

21. *Walpole Memoirs, George II*, vol. 2, p. 246; *CJ*, vol. 27, pp. 706, 715, 734, 735, 788, 816, 826, 830, 841, 910–11. Metcalf notes that Pitt's resignation helped to stall proceedings on the Knowles inquiry, coming as it did only shortly after Pitt had ordered the submission of all papers relating to Knowles—*Royal Government*, pp. 135–36. A cartoon of this time, *The Temple and Pitt*, clearly bracketed Beckford with the pro-Pitt "patriots" against Fox—F. G. Stephens and E. Hawkins, eds., *Catalogue of the Prints and Drawings in the British Museum* (London, 1877), vol. 3, p. 1179.

22. *The City Farce, as it was acted last week in Guildhall* (London, 1757), which appeared in issue 24 of the anti-Pitt organ, *The Test;* East Sussex Record Office, SAS-RF 20/5, letter C. Notably, Beckford's response to the indifference of the citizenry was to call in a "bookseller" to woo them with stories from history, which probably reflects the impact of his published speeches and the *Monitor*. For Pitt's attempts to woo the City, see Peters, *Pitt and Popularity*, esp. chapter 2.

23. East Sussex Record Office, SAS-RF/21 (uncatalogued papers), Charles White to Rose Fuller, 19 Mar. 1757; William Gale to same, 3 May 1757; James Prevost to same 4 May 1757; Edward Morant, 13 May 1757; John Morse to same, 5 June 1757; William Wynter to same, 25 June 1757. London agent John Gray judged the agency affair to be so sensitive that he would not communicate the Alderman's thoughts on the matter in a letter to Stephen Fuller on 4 Jan. 1757—Somerset Heritage Centre, DD/DN/497. Planter William Lewis later noted that Francis Beckford had been part of the pro-Stanhope campaign and that he was "under an obligation" to him. He also advised that Halifax must speak up for Stephen Fuller, "he being so great a friend of your brother's"—East Sussex Record Office, SAS-RF/21, Lewis to Rose Fuller, 6 June 1757. Governor Moore had dealt a severe blow to the Kingstonians in December 1756 by suspending seven councillors—Metcalf, *Royal Government*, pp. 142–44.

24. East Sussex Record Office, SAS-RF 21 (uncatalogued papers), Thomas Fearon to Rose Fuller, 25 June 1757. Beckford was, however, keen that he was not out of pocket while securing the island's advancement. In November 1756, declaring, "I have always and still continue to support my country to the utmost of my power," he refused to pay the £91 bill from solicitor Paris for the costs of defending the twenty secluded members, observing that Paris "knows how to draw out a long and expensive bill as well as to manage every affair with assiduity and address"—East Sussex Record Office, SAS-RF 19/48, Beckford to Rose Fuller, 20 Nov. 1756.

25. TNA, PRO 30/8/19, fol. 42, William Beckford to William Pitt, 20 Sept. 1757; East Sussex Record Office, Fuller Mss SAS-RF 17/335, William Beckford to

Rose Fuller, 1 Oct. 1757. Significantly, Beckford stressed to Pitt that Haldane's Scottishness was not at issue and that the key need was to retain the civil concord of the island in the wake of Knowles.

26. *Pitt Correspondence*, vol. 1, pp. 278–80.

27. *Journals of the Boards of Trade*, 1754–58, p. 374; East Sussex Record Office, SAS-RF/21 (uncatalogued papers), William Lewis to Rose Fuller, 7 Jan. 1758; Somerset Heritage Centre, Fuller Mss, DD/DN/501, Haldane entertainment papers; *Whitehall Evening Post*, 13–15 June 1758; *Lloyd's Evening Post*, 12–14 June 1758. Lingering Jamaican divisions were still evident in January 1758 when Beckford and Fuller were seen to espouse "the Spanish Town party" when seeking to block a proposal to establish a grand court at Kingston—*Acts of the Privy Council, Colonial*, unbound papers, p. 329. In contrast to William, brother Francis again let the side down, excusing himself from the Haldane entertainment on grounds that he had "now retired for the summer into the country"—DD/DN/501, Francis Beckford to Stephen Fuller, 5 June 1758.

28. *Pitt Correspondence*, vol. 1, pp. 327–30. Beckford was keen on African gains, lecturing Pitt on 12 June 1758 on the real importance of the seizure of Fort Louis in Senegal, as a break on French ambitions on the West African coast. Contrary to reports that this success was "trifling," he asserted that African trade was "a commerce more beneficial than any in the known world" and that the French commercial sector would be discouraged—TNA, PRO30/8/19, fol. 44. In a more candid exchange with Malachy Postlethwayt, Beckford confessed that he had been concerned that the Africa expedition had sailed on false pretences as a private "scheme of trade" rather than aimed to the public benefit, but "as it has succeeded I shall say no more on that head." In March 1759 Postlethwayt sought to gain Pitt's favor by claiming the support of Beckford—TNA, PRO30/8/53, fols. 26–27, Postlethwayt to Pitt, 16 Mar. 1759.

29. TNA, PRO30/8/19, fol. 46, William Beckford to William Pitt, 26 Aug. 1758; *Pitt Correspondence*, vol. 1, pp. 352–54; Metcalf, *Royal Government*, 141. Beckford recommended a direct attack on Martinique, for "a general must fight his men off directly, and not give them time to die by drink and disease." In January 1759, an unsuccessful attempt at Martinique was made but the island not secured until Rodney's attack in January 1762.

30. *Walpole Memoirs, George II*, vol. 3, p. 37; *Walpole Correspondence*, vol. 21, p. 257; *Pitt Correspondence*, vol. 1, p. 376. After "constantly ruminating on our present situation" since his return to Fonthill, Beckford thought that the seizure of Quebec, followed up by that of Montreal, would effectively end French interest in Canada. He called for the use of provincial troops and for the use of the

St. Lawrence River, as overland campaigns through forest and mountain had undermined all previous attempts. Regular troops were also not seen as effective fighters in the woods, and "the Indian yell is horrid to their ears, and soon throws them into confusion." For the importance of Pitt's assurances that imperial warfare would be a cost-effective means to check French power, see Gould, *Persistence of Empire*, chapter 2.

31. Add. Mss 6839, Symmer to Mitchell, 13 Mar. 1759; *Walpole Memoirs, George II*, vol. 3, pp. 53–55; TNA, PRO30/8/19, fols. 48, 107, 115, William Beckford to William Pitt, 24 Mar. 1759, and n.d.

32. *London Chronicle*, 27 Feb.–1 Mar. and 5–7 Apr. 1759, Two Letters from a Wiltshire MP to the *Monitor*.

33. Wiltshire and Swindon History Centre, Savernake Mss 9/34/07, Wiltshire militia papers; *Annual Register*, 1759, p. 107; TNA, PRO30/8/19, fols. 50, 51, 53–55, William Beckford to William Pitt, 18 Sept., 1 and 11 Oct. 1759; T. W. Copeland, ed., *The Correspondence of Edmund Burke* (Cambridge, 1958), vol. 1, p. 133. Beckford was one of ten captains under the command of Colonel Bruce, with a company of about seventy men. He echoed a truly Jamaican sentiment that "security cannot be purchased at too dear a rate" and was even keen to see action against the French in their current weakened state. For several years he had also been keen to see reform of the City militia, c. 1755–61—Bodl. microfilms, Bowood Mss, vol. 78, fols. 169–70, John Patterson to Ld. Shelburne, n.d.

34. P. Toynbee and L. Whibley, eds., *Correspondence of Thomas Gray* (Oxford, 1971), vol. 2, p. 651; T. Cadell and W. Davies, eds., *The Letters of Mrs E. Montagu* (1809), vol. 4, p. 246. Montagu thought Beckford's characterization of the French lying at Britain's feet might have been inspired by the statue of St. George at Charing Cross. Beckford's commitment to the war effort was attested by the £100,000 he raised for the government loan of 1759, although this remains one of his rare interventions as a financier—L. Namier, *The Structure of Politics at the Accession of George III*, 2nd ed. (London, 1968), p. 55.

35. TNA, PRO30/8/19, fols. 57, 59, 61, William Beckford to William Pitt, 19, 26 Feb., 22 Mar. 1760.

36. Edward Long, *The History of Jamaica* (London, 1774), vol. 2, pp. 448–50; TNA, PRO30/8/19, fol. 123, Maria Beckford to Hester Pitt, 23 June 1760; PRO30/8/98, fol. 299, minutes of meeting of planters and merchants, 16 Oct. 1760; M. Craton, *Testing the Chains: Resistance to Slavery in the British West Indies* (Ithaca, 1982), pp. 125–39; Burnard, *Mastery, Tyranny and Desire*, pp. 170–74. The Beckfords were not listed in the committee named to approach Pitt to represent their concerns, but it is clear that Beckford liaised closely with

the ministry on the island's militia matters. An undated letter to Jamaica agent Lovell Stanhope included Beckford's directions of which issues to raise with Pitt regarding the Jamaica garrison. He also defended the island's actions, and was ready to accelerate the securing of barracks for new troops—THA, PRO30/8/98, fol. 336.

37. Phillimore, *Memoirs and Correspondence of Lord Lyttelton*, vol. 2, p. 622; TNA, PRO30/8/19, fols. 63, 65, William Beckford to William Pitt, 1 Sept., 18 Oct. 1760; *Walpole Memoirs, George III*, vol. 1, p. 18. On the death of Haldane, Beckford had sought to establish Henry Moore as a permanent governor, but Pitt and Halifax favored the experienced governor (and long-term Pittite) Lyttelton—Metcalf, *Royal Government*, p. 152. Lyttelton's brother thought Beckford "a strange fellow."

38. J. Carswell and L. A. Dralle, eds., *The Political Journal of George Bubb Dodington* (Oxford, 1965), p. 417; *Walpole Correspondence*, vol. 21, p. 518.

39. *London Chronicle*, 3–5 Mar. 1761; *Gentleman's Magazine* (April 1761), pp. 158–59. In his acceptance speech he insisted that he has not solicited votes either in 1754 or on this occasion, evidently to justify his stance on parliamentary reform. John Brewer has argued that Beckford's stance on the issue in 1761 was "highly uncharacteristic, if not unique"—*Party Ideology and Popular Politics at the Accession of George III* (Cambridge, 1976), p. 215.

40. *London Chronicle*, 5–8 Sept. 1761. Note Horace Walpole's alarmist response to the 1761 elections, which saw the candidacy of "West Indians, conquerors, nabobs and admirals"—P. Lawson and J. Phillips, "Our Execrable Banditti: Perceptions of Nabobs in Mid-Eighteenth-Century Britain," *Albion*, vol. 16 (1984), p. 225. In fact, the number of West Indians had dropped from the thirteen returned in 1754 to only eleven in 1761—L. Namier and J. Brooke, eds., *The History of Parliament: The House of Commons, 1754–90* (London, 1964), vol. 1, pp. 156–57.

41. *Walpole Memoirs, George III*, vol. 1, p. 58; *Walpole Correspondence*, vol. 9, pp. 388–89; Toynbee and Whibley, *Correspondence of Thomas Gray*, vol. 2, p. 757. Bute's hostility toward Beckford in August 1761 is suggested by his comment to Lord Devonshire that Pitt had ceased to insist on the retention of Guadeloupe to humor the Alderman—P. Brown and K. Schweizer, eds., "The Devonshire Diary," *Camden Society*, 4th ser., vol. 27 (1982), p. 109.

42. *A Letter to the Right Honourable W—— P——, by a Citizen* (London, 1761); *A Letter from a Right Honourable Person* (London, 1761). Horace Walpole thought that Pitt's pension was a huge embarrassment for Pitt's allies and that "possibly even Beckford may blush"—*Walpole Correspondence*, vol. 38, p. 132.

43. *Pitt Correspondence*, vol. 2, p. 165; *Walpole Memoirs, George III*, vol. 1, p. 70. In his letter of 6 Nov. 1761, Beckford urged Pitt to attend the Guildhall, observing once again, "as you cannot say any one prediction of mine has proved false, so I hope you will give me an opportunity of being declared a true prophet in the present case."

CHAPTER 5: THE FRIEND OF LIBERTY

Epigraph: Account of Beckford's speech on the Address, 1761, Add. Mss 38334, fol. 29.

1. Beckford's importance as a radical leader was highlighted by Lucy Sutherland's Creighton lecture of 1958, which can be found as "The City of London and the Opposition to Government, 1768–1774: A Study in the Rise of Metropolitan Radicalism," in A. Newman, ed., *Politics and Finance in the Eighteenth Century* (London, 1984), pp. 115–47. Subsequent works that have used the 1761 speech to highlight the anti-aristocratic tone of oppositional politics in the 1750s and 1760s include J. Brewer, *Party Ideology and Popular Politics at the Accession of George III* (Cambridge, 1976), p. 215; K. Wilson, *The Sense of the People: Politics, Culture and Imperialism, 1715–85* (Cambridge, 1995), pp. 199–20; and Bob Harris, *Politics and the Nation* (Oxford, 2002), p. 98. For contextualization of many of Beckford's political interventions in the 1760s, see P. D. G. Thomas, *George III: King and Politicians, 1760–70* (Manchester, 2002).

2. For an excellent survey of Caribbean responses to controversial metropolitan legislation, see A. O'Shaughnessy, *An Empire Divided: The American Revolution and the British Caribbean* (Philadelphia, 2000), esp. chapters 4 and 5. For landmark studies of the interaction of colonial and domestic discontents, see C. Robbins, *The Eighteenth-Century Commonwealthsman* (Cambridge, Mass., 1959); Brewer, *Party Ideology*, esp. chapter 10; J. Bradley, *Religion, Revolution and English Radicalism* (Cambridge, 1990); M. Jacob and J. Jacob, eds., *The Origins of Anglo-American Radicalism* (London, 1984). More recently, Kathleen Wilson has been less convinced of the impact of colonial arguments on domestic radical thought—*Sense of the People*, chapter 4; and Eliga Gould has reminded us of the importance of popular support for British imperial policy—*The Persistence of Empire* (Chapel Hill, 2000). J. G. A. Pocock has also emphasized the varieties of republican thought in the eighteenth-century Atlantic world—*The Machiavellian Moment* (Princeton, 2003), pp. 553–83.

3. Add. Mss 38334, fol. 29, account of Beckford's speech on the address, November 1761. In a subsequent debate of January 1762, Grenville insisted to

Beckford that no assurances had been given to the City that there would be no war against Spain—*Walpole Memoirs, George III*, vol. 1, p. 107.

4. *Walpole Memoirs, George III*, vol. 1, pp. 72–73, 77, 89, 95.

5. *London Chronicle*, 4–6 Mar. 1762; *Gentleman's Magazine* (1762), pp. 155–56; TNA, PRO30/ 8/ 19, fol. 75. Later that year the *Chronicle* attacked the sugar trade in general, arguing that it led to enslavement and that great fortunes were being made at the cost of home consumers—19–21 Aug. 1762. Peters notes that it had moved away from its previously pro-Pittite stance in 1761–62—*Pitt and Popularity*, p. 278. The leading West Indian merchant firm of Drake-Long in London was pessimistic regarding the sugar market in February 1762 at the prospect of peace. Their best hope was for a decrease in the supply of sugar to Europe and an upturn in the North America trade with the shift of war to the south—Bodl., Mss Clarendon dep. c. 360/ 1, bundle 7.

6. *Walpole Correspondence*, vol. 22, p. 39; Add. Mss 41347, fol. 131, Samuel Martin Sr. to Samuel Martin Jr., 20 Mar. 1762. Writing from Antigua, Martin was profoundly suspicious of Jamaican self-interest, believing that the Jamaicans had no wish to enlarge the British sugar market due to the challenges of cultivation on the island.

7. Attacks on Beckford and other opposition figures in 1762 are usefully collated in *The True Flower of Brimstone: extracted from the Briton, North Briton, and Auditor* (London, 1763), esp. pp. 5–12. It was reissued in 1766 as *A Collection of all the Remarkable and Personal Passages in the Briton, North Briton and Auditor* (London, 1766). Further critiques of Beckford in the spring of 1762 include John Shebbeare's *History of the Sumatrans*, which, in another pro-Bute tale, depicted the Alderman as Rhum-kikh, "an half-witted politician, self-conceited, headstrong, turbulent and ambitious," who sought the support of the mob. A pictorial reference to this intense media battle comes with *The Fishermen* of August 1762, which includes a depiction of Beckford's ally Arthur Beardmore, and the *Auditor*'s Arthur Murphy—F. Stephens and E. Hawkins, eds., *Catalogue of the Prints and Drawings in the British Museum* (London, 1877), vol. 4, pp. 91–92.

8. Wiltshire Record Office, Savenake Mss 9/ 35/ 97, William Beckford to Ld. Aylesbury, 25 July 1762. Beckford declined to serve beyond three years as a militia officer due to "unavoidable" other duties, but he still took pride in having reached "the height of an emeritus [officer]." Beckford's company disbanded on 11 January 1763 and visited Fonthill to receive bounties and clothing—*Salisbury Journal*, 3 Jan. 1763. The Bruce papers refer to the further existence of Captain Beckford's company in 1766–67.

9. F. G. Stephens and E. Hawkins, eds., *Catalogues of the Prints and Drawings in the British Museum* (London, 1893), vol. 4, pp. 188–90; *London Chronicle*, 23–25, 28–30 Sept. 1762; *London Evening Post*, 28–30 Sept. 1762. Beckford had notified both his ward and the court of aldermen that he wished to step down. On election day he insisted that he would have declined the mayoralty if the livery had allowed him to speak, due to ill health "for some years past" and "the multiplicity of business which he had on his hands." Horace Walpole at the time reported that "Pitt from the bosom of his retreat has made Beckford mayor" and later suggested that the City had made Beckford mayor against his will as "a mark of their good-will to his friend Mr Pitt"—*Walpole Correspondence*, vol. 38, p. 183; *Walpole Memoirs, George III*, vol. 1, p. 153.

10. *London Chronicle*, 9–11 Nov. 1762; *Gentleman's Magazine* (1762), p. 549; Guildhall Library Mss 16967/11, pp. 6–12. It was reported that Beckford had bought a "fine set of Flanders mares" from the Dutch ambassador to draw the state coach—*London Chronicle*, 23–26 Oct. 1762. On 8 November an elegant entertainment was held at the Mansion House after Beckford was sworn in at Guildhall; another grand celebration took place at Guildhall in the wake of his inauguration at Westminster the following day.

11. *The Briton*, no. 25, 13 Nov. 1762. For a full critical edition, see B. Gassman, O. Brack, and L. Chilton, eds., *The Works of Tobias Smollett: Poems, Plays and the Briton* (Athens, Ga., 1993), esp. pp. 362–66. By the end of the month, another attack on West Indian corruption had appeared with Charles Johnstone, *The Reverie: or a Flight to the Paradise of Fools* (London, 1762), which focused on the manifold tribulations of Mr. Sugarcane, from love to politics. Further editions of this work appeared in 1764, 1767, and 1776.

12. P. Yorke, ed., *The Life and Correspondence of Philip Yorke, Earl of Hardwicke* (New York, 1977), vol. 3, pp. 436, 438; *Walpole Memoirs, George III*, vol. 1, p. 174. Burke noted on 25 Nov. "a little grumbling by Beckford" in response to the Address, but little opposition in general—T. W. Copeland, ed., *The Correspondence of Edmund Burke* (Cambridge, 1958), vol. 1, p. 157. Significantly, Burke suggested that Beckford could have been more active against the treaty, for on 9 Dec. 1762 he expected Beckford to present a petition of disgruntled merchants, angered by the proposed loss of West Indian islands to the French. He also noted on 12 Dec., after Pitt had defended himself over the peace for some three and a half hours, that the Commons "would not hear Beckford."

13. *North Briton*, no. 39, 26 Feb. 1763. Another possible sign of Beckford's accommodation with the ministry came in March 1763, when Smollett took Beckford's side in attacking Shebbeare's *History of the Sumatrans*, hinting that

Shebbeare had "particular obligations" to the lord mayor—*The Critical Review*, vol. 15 (1763), pp. 209–10.

14. *A Genuine Narrative of the Life and Actions of John Rice, broker* (London, 1763); TNA, PRO30/8/26, fol. 70. The tract's emphasis on Beckford's "useful and polite literature in his younger years" can be read as a direct retort to Smollett's barbs regarding his Creolian roots. Beckford did not neglect his traditional City roots either, for he attended the family parish of St. Mary at Hill in December 1762. The parish erected a sword-iron (an ornamental holder for the ceremonial civic sword) to "accommodate him agreeable to his dignity" during his visit, the total cost of which came to over £40—Guildhall Library Mss 1240/2, entry of 15 Dec. 1762, 1239/4, p. 40. His liberality in office soon became proverbial: "I labour not, yet eat and drink/As well as Beckford when Lord Mayor"—Thomas Mozeen, *Fables in Verse* (London, 1765), vol. 1, p. 57.

15. Yorke, *Life and Correspondence of Hardwicke*, vol. 3, p. 525; *Pitt Correspondence*, vol. 2, p. 235; British Museum, satire no. 4065; D. Fenning, *The Young Man's Book of Knowledge* (London, 1764), dedication, dated 16 July 1764; *Public Advertiser*, 23 Mar. 1768. Following Secretary Egremont's death in August 1763, it was suggested that Pitt was to meet Bute at Beckford's Soho Square home, but Bute later decided to visit Pitt at his Jermyn Street house—John Almon, *The History of the Late Minority* (London, 1766), p. 216. A Horace Walpole letter of 1 September suggests that either Newcastle or Beckford advised Pitt to make tough demands for coming into office—*Walpole Correspondence*, vol. 22, p. 160. Beckford received the thanks of both the aldermen and the common council for his term of office, and these thanks were printed.

16. R. Hoffman, S. Mason, and E. Darcy, eds., *Dear Papa, Dear Charley: The Peregrations of a Revolutionary Aristocrat* (Chapel Hill, 2001), p. 340; *Walpole Memoirs, George III*, vol. 1, p. 249; J. R. G. Tomlinson, ed., *Additional Grenville Papers, 1763–65* (Manchester, 1962), p. 321; Add. Mss 30867, fol. 242, William Beckford to John Wilkes, Dec. 1763; *A Letter to the Common Council of the City of London* (London, 1764), pp. 4–5. Grenville described Beckford's speech on the Address to the King as "angry observations."

17. TNA, PRO30/8/63, fol. 249, Lord Temple to Hester Pitt, n.d.; PRO30/8/19, fol. 78, Beckford to William Pitt, "1763."

18. TNA, PRO30/8/63, fol. 249, Lord Temple to Hester Pitt, n.d.; Beinecke Library, General Mss 102, b. 4, folder 84, William Beckford to [John Curtis], 29 Dec. 1764; *Newport Mercury*, 27 Feb. 1764. His decision to travel may even have been sparked by a jibe from an island agent in February 1760, who contested the views of Beckford and Fuller on the state of the island's currency by

suggesting that they had not been on the island "for many years"—*Journal of the Commissioners of Trade and Plantations*, 1759–63, pp. 90–92. Marie Peters notes Beckford's absence from civic councils from November 1763 to 1765 and links this to his political isolation alongside Pitt. She ascribed the final demise of the *Monitor* by March 1765 to a simultaneous "disjunction between City and national politics"—*Pitt and Popularity*, pp. 263–64.

19. O'Shaughnessy, *Empire Divided*, esp. chapter 5; Jack P. Greene, "Liberty, Slavery and the Transformation of British Identity in the Eighteenth-century West Indies," in *Slavery and Abolition*, vol. 21 (2000), pp. 1–31. On 7 March 1764 Beckford immediately responded to the announcement of Grenville's plans to tax America, expressing hope that "regard would be had to American legislatures"—L. Namier and J. Brooke, *Charles Townshend* (London, 1964), p. 114.

20. O'Shaughnessy, *Empire Divided*, pp. 65–67. In fact, in August 1764 Beckford was prepared to approach Jenkinson and Grenville for aid in freeing ships detained at Liverpool—Add. Mss 57809, fol. 139, Charles Jenkinson to William Beckford, 14 Aug. 1764.

21. Worcestershire Record Office, Lyttelton papers, box 17, vol. 2, Stephen Fuller to Governor Lyttelton, 24 Apr. 1764; copy of letter from Jamaican committee of correspondence to Stephen Fuller, endorsed as sent December 1764. Fuller had to beat off challengers Colonel Morrison (the assembly's choice) and Joseph Pickering, agent for Barbados (who was supported by Lovell Stanhope)—L. Stanhope to Governor Lyttelton, 12 Mar. 1764. For a detailed discussion of the Lyttelton-Olyphant affair, see Metcalf, *Royal Government*, 163–66. Greene sees the 1764–66 battle as more serious than that surrounding Knowles.

22. *Walpole Correspondence*, vol. 38, pp. 487, 499; Jared Ingersoll, *Mr. Ingersoll's Letters relating to the Stamp Act* (New Haven, Conn., 1766), p. 15; *HMC 8th report*, appendix, p. 190; John Free, *The Voluntary Exile* (London, 1765), p. 35. Townshend was said to have been "much hurt" by Beckford's outburst on 23 January, and left the House soon afterward. In these debates, Beckford accepted that Britain had a right to impose "external" taxation, instancing his approval of the 1764 sugar regulation. However, Grenville and Yorke countered him by asserting Britain's power to tax Ireland and the colonies—*Camden Miscellany*, vol. 23 (1967), pp. 256–57. Beckford's stance on the Stamp Act increased his prominence in the American press, leading to many more citations (usually from London press reports) from 1765 until his death—for example, *Newport Mercury*, 6 May 1765. For the sensitivity of the Jamaican assembly to their

status as "natural, free-born subjects of England" who had conquered the island, see their defiant resolutions of 1722—F. Cundall, *The Governors of Jamaica in the First Half of the Eighteenth Century* (London, 1937), p. 96.

23. R. Phillimore, ed., *Memoirs and Correspondence of George Lyttelton from 1734 to 1773* (London, 1845), vol. 2, p. 665.

24. Worcestershire Record Office, Lyttelton Mss, box 17, vol. 2, Lovell Stanhope to committee of correspondence, 9 Apr. 1764. Beckford argued that in the event of the king's death Parliament was a far better trustee of the powers of the regency than an appointed council, should "that grievous calamity befall us." Horace Walpole dismissed Beckford's arguments as "nonsense" and observed that he was only supported by "mad" Nicholson Calvert—*Walpole Memoirs, George III*, vol. 2, p. 76.

25. *Walpole Memoirs, George III*, vol. 2, pp. 167, 204, 206, 224–25; *HMC Sackville (9th report, vol. 3)*, p. 22; *New York Mercury*, 28 Apr. 1766; M. Peters, *The Elder Pitt* (Harlow, 1998), pp. 154–56. A report of December 1765 suggested that Beckford had informed Newcastle's contacts that Pitt was censorious of the late administration and well inclined toward Newcastle and Rockingham—*Walpole Correspondence*, vol. 22, p. 382.

26. *HMC Sackville (9th report, vol. 3)*, p. 24; TNA, PRO30/ 8/19, fol. 80, William Beckford to William Pitt, 18 Apr. 1766; *Pitt Correspondence*, vol. 2, pp. 417–19; P. Langford, *The First Rockingham Administration, 1765–66* (Oxford, 1973), pp. 203–5; F. Armytage, *The Free Port System in the British West Indies: A Study in Commercial Policy, 1766–1822* (London, 1953), pp. 28–51. In late April 1766 Beckford and Burke ridiculed Grenville for suggesting that any act was sacred when he defended the navigation laws. However, Pitt and Beckford were seen to have lost support in the City over the free ports scheme—*Walpole Memoirs, George III*, vol. 2, pp. 224–25. Beckford's ally Rose Fuller chaired the committee on the free ports bill.

27. Metcalf, *Royal Government*, pp. 162–69; Worcestershire Record Office, Lyttelton papers, box 17, vol. 1, petition of Middlesex jury, 28 Feb. 1766; *Acts of the Privy Council, Colonial Series*, 1745–66, p. 712. By November 1766, the Jamaican assembly had unanimously resolved: "That this House hath, as representatives of the people of this island, all the privileges that the House of Commons hath as representative of the people of Great Britain"—Metcalf, *Royal Government*, p. 169.

28. TNA, CO30/8/19, fols. 87, 89, William Beckford to Lord Chatham, 28 July, 9 Aug. 1766; Bodl., Ms Eng. Lett. c. 386/1, fols. 12–13, William Beckford to Captain Cole, Aug. 1766; Add. Mss 41347, fol. 234, Samuel Martin Sr. to Samuel

Martin Jr., 10 Aug. 1766. The reference to *faece Romuli* comes from Cicero's letter to Atticus, 2.1.8. In his letter to Cole, Beckford dismissed two recent unnamed works, averring that "part of the contents I know to be false." One of these must be Tobias Smollett's *Continuation of the Complete History of England* (London, 1766), in which Beckford was vilified as "a native of Jamaica, proud, violent, and obstinate, who by means of an ample fortune and extensive commerce had acquired considerable influence in the City, without any personal address or any superiority of understanding"—vol. 2, p. 328. Pitt's peerage must have rankled if Beckford had recalled an exchange on 13 June 1758, when Pitt defended both his ally and the status of an alderman, suggesting that it was a title "he should be more proud of than that of a peer"—T. Cadell and W. Davies, eds., *The Letters of Mrs. E. Montagu* (London, 1809), vol. 4, pp. 80–81. Montagu had reported that even the City "ungratefully say, it was too gross."

29. TNA, CO30/8/19, fol. 93, William Beckford to Lord Chatham, Sept. 1767. For a detailed survey of this ministry, see J. Brooke, *The Chatham Administration, 1766–68* (London, 1956).

30. TNA, CO30/8/19, fol. 91, William Beckford to Lord Chatham, 15 Oct. 1767. For studies of the political impact of the East India debates of the 1760s, see Namier and Brooke, *Charles Townshend*, pp. 155–72; L. Sutherland, *The East India Company in Eighteenth-Century Politics* (London, 1952).

31. Copeland, *Correspondence of Edmund Burke*, vol. 1, p. 281; *HMC Lothian*, pp. 272–74; *HMC Sackville (9th report, vol. 3)*, p. 25; *Walpole Memoirs, George III*, vol. 2, pp. 268–69, 279–80.

32. *Walpole Memoirs, George III*, vol. 2, pp. 287–88, 295–96; Sheffield Archives, Wentworth Woodhouse Muniments, WWM/R/1/726, Duke of Newcastle to Lord Rockingham, 9 Dec. 1766; *HMC Sackville (9th report, vol. 3)*, pp. 26–27; *HMC Lothian*, p. 275; *Pitt Correspondence*, vol. 3, pp. 176, 201; Bodl. microfilms, Bowood Mss, vol. 34, fol. 61, William Beckford to Lord Shelburne, 14 Feb. 1767; Copeland, *Correspondence of Edmund Burke*, vol. 1, pp. 298–99, 303, 310; TNA, PRO30/70/3, no. 138, William Beckford to Lord Chatham, 12 Mar. 1767. Beckford's first speech of the session is not dated, but was possibly on 9 December, when he moved the inspection of charters and attacked the new adventurers. On 6 January 1767, it was reported that Pitt had left the management of the East India business to Beckford, who is "first in his confidence," but "it is not a little humiliating that the E. of Chatham should be reduced to trust his cause to such an advocate." The debate was also notable for Beckford's closer political ties with Lord Shelburne, to whom he wrote in February for a sight of his proposals, stressing, "I love to talk and act with consistency and precision; I am at

a loss for want of it." On 28 April, Burke reported that Beckford had eight proposals to table, but these were shelved on 1 May when it was announced that an accommodation between the ministry and the company was likely.

33. *Pitt Correspondence*, vol. 3, pp. 176, 201, 251; Bodl. microfilms, Bowood Mss, vol. 34, fol. 61, William Beckford to Lord Shelburne, 14 Feb. 1767. In the summer of 1766 Beckford had been glad to hear of new appointments, including that of "our friend Charles" Townshend as chancellor but responded to Townshend's key speech of 13 May 1767 (announcing the new duties and American customs board) by calling for a more indulgent approach toward the colonists. In 1770, he would oppose all the Townshend duties on principle— TNA, PRO30/8/19, fol. 89, William Beckford to Lord Chatham, 9 Aug. 1766; Brooke, *Chatham Administration*, pp. 136–38. Beckford's exasperation with the North Americans was echoed in other West Indian circles, such as those of the Pinneys of Bristol, where the northerners were seen as "more disposed to bully than petition" in December 1765—Arts and Social Sciences Library, University of Bristol, DM58, vol. 3, p. 239.

34. TNA, PRO30/8/19, fol. 93, William Beckford to Lord Chatham, Sept. 1767; *A Catalogue of the Paintings, Sculptures, Architecture, etc . . . now exhibiting by the Free Society of Artists* (London, 1767), p. 12; *Political Register*, vol. 1 (June 1767), p. 65; Wiltshire Record Office, Savenake Mss 9/34/1, William Beckford to Lord Bruce, July 1767. Beckford styled himself as "an obedient subaltern" to his former militia commanding officer and promised to "cheerfully obey the commands of my superior officers" in "the old interest of the county." Despite such loyalty, the same month it was reported that Chatham had even refused to open a "letter of business" from Beckford—J. Black, *Pitt the Elder* (Cambridge, 1992), p. 274. The statue, which now stands in the Ironmongers' Hall, had been in production for at least two years—P. J. Grosley, *A Tour to London* (London, 1772), vol. 1, pp. 202–3. A payment of £150 by Beckford to Moore was made on 21 May 1767—Hoare's Bank Mss, ledger D, fol. 288. For discussion of the likely depression of his ally Pitt (who clearly shared many of the Alderman's symptoms), see Edward Pearce, *Pittt the Elder: Man of War* (London, 2010), pp. 341–46.

35. *Walpole Correspondence*, vol. 22, p. 584; *Walpole Memoirs, George III*, vol. 3, pp. 109, 111; Newman, *Politics and Finance*, pp. 124–25. Peter Thomas notes that opposition to the measure increased when Dowdeswell further proposed a clause to exclude revenue officers from voting—*George III: King and Politicians*, pp. 184–85. Critics of the bill also attacked the West Indians as boroughmongers—Brooke, *Chatham Administration*, p. 337. The idea of requiring a

double oath from MPs was supported by Beckford in January 1760 in connection with their property qualifications—P. Brown and J. Schweizer, eds., "The Devonshire Diary 1759–62," *Camden Society*, 4th ser., vol. 27 (1982), p. 35.

36. Sutherland argued, in part by reference to Beckford's recent activity, that there would have been a renewed alliance between the City and parliamentary opposition groups even without the appearance of Wilkes—Newman, *Politics and Finance*, pp. 124–26. For Wilkes's candidacy in the City election, see Arthur Cash, *John Wilkes: The Scandalous Father of Civil Liberty* (New Haven, 2006), pp. 204–8.

37. *Public Advertiser*, 11, 14 Mar. 1768; *Political Register*, vol. 2. (Jan. 1768), pp. 42–43; *Now or Never, Old England for Ever* (London, 1768); *City Races* (London, 1768). *Now or Never* backed Beckford and the three other sitting MPs as in the interest of Old England, and Trecothick was listed as on his own as representative of New England. Mid-poll adverts suggested that Beckford's supporters were working in tandem with those of Mayor Thomas Harley and father of the City Sir Robert Ladbroke—*To the Worthy Liverymen of the City of London* (London, 1768). In order to circumvent accusations that his American loyalties were inimical to the national interest, pro-Trecothick supporters stressed his positive qualities as a merchant, who must be supported "if his fortune be ample, his mind enlarged and his soul independent." His rivals duly asked how could any merchants "under the influence of a few North American houses" support "a gentleman educated, apprenticed, married, and many years resident in Boston with his family, and [with] commercial connections in that town"? It was also reported that the City election was being closely watched in the colonies—*Public Advertiser*, 16, 18, 21 Mar. 1768. Within weeks of the election, Trecothick's name appeared alongside that of Beckford's as fellow petitioners in favor of the Jamaican counties act of 1758, which was seen to protect Spanish Town interests—TNA, CO137/34, nos. 139–41. Across the Atlantic, there was delight at the return of "Beckford, a Jamaica-man, and Trecothick, a Bostonian . . . and the wisdom of that choice has since conspicuously manifested itself by the actions of those worthy patriots"—*The Defence of Injured Merit Unmasked* (American imprint, 1771), p. 1.

38. *Public Advertiser*, 19, 22, 23 Mar. 1768; [William Beckford], *To the Worthy Liverymen of London* (London, 1768). He also defended his vote for land tax cuts to support the poor, observing that probably "few private men" would pay more than him. Significantly, his failure to mount a defense of being pro-colonist was noted by a critic on 23 March, who also called upon the "hundreds of the members who have sat in Parliament with him" to testify to his mob-friendly

speeches. Critics went on to suggest that he was anti-London, rather than antimonopoly, in opposing the East India Company, identifying him as the member who had urged the House to look to the "rising sun" for heavy taxes.

39. *Boswell in Search of a Wife, 1766–1769*, ed. F. Brady and F. A. Pottle (New Haven, 1957), p. 152; *Walpole Memoirs, George III*, vol. 3, pp. 126–27. Boswell regarded the poll as a "really grand" event, with the candidates on a raised platform all demonstrating "true London countenances." One account suggested that a candidate was saved from "the resentment of the mob" by Wilkes's departure and by the fact that he "sheltered himself by Mr. Beckford's presence"—*Political Register*, vol. 2 (1768), p. 328.

40. TNA, PRO30/8/19, fols. 96, 98, William Beckford to the Countess of Chatham, 24 Mar. 1768; Countess of Chatham to Beckford, n.d. Several tracts attacked Beckford for self-interest and predicted that he would desert the Londoners to back Pitt and Bute in hopes of a peerage. The election also saw a reprint of the *City Farce* of 1757—D. W. Nichol, ed., *The New Foundling Hospital for Wit* (London, 2006), vol. 1, pp. 94–104, 113–17, 231–38. Beckford was also charged with gaining £2,500 from a £30,000 investment in a recent government subscription. His personal accounts do not reveal this, although they provide evidence of investments in other periods, including shortly before Chatham took office—Hoare's Bank Mss, ledger C, fols. 178v–179. For certain, Beckford did seek personal favors from Pitt. Although "exceedingly unwilling to break in on the retirement of my much respected friend," he pressed Lady Chatham on 24 March 1768 about the possible preferment of Charles Wake, whose advancement he sought for two years. She would not raise business with her husband but sent congratulations to Beckford on his election—TNA, PRO30/8/19, fol. 96.

41. Prince Hoare, *Memoirs of Granville Sharp* (London, 1820), pp. 48–49; Gloucestershire Record Office, D3549/13/1/B16, Sharp correspondence, alphabetical sequence; G. Gerzina, *Black London: Life before Emancipation* (New Brunswick, N.J., 1995), p. 104. Christopher Brown identifies growing concern over the number of Africans in England in the 1760s, although he regards the American Revolution as the true turning point for the abolitionists in their struggle to gain public support in Britain—*Moral Capital: Foundations of British Abolitionism* (Chapel Hill, 2006).

CHAPTER 6: THE CULTURAL CHAMELEON

Epigraph: *A Genuine Narrative of the Life and Actions of John Rice*, broker (London, 1763), pp. 27–28.

1. *Walpole Correspondence*, vol. 31, p. 431. Relatively little work has been completed on the reception of the West Indians in Britain, although for an illuminating surveys of their cultural immersion, see A. O'Shaughnessy, *An Empire Divided: The American Revolution and the British Caribbean* (Philadelphia, 2000), chapter 1; C. Taylor, "The Journal of an Absentee Proprietor, Nathaniel Phillips of Slebech," in *Journal of Caribbean History*, vol. 18 (1983), pp. 67–82; John Gilmore, *The Poetics of Empire: A Study of James Grainger's The Sugar Cane (1764)* (London, 2000), esp. pp. 36–53. The Indian Nabobs have received more coverage, especially for the post-1780 period—P. Lawson and J. Phillips, "Our Execreable Banditti: Perceptions of Nabobs in Mid-Eighteenth-Century Britain," *Albion* 16 (1984), pp. 225–42; C. McCreery, "Satiric Images of Fox, Pitt and George III: The East India Bill Crisis, 1783–4," *Word and Image* 9 (1993), pp. 163–85; M. Edwardes, *The Nabobs at Home: British Society and the Wealth of the Indies, 1750–1850* (London, 1991); N. Dirks, *The Scandal of Empire: India and the Creation of Imperial Britain* (Cambridge, Mass., 2006); T. Nechtman, *Nabobs: Empire and Identity in Eighteenth-Century Britain* (Cambridge, 2010).

2. K. Wilson, *The Island Race: Englishness, Empire and Gender in the Eighteenth Century* (London, 2003), esp. pp. 129–68. For the fullest review of the Alderman's cultural patronage and importance, see Philip Hewat-Jaboor, "Fonthill House: One of the Most Princely Edifices in the Kingdom," in D. Ostergard, ed., *William Beckford, 1760–1844: An Eye for the Maginificent* (New Haven, 2001), pp. 50–71. On Fonthill, see also John Harris, "Fonthill, Wiltshire—I: Alderman Beckford's Houses," *Country Life*, vol. 140 (1966), pp. 1370–74. O'Shaughnessy has argued that the metropolitan social success of the absentees, especially when compared to the North Americans, "defies claims of a closed elite in eighteenth-century Britain"—*Empire Divided*, pp. 10–15.

3. For an overview of patterns and processes of elite house-building, see R. Wilson and A. Mackley, *Creating Paradise: The Building of the English Country House* (London, 2000). For the importance of the arts within Georgian society, see J. Brewer, *The Pleasures of the Imagination* (London, 1997).

4. R. J. Dircks, ed., *The Memoirs of Richard Cumberland* (New York, 2002), pp. 111–12. For the early improvements, see Hewat-Jaboor, "Fonthill House," pp. 52–53. The clearest connections Beckford forged with the county elite before 1755 came through political associations, most obviously George Bubb Dodington and Lord Shaftesbury—see J. Carswell and L. A. Dralle, eds., *The Political Journal of George Bubb Dodington* (London, 1765), p. 167. He also entertained West Indians and family members in Wiltshire—D. Crossley and R. Saville, eds., "The Fuller

Letters, 1728–55: Guns, Slaves, and Finance," in *Sussex Record Society*, vol. 76 (1991), p. 268. For the debate on the openness of aristocratic society, see L. and J. Stone, *An Open Elite? England, 1540–1880* (Oxford, 1984); E. and D. Spring, "The English Landed Elite, 1540–1879: A Review," *Albion*, vol. 17 (1985), pp. 149–66. For discussion of the mobility of the London elite, see H. Horwitz, "The Mess of the Middle Class Revisited: The Case of the Big Bourgeoisie of Augustan London," *Continuity and Change*, vol. 2 (1987), pp. 263–96; P. Gauci, *Emporium of the World* (London, 2007), esp. chapters 5 and 6.

5. *The Public Advertiser*, 18, 20, 27 Feb. 1755. Suspicion fell on a group of workmen, who were reported to have started a fire in a hearth whose chimney had been blocked up, although they claimed that they had quenched it before they left. Later reports suggested that Beckford's books and writings had been saved, along with most of his plate.

6. *Walpole Correspondence*, vol. 35, pp. 211; J. J. Cartwright, ed., "The Travels through England of Dr. Richard Pococke, vol. 2," in *Camden Society*, n.s., vol. 44 (1889), p. 47; *Public Advertiser*, 20 Feb. 1755; M. Brownell, *The Prime Minister of Taste* (New Haven, 2001). Overall, it was thought that only £6,000 worth of goods was insured. Ronald Paulson records that Beckford paid £273 for the Hogarths at the auction in February 1745, and bought fourteen other paintings. However, it does not appear that Beckford collected Hogarth systematically, or shared his friendship (based on the fact that he did not inform the artist that the *Rake's Progress* had survived the fire)—*Hogarth* (Cambridge, 1992), vol. 2, pp. 236–37; vol. 3, pp. 176–78. The "very curious organ" was said to have taken over six years to make, at a reported cost of over £2,500—*Read's Weekly Journal*, 7 July 1753.

7. *London Evening Post*, 25–27 Feb. 1755; *Walpole Correspondence*, vol. 35, p. 211. The story of Beckford's equanimity in the face of adversity first appeared in the press in 1757.

8. *Public Advertiser*, 25 Jan. 1755; *Walpole Correspondence*, vol. 35, p. 211; M. Fraser, D. Beckford Stanton, and J. Fox, "William Beckford's Half-Siblings and Their Descendants," *Beckford Journal*, vol. 10 (2004), pp. 14–29. Brother Richard Beckford had also been unconventional in his domestic arrangements, and fathered William Beckford the historian after a union with Elizabeth Hay, "whom I have esteemed and do esteem in all respects as my wife"—TNA, PCC, will of Richard Beckford, proved 1756.

9. TNA, PCC, will of Francis March, proved 1752; *Public Advertiser*, 25 Jan. 1755, 17 June 1756. The press report suggested that the couple would be married "speedily" in January 1755, but the ceremony was probably postponed by the Fonthill fire. The couple did sign a prenuptial agreement, through which

Maria accepted a settlement of some £850 per annum in lands in event of William's death—TNA, C12/1325/21, testimony of Maria Beckford. Evidence of the close bond between the Marches and the Beckfords can be found as early as the mid-1730s, when Francis March acted a power of attorney on the island for Thomas Beckford of London, and he also attested to a grant of attorney powers from Richard Beckford to his brother William—JA, 1B/11/24, vol. 28, fols. 58–59, 177.

10. TNA, PRO30/8/19, fols 117, 120, Maria Beckford to Hester Pitt, 17 June 1758, 15 Sept. 1759. This pattern of City and country residence was very common for the upper classes, but it may have fulfilled a peculiar function for the Alderman, permitting him to visit his illegitimate children in London. He was even prepared to go to some lengths for their provision, embarking on a trip to Hamburg to settle his son in trade—East Sussex Record Office, Fuller Mss 19/78, John Pennant to Rose Fuller, 29 June 1757. Maria later reported that "the weakly constitution" of their son William argued for his education at Fonthill—TNA, C12/1325/21, testimony of Maria Beckford.

11. Wiltshire and Swindon Archives, parish register transcripts, Fonthill Gifford; *Pitt Correspondence*, vol. 2, pp. 11–12 (although this letter is dated 7 Jan. 1760 in the printed edition, its contents suggest that it must have been written in September 1760). Beckford also hoped that Pitt would advise him on Fonthill but accepted that Pitt would not enjoy its comforts "until you have first procured for your country a safe, honourable and lasting peace." For the acceptable "familial" character of political activity by elite women, see Elaine Chalus, *Elite Women in English Political Life, c. 1754–1790* (Oxford, 2005).

12. TNA, PRO30/8/62, fols. 44–45, Lord Temple to Hester Pitt, 22 July, 1762; PRO30/8/26, fols. 65–66, J. Cathcart to Hester Pitt, 7 Aug. 1762; PRO30/8/61, fols. 71–72, Lord Temple to William Pitt, 7 Sept. 1762. Both Pitt and his wife were "laid up" with illness at Fonthill. Cathcart also reported that Hester had commended Maria's fine hospitality and "the perfection of her son" as he neared his second birthday. Temple evidently saw the original plans for Fonthill and, noting the lack of stables, argued for the addition of "two more offices with the same colonnade."

13. The figure for rental income on his Wiltshire (£3,944), Hertfordshire, and Bedfordshire (£1,873) properties comes from a survey completed on his death—TNA, C12/1321/8, 1st and 2nd schedule. For discussion of the fundamental economic challenges facing the planter, see D. Hall, "Incalculability as a Feature of Sugar Production during the Eighteenth Century," *Social and Economic Studies*, vol. 10 (1961), pp. 340–52.

14. JA, 1B/11/4, vol. 3. fol. 2; 1754 land survey; J. Beckett, "Landownership and Estate Management," in G. Mingay, ed., *The Agrarian History of England: Vol. 6, 1750–1850* (London, 1963), pp. 618–30. The shipments of plantation produce went mainly to London (65 percent) and Bristol (24 percent), with only 8 percent remaining in Jamaica (and 4 percent to unspecified destinations). The Jamaica survey of 1754 revealed that Beckford's three brothers had an additional 20,000 acres on the island—Bodl., Ms Eng. Misc. c. 888, fol. 15. The calculations for the value of sugar come from the papers of future colonial agent Stephen Fuller, where each hogshead was reckoned in 1752 at J£20 before freight, duty, and sundry other expenses, including merchant commissions, were added (which added another 28 percent to the cost)—Somerset Heritage Centre, DD/DN/513, agent papers. The figure for income must be regarded only as a general guide, for, as Edward Long was keen to point out in 1774, the quality of each hogshead could vary greatly—*The History of Jamaica* (London, 1970), vol. 1, p. 463. For London sugar prices, see Richard Sheridan, *Sugar and Slavery* (Kingston, 1974), pp. 496–99.

15. Sources for Beckford's holdings are incomplete, but table 6.1 provides coverage of his major estates. Of the estates he held from his father, he appears to have bought out any co-partners by 1754 and may have sold Guanaboa in St. Catherine's, for no mention of it is made in his agents' accounts after 1754. He may also have absorbed other holdings into these ancestral plantations. For instance, Limehall, repossessed in 1758, may be included in neighboring Rock River, although his agents later listed its slaves separately in 1779—TNA, C107/143, plantation accounts 1779. Of the major post-1740 purchases, the estates in St. Thomas-in-the-East probably resulted from earlier Beckford moves against the Stoakes family, for William and his brothers had seized the Stoakes's plantations there in 1736 to pay off a £10,880 debt arising from their father's loan of £7,200 in 1729—JA, 1A/3, liber 35, fols. 1–9. For Boyd Alexander's map of William Thomas Beckford's estates, see Bodl., Ms Top. Gen a. 23, fol. 2.

16. B. W. Higman, *Jamaica Surveyed* (Kingston, 1988), pp. 99–101. Beckford issued a power of attorney to three of his agents on 15 April 1762 to manage Drax Hall—JA, 1B/11/24, vol. 51, fol. 54. Speaker Peter Beckford had purchased 1,000 acres of this estate in 1715, but the estate seized in 1762 was perhaps 3,000 acres. D. V. Armstrong has demonstrated a significant increase in yield after Beckford's seizure, from c. £6,600 to almost £12,000 annually across the years 1763–80—*The Old Village and the Great House* (Urbana, 1990), pp. 26–27, appendixes 1 and 2. Beckford secured few new land patents after 1745: only a 300-acre site in Clarendon in 1750, and a 50-acre plot in St. John's in

1768—JA, 1B/11/1, vol. 26, fol. 46; vol. 32, fol. 25. For a contrasting attitude toward absentee investment at this time, see the example of the Lascelles family, which eschewed land ownership on Barbados for over a century—S. Smith, *Slavery, Family and Gentry Capitalism in the British Atlantic* (Cambridge, 2006), chapter 7.

17. Lincolnshire Archives, Monson Mss 31/86. Alongside John Cope, Lewing and Mason were the recipients of instructions from Richard for the management of his estate when he left for Britain in April 1754, and they acted for the trustees of Richard's estate on his death. The Alderman continued to deal in slaves as late as October 1758, when he sold a three-quarters share in ten slaves "and their future increase" for J£400—JA, 1A/3/13, fol. 163.

18. JA, 1B/11/24, vol. 49, fols. 18, 53, 54; TNA, C12/1321/8, Beckford accounts, 2nd schedule, 1769–70. John Mcleod also featured in the power of March 1761, but not in that of April 1762. A separate power was granted for Drax Hall, and Beckford appointed a third manager, Dr. John Gordon, then of St. Mary's (whose bills came to over £1,600 in 1769–70). It is unclear whether William paid them a salary, but brother Richard Beckford had paid Richard Lewing J£200 per annum and Mason J£100—JA, 1B/11/24, vol. 56, fol. 59v. Lewing also acted as deputy for the family's patent of the office of island secretary and was ready to take a smaller share of its profits from the Alderman due to "the other advantages I enjoyed from him"—C107/143, Lewing to John Beckford, 17 Mar. 1773. Evidence of direct contact between the Alderman and the agents comes from Thomas Collett, who reported in 1770 that the Alderman would write to Lewing and Gordon to appoint a surgeon for the plantations, after an approach from Wiltshire neighbor and banker Henry Hoare—Hoare's Bank Mss, private letters 1758–71, Thomas Collett to Charles Wray, 28 Feb. 1770; John Ansty Austen to Henry Hoare, 17 Nov. 1769. The importance of continuity in the management of the family's Jamaica estates was impressed on the Alderman's son in 1794, when Thomas Wildman recalled: "I always remember your mother's observation about changing, but the time is come now when new agents we must have"—Bodl., Ms Eng. Lett. 501, fol. 14v.

19. Guildhall Library Mss 2480, p. 1020; *House of Lords Appeals: Richard Beckford vs. William Beckford* (London, 1782), p. 3; [John Railton], *Introduction to an Extract, entitled Zealous Remonstrances* (London [1758?]). Collett may have come into contact with the Beckfords via Solomon Ashley, who served alongside Collett in 1749–52 as a director of the Company of Mine Adventurers of England and as a commissioner for the creditors and proprietors of the Royal Africa Company. A more direct contact with the Alderman came through the Society for

the Free British Fishery, whose board Collett attended from 1752. By March 1756 Collett was undertaking business with the Alderman, signing a bond for the repayment of a loan of £8,000—Beinecke Library, General Mss 102, b. 4, folder 116.

20. Hoare's Bank Mss, ledger 64, fol. 427v; TNA, C12/1325/21, testimonies of David Evans and Richard Beckford. The first reference to his Liverpool agent, Richard Savage, in these accounts is August 1761. The first appearance of his Bristol agent Mr. [Michael] Atkins comes in October 1761, and John Curtis would also act for him there by July 1765 (Atkins having died by 1763)—Beinecke Library, General Mss 102, b. 4, folder 77. Although Beckford always recorded his main London address as Soho Square from 1751, his Beckford partnerships were all based in Nicholas Lane. The first, "Beckford, Collett and Evans," was based there in 1763–67 and was succeeded by "Collett and co." in 1767–72. David Evans was a merchant of St. Clements Eastcheap, who attested to knowing Alderman Richard Beckford well in 1756—TNA, PCC, will of Richard Beckford, proved 1756.

21. Hoare's Bank Mss, ledger 64, fols. 426v–427v; ledger B, fols. 46v–47, 398v–399; ledger C, fols. 177v–179; ledger D, fols. 288, 312v–314. It is unclear whether Hoare's handled all of the Alderman's financial dealings, but his accounts there cover payments in 1761–70 from London, Liverpool, and Bristol, which were usually paid in bills of exchange. The Alderman's name does not appear as an owner of slave ships or as an investor in the trade, although the vessels *Beckford* and *Richard and Julines* were involved (although neither were owned by the family at the time)—D. Eltis, S. Behrendt, D. Richardson, H. Klein, *The Transatlantic Slave Trade: A Database on CD-Rom* (Cambridge, 1999), voyages 75118, 76948, 77621, 78280. The strong returns in 1762 are not far from the £40,000 estimate which Beckford himself made at the end of the decade as his son's likely inheritance—*HMC Cathcart*, p. 25. For the bitter disputes over the estate after 1770, see B. Alexander, *England's Wealthiest Son* (London, 1962), chapter 3.

22. R. Wilson-North and S. Porter, "Witham, Somerset: From Carthusian Monastery to Country House to Gothic Folly," *Architectural History*, vol. 40 (1997), pp. 81–98. Some work was under way at Witham by c. 1764, and recent research suggests that the shell of the structure may have been completed by 1770. Letters from Beckford at Witham first appear in the summer of 1764—Essex Record Office, Mildmay Mss, D/DQ, 10/1, Beckford to John Curtis, 23 Aug. 1764. He also proudly took Lord Shelburne there in September 1767, when the peer reported "Fonthill and Witham are very magnificent, but the latter in the best taste"—Bowood Mss, Countess of Shelburne's Diary, vol. 3, p. 295.

23. *London Daily Advertiser*, 27 Sept. 1762; *London Chronicle*, 23 Sept. 1762; Wilson-North, "Witham, Somerset," p. 93. Although several accounts have suggested that Lord Egremont sold Witham to Beckford, John Pennant bought the property in 1761 and must have sold it to Beckford the following year. This John Pennant (d. 1782) was son of Edward Pennant (1672–1736), a Clarendon planter and chief justice of Jamaica. John had returned to England in the later 1730s, and his brother, Sir Samuel (d.1750), a member of Beckford's livery company, became lord mayor of London in 1749. John's son, Richard (later Lord Penrhyn), was cited as "of Witham Park" in 1763—*The Complete Pocket-Book* (London, 1763), p. 141.

24. Beinecke Library, General Mss 102, b. 4, folders 77–78, Beckford to John Curtis, 29 June, 23 July, 31 Aug. 1765, June 1766; Hoare's Bank Mss, ledger C, fol. 178, ledger D, fol. 313; *Victoria County History, Bedfordshire* (London, 1912), vol. 3, pp. 369–75. The original Witham mortgage was secured with a Mr. Grenville, who transferred it to Hoare in June 1766. In July 1763 Beckford had expressed satisfaction to his Bristol agent, whose sugar accounts made for "agreeable" reading, and this may have given him confidence to purchase Eaton Bray. However, his desperation to exploit his English estates to the full is suggested by his attempts to offload venison to caterers in Bristol or the Hot Wells—Essex Record Office, D/DQ, 10/1, Beckford to John Curtis, 23 Aug. 1764.

25. TNA, PRO30/8/63, fol. 249, Lord Temple to Hester Pitt, n.d.; Essex Record Office, D/DQ, 10/3, Beckford to John Curtis, 25 Aug. 1764; Beinecke Library, General Mss 102, b. 4, folder 84, Beckford to [John Curtis], 29 Dec. 1764. It is possible that the elaborate estate plan for Drax Hall (including the image of the great house) was prepared in expectation of Beckford's arrival. One of Beckford's most pressing island concerns at this time lay with a dispute over 1,300 acres in St. Mary's parish. In November 1763 the governor and council had reversed the judgment of the Jamaican supreme court which had granted Beckford's action of trespass against Samuel Jeake on this estate. The Privy Council committee subsequently upheld the judgment of the governor and council against Beckford in July 1764—*Acts of the Privy Council, Colonial Series*, 1745–66, pp. 682–83. Julines Beckford had returned to Jamaica by 1762 and died there in 1765.

26. Bodl., Clarendon Mss dep. c. 376, Florentine Vassall to J. F. Barham, 19 May 1767, 11 Oct. 1768. In common with other absentees, Vassall could be most censorious of overseers/agents in Jamaica, but also recognized their difficulties, suggesting that for a friend based on the island to send "any sort of

intelligence" to an absentee was "a very unpardonable fault to attorneys and overseers." In less forgiving moments, he regarded overseers as "in general a set of very undeserving fellows" and argued that upright specimens "don't abound in this country, and them sent from home are most of them soon corrupted." Beckford never aired such dissatisfaction with his island agents, but he may well have felt his presence was needed to support them. Ill health did revisit him in June 1765, when he described himself as "very much out of order with a fever, and still continue low and languid, but I hope the regimen I am now in will restore me"—Beinecke Library, General Mss 102, b. 4, folder 78. He wrote his last will on the nineteenth of that month—TNA, PCC, will of William Beckford, proved 1770.

27. Hoare's Bank Mss, Money Lent Book 1743–73, fols. 110v–111; private letters 1758–71, Henry Hoare to Captain Collett, 8 Jan. 1771; Edward Long, *The History of Jamaica* (London, 1970), vol. 2, p. 242. Boyd Alexander suggested that the Alderman's proposal for his natural son John to undertake a Jamaican office in the later 1760s may have aimed to secure a close relative as an agent on the island—*England's Wealthiest Son*, p. 55. For the growing acceptance of debt among large landowners in Britain, see Beckett, *Agrarian History*, pp. 634–40.

28. C. Petley, "Home and this Country: Britishness and Creole Identity in the Letters of a Transatlantic Slaveholder," *Atlantic Studies*, vol. 6 (2009), pp. 43–61. Edward Long personified the cultural sensitivities of white Jamaicans, vilifying the absentees for excess but also keen to boast of island improvements—*History of Jamaica* (London, 1970), vol. 2, pp. 21–22, 256–57. For discussion of the decidedly mixed British responses to the new "classical" public square at Spanish Town, erected in the 1760s and 1770s, see J. Roberston, *Gone Is the Ancient Glory: Spanish Town, Jamaica, 1534–2000* (Kingston, 2005), chapter 4.

29. *Vitruvius Britannicus, or the British Architect* (London, 1767), vol. 4, p. 9, and plates 82–87; Hewat-Jaboor, "Fonthill House," pp. 50–71; Wilson and Mackley, *Creating Paradise*, pp. 240–41. The architect of Fonthill has been identified as a Mr. Hoare, "a builder in the City," and Houghton Hall is generally thought to be its most direct inspiration—Howard Colvin, *A Biographical Dictionary of British Architects, 1600–1840*, 3rd ed. (New Haven, 1995), p. 499.

30. *Wiltshire Gazette*, 21 Feb. 1924, letter of Robert Drysdale to James Nairne; Shelburne Diary, vol. 5, pp. 4–5. Drysdale noted in October 1768 that the house was "not yet quite finished" after fourteen years, identifying the bedroom as the key remaining project, where the painting alone cost the alderman "about £10,000"—*Wiltshire Gazette*, 14 Feb. 1924, Drysdale to Nairne, 13 Oct. 1768. The

house was not always seen to its best advantage by visitors, for when Mrs. Powys visited in 1776, the housekeeper took her party through the "dark and gloomy hall" in the basement, and then to attic, before revealing the principal floor "where is displayed the utmost profusion of magnificence, with the appearance of immense riches, almost too tawdrily exhibited"—E. J. Climenson, ed., *Passages from the Diaries of Mrs Philip Lybbe Powys of Hardwick House, Oxon, 1756–1808* (London, 1899), pp. 166–67.

31. *Wiltshire Gazette*, 21 Feb. 1924, letter of Robert Drysdale to James Nairne; Shelburne Diary, vol. 5, pp. 4–5; F. Cundall, *The Governors of Jamaica in the First Half of the Eighteenth Century* (London, 1937), p. 24. Drysdale's attribution of pictures of the two Peter Beckfords to Hoare may be linked to the payment of £42 to "Wm. Hoare" in Jan. 1767—Hoare's Bank Mss, ledger C, fol. 178v. No trace of the Casali of William and Maria Beckford has been found. For the dynastic paintings commissioned by "Vathek" Beckford, see M. Hamilton-Phillips, "Benjamin West and William Beckford: Some Projects for Fonthill," *Metropolitan Museum Journal*, vol. 15 (1980), pp. 157–74. Evidence of his retention of African servants comes from a letter he penned at Fonthill in July 1765, when he discussed "a black fellow who is turned out a very bad servant and a thief." Showing little patience, Beckford resolved to use "some artifices" to have him shipped back to Jamaica—Bodl., Ms Eng. Misc. d. 1459, fol. 40. The body of "a black" was said to have been consumed in the fire of 1755—*Public Advertiser*, 20 Feb. 1755. Brother Richard Beckford had also brought African servants with him on his return to England in 1754, and baptized two of them during the trip—Cambridgeshire County Record Office, P1/1/2, baptismal entries for Great Abington parish, 15 June 1755. For the discussion of the depiction of African servants in elite portraits, see S. Amussen, *Caribbean Exchanges: Slavery and the Transformation of English Society, 1640–1700* (Chapel Hill, 2007).

32. *Wiltshire Gazette*, 14 Feb. 1924, Drysdale to Nairne, 13 Oct. 1768; Keble College, Oxford, Wilson papers, file Bonham 930, Beckford to Wilson, 11 Oct. 1769; Reginald Heber, *Historical List of Horse-matches Run* (London, 1764), p. xiii; Bowood Mss, Countess of Shelburne's diary, vol. 3, p. 91; Robert Dossie, *Memoirs of Agriculture, and other Oeconomical Arts* (London, 1782), vol. 3, p. 448. For doubts on the extent of the Alderman's impact on the Fonthill landscape, see Laurent Châtel, "The Mole, the Bat, and the Fairy, or the Sublime Grottoes of Fonthill Splendens," *Beckford Journal*, vol. 5 (1999), pp. 53–74. For a more positive view, see T. Mowl, *William Beckford: "Composing for Mozart"* (London, 1998). Maria Beckford observed that Fonthill's pleasure grounds and park

covered over two hundred acres, although only one hundred were said to be "ornamental"—TNA, C12/1325/21, testimony of M. Beckford.

33. *Wiltshire Gazette*, 14 Feb. 1924, Drysdale to Mairne, 13 Oct. 1768; LMA, Willis collection, Q/WIL/26, William Beckford to William Thomas Beckford, December [1768?]. The Alderman's concern for the health and upbringing of William Thomas is also reflected in the remark of Henry Hoare in January 1771, who thought that "our departed friend . . . would not be pleased at the conduct of a certain person," noting the son's "going to operas (to learn songs) and nocturnal meetings"—Hoare's Bank Mss, private letters, 1758–71, Hoare to Capt. [Thomas] Collett, 8 Jan. 1771. The strictness of Beckford, and his emphasis on religious duty, may reflect the waywardness of his own bachelorhood. He was prepared to acknowledge his own "impiety" but did not regard himself as blasphemous—R. Gore-Brown, *Chancellor Thurlow* (London, 1953), pp. 41–42. For an account of young Beckford's "solitary childhood" at Fonthill, see B. Fothergill, *Beckford of Fonthill* (Stroud, 2005), chapter 2.

34. TNA, PRO30/8/26, fol. 70, J. Cathcart to Hester Pitt, 26 Feb. 1763; *Wiltshire Gazette*, 14 Feb. 1924, Drysdale to Nairne, 13 Oct. 1768; Hampshire Record Office, COPY/814/1, Morant Diary. The tutor thought such visitors "no very gay company for a young lady," although perhaps for a "philosopher" like his charge, Miss March. The Morant diary gives a very full picture of the sociability of the absentees. For instance, in the early months of 1762, Morant's recorded meetings in London with the Pennants, Beckfords, Dawkinses, and Vassalls.

35. Bowood Mss, Countess of Shelburne's diary, vol. 5, pp. 2–5. Lady Shelburne noted that Beckford kept part of the old house of Sir William Wyndham at Witham as a residence until his new house was finished. Beyond Witham, there were also trips to Stourhead, Wardour, and Longleat. Although tutor Drysdale regarded Fonthill as having a somber environment, Shelburne acknowledged its "gaiety," which rendered Longleat "very melancholly to Miss March." Edward Morant stayed at Fonthill only a few weeks after Shelburne and also visited Mr. Hoare and Witham. He visited again in September 1770 and spent five days, undertaking a great deal of shooting and visiting Wardour Castle—Hampshire Record Office, COPY/814/1, Morant Diary, August 1769, 1770.

36. TNA, C12/1321/8, schedules 2, 4, passim. Notable payments include sums to Casali "for a picture" (£14–14) on 23 Sept. 1769; to Moore on 25 Jan. 1770 (£400); to Chippendale "on account for glasses" on 10 Nov. 1770 (£300), and further sums for glasses on 16 Jan. 1771 (£300), on 29 Jan. 1771 (£400), and

on 1 Feb. 1771 (£500). Not only did he expend large sums on the establishment of his natural children, but he was even prepared to support them if they went against his wishes, as his son John did by entering the army—TNA, C107/143, Richard Lewing to John Beckford, 27 Dec. 1770.

37. TNA, C12/1321/8, schedule 2, item listed 23 Jan. 1770.

CHAPTER 7: APOTHEOSIS

Epigraph: Inventory of slaves, Dank's plantation, Clarendon, Jamaica, JA, IB/11/3, vol. 55, fol. 94.

1. T. Burnard, "Slave Naming Patterns: Onomastics and the Taxonomy of Race in Eighteenth-Century Jamaica," *Journal of Interdisciplinary History*, vol. 31 (2001), pp. 325–46. The inventory was completed on 5 Oct. 1774, but there is no clue as to the date when the two slaves were named. Although slaves might retain both African and European names, Burnard argues for the superior influence of whites in the naming process. The naming of Beckford's slaves may reflect the Alderman's more obvious public alignment with Wilkes in 1769–70.

2. J. Wright, ed., *Sir Henry Cavendish's Debates of the House of Commons* (London, 1840–43)—hereafter *Cavendish Debates*. Lucy Sutherland's remains the most authoritative review of Beckford's importance among the metropolitan radicals—"The City of London and the Opposition to Government, 1768–1774," in A. Newman, ed., *Politics and Finance in the Eighteenth Century* (London, 1984), pp. 115–47. For important subsequent studies of London radical politics in the later 1760s, see J. Brewer, *Party Ideology and Popular Politics at the Accession of George III* (Cambridge, 1976), esp. chapters 9 and 10; P. D. G. Thomas, *John Wilkes: A Friend to Liberty* (Oxford, 1996).

3. *Calendar of Home Office Papers, 1766–69*, p. 347; *Cavendish Debates*, vol. 1, pp. 10, 21, 26; G. Rudé, *Wilkes and Liberty* (London, 1983), pp. 49–56. Beckford's eagerness to reconcile the coal-heavers can be linked to his aldermanship of Billingsgate, the site of the City coal market. In an earlier demonstration of his status on the dockside, in 1756 he had been presented with a book as "the worthy governor" of the Fellowship of Billingsgate Porters—Guildhall Library Mss 1703.

4. Bodl. microfilms, Bowood Mss 34, fol. 61, William Beckford to Lord Shelburne, 1 Oct. 1768; *Wiltshire Gazette*, 14 Feb. 1924, letter of tutor Drysdale, 13 Oct. 1768.

5. *Cavendish Debates*, vol. 1, pp. 47, 49, 61, 62, 64, 75, 82, 95, 111, 113.

6. Ibid., p. 50.

7. Ibid., vol. 1, pp. 85, 89; Beinecke Library, General Mss 102, b. 4, folder 84, William Beckford to Lord Chatham, 9 Dec. 1768; TNA, PRO30/8/10, fol. 55, Lady Chatham to William Beckford, 9 Dec. 1768. Even the plea of "your old inalterable friend" was insufficient to gain him a weekend audience at Hayes, although Chatham hoped that Beckford would understand "both as a physician and as a friend." The failure of Beckford's motion was noted by Benjamin Franklin and seen as a missed opportunity to expose ministerial culpability in directing the actions of American governors, who had in turn sparked angry demonstrations—W. B. Willcox, ed., *The Papers of Benjamin Franklin* (New Haven, 1972), vol. 15, p. 287.

8. *Cavendish Debates*, vol. 1, pp. 117, 118, 121, 128, 130–31, 133, 140, 150, 157–58.

9. Ibid., vol. 1, pp. 185, 187, 189, 190, 203, 208–9. On 8 Feb., his stance earned him the countercharge that he was encouraging the colonists to defy the Navigation Laws, which he vigorously denied and simply asserted that he had "foretold what would be the effect of your measures." He also cited the Spanish writer Geronimo de Ustariz, whose work had been translated into English in 1751 at the behest of the Prince of Wales—*Whitehall Evening Post*, 30 May–1 June 1751. Ustariz had advocated a leading role for the state in encouraging domestic industry and the circulation of trade. The Massachusetts assembly later saw fit to record an account of Beckford's and Trecothick's actions in the Commons on 25 Jan. 1769, when Beckford had presented the petition from the colony—*Journal of the Honorable House of Representatives of His Majesty's province of the Massachusetts-Bay* (Boston, 1769), p. 83.

10. *Oxford Magazine*, vol. 2, pp. 77–79. For a full description of "The Conference," see F. G. Stephens and E. Hawkins, eds., *Catalogue of the Prints and Drawings in the British Museum* (London, 1893), vol. 4, pp. 501–2.

11. *Cavendish Debates*, vol. 1, pp. 228–29, 268–69, 274, 280–81, 304–5. In debate on the Nullum Tempus bill on 24 Feb., he was against the general principle of the bill but argued strongly for the discovery of estates concealed from the Crown, regarding the property of the Crown as the property of the people (for which the Crown was a trustee)—pp. 241, 245.

12. *Cavendish Debates*, vol. 1, pp. 228, 360, 364–65; *Oxford Magazine*, vol. 2, p. 156.

13. *Cavendish Debates*, vol. 1, pp. 370–72. *Walpole Memoirs, George III*, vol. 3, pp. 237–38. He also took government supporters in the City to task over their loyal procession and address to the king on 22 March, likening them to the minions of the despotic king of Morocco ahead of a "massacre."

14. *Cavendish Debates*, vol. 1, pp. 399–400, 428. In his speech of 13 April, Beckford had attacked Grafton more directly by reference to Rehoboam, who had lost ten of the twelve tribes after rejecting the advice of his father's counsellors in favor of that of younger men (that is, Grafton). Although a sentinel against corruption, Beckford conceded on 17 April that Britain was not as sunk in luxury as the French—*Cavendish Debates*, vol. 1, p. 388.

15. W. P. Treloar, *Wilkes and the City* (London, 1917), pp. 52–54; L. Sutherland, ed., *The Correspondence of Edmund Burke* (Cambridge, 1960), vol. 2, p. 34. Among many grievances, the City petition denounced the peculation of Henry Fox as paymaster and his ennoblement as Baron Holland in 1763. Lord Holland subsequently appealed to Beckford's testimony for exoneration of the charges levied against him—John Noorthouck, *New History of London* (London, 1773), chapter 15. Relations between Beckford and the Rockinghams were still strained at this time, for Horace Walpole reported in April 1769 that Beckford and Barré had "abused" the Rockinghamites over the bill to make the militia perpetual—*Walpole Memoirs, George III*, vol. 3, p. 236.

16. Sutherland, *Correpondence of Edmund Burke*, vol. 2, p. 90; *Walpole Correspondence*, vol. 23, pp. 131–32; Bowood House, Countess of Shelburne's Diary, vol. 5, pp. 4–9, 15. Barré and Townsend had visited Bowood in late July, and Shelburne visited Fonthill for an extended stay right after this. Burke saw Beckford as a key figure behind the petitioning meeting at Devizes—Countess of Shelburne's Diary, vol. 2, p. 50. In late October Beckford reported that he was organizing the publication of grievances within Wiltshire—Bodl. microfilms, Bowood Mss, Beckford to Shelburne, 24 Oct. 1769.

17. TNA, C12/1321, 2nd schedule, entry 4 Oct. 1769; Keble College, Oxford, Wilson papers, File Bonham 930, Beckford to Thomas Wilson, 9 Sept. 1769. The thirty-six prints cost £9, 9s.

18. Add. 57827, fol. 98, account sent to Earl Temple; Keble College, Oxford, Wilson papers, File Bonham 930, Beckford to Thomas Wilson, 11 Oct. 1769; *HMC Sackville (9th report, vol. 3)*, p. 29; TNA, PRO30/8/19, fol. 101, William Beckford to Lord Chatham, 16 Oct. 1769. Beckford subsequently attributed his election to the "management" of sheriff Townsend—Bodl. microfilms, Bowood Mss, vol. 34, fol. 65, Beckford to Shelburne, 24 Oct. 1769. The "regular conduct" of the livery, over several hours, was commended by Lord Temple's correspondent.

19. Bodl. microfilms, Bowood Mss vol. 34, fol. 67, William Beckford to Lord Shelburne, 30 Oct. 1769; Bowood House, Countess of Shelburne's Diary, vol. 5, pp. 59–62; *Correspondence of John, Fourth Duke of Bedford* (London, 1846), vol. 3, p. 410; *Walpole Correspondence*, vol. 39, p. 119. Walpole saw Lord Temple's

efforts to dine on 9 Nov. as a significant favor to Beckford. Boswell was at the dinner and speculated that Paoli was not there because he wanted to avoid prominent Whigs, such as Catherine Macaulay—R. C. Cole, *Boswell's Correspondence* (New Haven, 1997), vol. 7, p. 257. Beckford's costs for his lord mayor's day included the import of seven horses from Holland—TNA, C12/1321/8, 2nd schedule, payment of 15 Nov. 1769.

    20. *Hening's Statutes at Large* (Richmond, 1821), vol. 8, p. 425; Wilcox, *Papers of Benjamin Franklin*, vol. 17, p. 37; *Public Advertiser*, 18 Nov. 1769; Institute of Commonwealth Studies Library, London, microfilm M915, West India committee minutes, vol. 1, fols. 1–6; O'Shaughnessy, *Empire Divided*, chapter 5. In September 1769 a New York correspondent (briefed by English newspapers) identified Beckford and the sheriffs as "very popular partisans of Wilkes's cause" after their transmission of the petition to the Crown on 5 July—A. C. Flick, ed., *The Papers of Sir William Johnson* (Albany, N.Y., 1931), vol. 7, p. 156. The ballad in the *Public Advertiser* referenced both Beckford's grandfather, who "the beat the drum," and his father, who led "a mighty band of swarthy moors to war." American patriots were certainly keen to enlist Caribbean support at this juncture, for key centers such as Philadelphia exempted the West Indies from its trade boycotts of 1765 and 1769 (although they were included in the boycott of 1774)—M. Craig, "Grounds for Debate? The Place of the Caribbean Provisions Trade in Philadelphia's Prerevolutionary Economy," *Pennsylvania Magazine of History and Biography*, vol. 128 (2004), pp. 149–78.

    21. *The Town and Country Magazine* (London, 1770), vol. 2, p. 53; *The Freeholders Magazine, or Monthly Chronicle of Liberty* (London, 1769), vol. 1, pp. 112–13. More "official" mayoral portraits were also produced, such as the full-length John Dixon 1769 print with Magna Carta.

    22. *Cavendish Debates*, vol. 1, pp. 437, 442, 449–50, 480; Thomas, *George III*, pp. 211–16.

    23. *Freeholders Magazine*, vol. 1, pp. 324–25; *London Evening Post*, 10–13 Feb. 1770; CD, vol. 1, pp. 448–50. The dukes present were those of Portland, Richmond, Bolton, Queensbury, Manchester, and Northumberland. Edmund Burke, six alderman, and the two sheriffs were also there, as were "a great number of merchants with their ladies."

    24. *Cavendish Debates*, vol. 1, p. 489.

    25. Ibid., pp. 520–23.

    26. *Walpole Correspondence*, vol. 23, pp. 196–98, 199–200; *Walpole Memoirs, George III*, vol. 4, pp. 68–72. Walpole himself thought the City petition an

"outrageous paper" but was very keen that the ministry should show moderation and not inflame the people. The clash between Harley and Beckford was regarded by Conway as "a little scolding and giving the lie between Beckford and Harley." Harley suggested that a majority of aldermen had protested against the petition, prompting Beckford to ask why they had not been attending common hall to argue against it—*The London Museum* (London, 1770), p. 210.

27. *Pitt Correspondence*, vol. 3, p. 431; TNA, PRO30/8/19, fol. 103, William Beckford to Lord Chatham, 21 Mar. 1770.

28. *Freeholders Magazine*, vol. 2, pp. 73–75; *Walpole Correspondence*, vol. 23, p. 200.

29. *Pitt Correspondence*, vol. 3, p. 431; C. W. Everett, ed., *The Letters of Junius* (London 1927), pp. 231–32. Walpole still feared violence at such events and lamented how Chatham fomented trouble by "pressing a popular general" to head the procession—*Walpole Memoirs, George III*, vol. 4, p. 77.

30. *London Evening Post*, 10–12 Apr. 1770; *Independent Chronicle*, 11–13 Apr. 1770; *Town and Country Magazine*, vol. 2, p. 221; *Walpole Correspondence*, vol. 23, p. 205; Treloar, *Wilkes and the City*, pp. 105, 260. Wilkes had been imprisoned in June 1769 for publishing scandalous literature.

31. *Cavendish Debates*, vol. 1, p. 549; vol. 2, pp. 7–9. Boston patriots sent an account of the massacre to Beckford and other friends of America—*A Short Narrative of the Horrid Massacre in Boston* (Boston, 1770), p. 85.

32. *Salisbury Journal*, 21st May 1770; D. S. Taylor and B. B. Hoover, eds., *The Complete Works of Thomas Chatterton* (Oxford, 1971), pp. 579–83.

33. *Oxford Magazine* (London, 1770), vol. 4, pp. 186–88.

34. Doubts were subsequently cast on the authorship and accuracy of Beckford's recorded speech, and the published "text" was attributed by some to the Rev. Horne after he claimed it as "his composition" many years later—A. Stephens, *Memoirs of John Horne Tooke* (London, 1813), vol. 1, p. 157. However, the immediate responses of both pro- and anti-court figures suggest that the published text accorded with the mayor's oration. See the discussion of Lucy Sutherland in A. Newman, ed., *Politics and Finance in the Eighteenth Century* (London, 1984), p. 116.

35. *Correspondence of John, Fourth Duke of Bedford*, vol. 3, pp. 413–14; *Walpole Correspondence*, vol. 23, pp. 215–16. Rigby observed that very few aldermen attended the civic procession and not many common councillors either. He also suggested that "the rabble was of the lowest sort, and no mobbing." Walpole later recorded that Beckford had invited the king to respond, and that the king had allowed the kissing of hands "notwithstanding the murmurs

of the courtiers who surrounded him"—*Walpole Memoirs, George III*, vol. 4, pp. 102–3.

36. *Oxford Magazine*, vol. 4, pp. 211–13. Also on 25 May, Townsend sent word to Chatham to confirm that Beckford's speech in *the Public Advertiser* "is verbatim," except that the words "and necessary" were left out before "revolution." He also reported that Beckford was in favor of the congratulatory address to the king, despite opposition of "the leading men and the common councilmen in general, i.e. of our friends." Wilkes had expressed reservations on the address in the common hall that day—*Pitt Correspondence*, vol. 3, pp. 460–61.

37. *Pitt Correspondence*, vol. 3, pp. 462–64; Bodl., Beckford Mss c. 84, fol. 11.

38. *Oxford Magazine*, vol. 4, pp. 213–15; *Walpole Memoirs, George III*, vol. 4, pp. 102–3. The audience of the 30 May was later commemorated by a radical cartoonist, who depicted the Lord Chamberlain holding a bridle to Beckford's mouth. Only three days after the audience, another supportive image portrayed him as immune to court bribery—Stephens and Hawkins, *Catalogue of the Prints*, vol. 4, pp. 622–24.

39. *Pitt Correspondence.*, vol. 3, p. 463; *Oxford Magazine*, vol. 4, p. 239; *The Court and City Magazine* (London, 1770), vol. 1, pp. 333–34; *Salisbury Journal*, 25 June, 1770. Amid much speculation concerning Beckford's illness, it was suggested that Beckford might have infected Rev. Horne, who in turn passed it to Thomas Oliver—*London Museum*, vol. 2, p. 57.

40. *Oxford Magazine*, vol. 4, p. 239–40; *Lloyd's Evening Post*, 22–25, 27–29 June 1770; *Court and City Magazine*, vol. 1, p. 328; *Freeholders Magazine*, vol. 2, pp. 210, 214, 242, 257–79; *Town and Country Magazine*, vol. 2, pp. 292–93; *London Museum*, vol. 2, pp. 48–49; D. S. Taylor and B. B. Hoover, eds., *The Complete Works of Thomas Chatterton* (Oxford, 1971), pp. 587–88, 713–18, 774–75. The National Portrait Gallery, London, has a copy of the Beckford medal by John Kirk in its primary collection (no. 5758) and several of the Beckford prints produced in 1769–70. The Museum of London Docklands also has bronze and white metal Beckford medals dated 1770 (nos. 11043–44); a blue stone intaglio engraved "Alderman Beckford for ever" (no. 15307); and a silver spoon with Beckford's profile, akin to those produced for Wilkes (no. 2003.74). At least four graphic prints commemorated his death within a few weeks of his passing— Stephens and Hawkins, *Catalogue of the Prints*, vol. 4, pp. 628–30.

41. *Walpole Correspondence*, vol. 23, p. 223; vol. 35, p. 339; R. Blunt, *Mrs Montagu, Queen of the Blues* (London, n.d.), vol. 1, p. 234. Horace Walpole's correspondent, Sir Horace Mann, had on the eve of Beckford's death dismissed him as "that furious lord mayor who avails himself of his occasional dignity to

create confusion," while praising the king for showing moderation in allowing Beckford to finish "his senseless harangue"—*Walpole Correspondence*, vol. 23, p. 219.

42. *HMC 10th report, vol. 1*, p. 426; Treloar, *Wilkes and the City*, p. 105; Wilcox, *Papers of Benjamin Franklin*, vol. 17, p. 181; Stephens and Hawkins, *Catalogue of Prints and Drawings*, vol. 4, p. 630; Flick, *Papers of Sir William Johnson*, vol. 7, pp. 869–70.

43. *London Evening Post*, 21–23, 23–26 June 1770; *Lloyd's Evening Post*, 20–22 June 1770.

44. *London Evening Post*, 3–5 July, 1770; *London Museum*, vol. 2, pp. 57, 119; Guildhall Library Mss 1240/2, St. Mary Hill vestry minutes, 26 June 1770; 952/2, p. 312, St. George Botolph Lane vestry minutes, 28 June 1770; 2480, Jewer epitaphs, p. 793. Edmund Burke noted in September that Trecothick was still attempting to deflect criticism that he had been lukewarm toward Beckford when accepting the mayoralty on 30 June. Trecothick's mistake had been to echo some praise for Sir Henry Banks, who was regarded of an acolyte of Alderman Harley—*London Museum*, vol. 2, p. 57. Burke thought that an opportunity had been missed "of taking the City out of the worst hands in the world and of putting it into good ones"—Sutherland, *Correspondence of Edmund Burke*, vol. 2, pp. 159–60.

45. *London Evening Post*, 28–30 June 1770; *Salisbury Journal*, 2 July 1770; *Oxford Magazine*, vol. 4, p. 240. The coaches were full of his closest personal servants, including his man of business, Captain Collett; his chaplain, Mr. Sclater; and his cook, Mr. Isadore. There is no evidence to corroborate the report that his heart was taken in a lead urn to Jamaica, but the story was repeated in several American newspapers.

CODA

1. *Town and Country Magazine*, vol. 2 (1770), pp. 416–17; LMA, Misc Mss/65/12, papers relating to the Beckford statue, 1770–72; P. Ward-Jackson, *Public Sculpture of the City of London* (Liverpool, 2003), pp. 163–66. The committee backed Moore over Carlini by eight votes to four. Other surviving models include those by Nathaniel Smith (now held at the Victoria and Albert Museum, Gallery 111) and John Flaxman—K. A. Esdaile, "Flaxman's Design for the Monument to Lord Mayor Beckford at the Guildhall," *Burlington Magazine*, vol. 45 (1924), pp. 80–82, 87. The finished statue was originally placed at the west end of the great hall. Other commemorative media include a Staffordshire earthenware figure, by the Wood factory of c. 1780 (currently housed in the Willetts

Collection of Brighton Museum and Art Gallery)—P. Halfpenny, *English Earthernware, 1740–1840* (Woodbridge, 1991), pp. 63, 66.

2. *Constitutional Gazette*, 23 Aug. 1775; *Pennsylvania Evening Post*, 18 Nov. 1775; John Baxter, *A New and Impartial History of England* (London, 1796); George Sael, *Moral Biography, or the Worthies of England Displayed* (London, 1798), pp. 32–34; *City Biography* (London, 1800), pp. 63–80; *The Britannic Magazine, or Entertaining Repository of Heroic Adventures* (1793–1807), vol. 10, pp. 193–95. As early as 1773, Beckford was depicted as a demagogue alongside Tyler, Cade, and Wilkes—M. D. George, *Catalogue of Political and Personal Satires in . . . the British Museum* (London, 1935), vol. 5, p. 111. Another version of the Beckford audience was published by T. Robbins in 1824 (copy in National Portrait Gallery, Heinz Library, biographical file of sitters, Beckford family). In *Punch* magazine for 23 Sept. 1876, Beckford was listed as one of the City's "famous" historical figures, alongside Whittington, Walworth, Tyler, and Wilkes. Images of Beckford also circulated in the American colonies—*Boston News-letter*, 30 May 1771; *Bowen's Columbian Museum* (Boston, 1798).

3. C. Brown, *Moral Capital: Foundations of British Abolitionism* (Chapel Hill, 2006); T. Nechtman, *Nabobs: Empire and Identity in Eighteenth-Century Britain* (Cambridge, 2010).

4. Richard Cumberland, *The West Indian: A Comedy* (London, 1792), esp. the prologue and pp. 15, 111; *Public Advertiser*, 26 Jan. 1771; R. J. Dircks, ed., *The Memoirs of Richard Cumberland* (New York, 2002), pp. 111–12. Within a year four editions of the play had been published, and it was also performed in Dublin, and in the colonies—*Hoey's Dublin Mercury*, 5–7 Mar. 1771; J. Flavell, *When London Was Capital of America* (New Haven, 2010), p. 104. For a much harsher colonial stereotype, see Samuel Foote's *The Nabob*, first performed in 1772. For the hardening of attitudes toward Caribbean slavery in late eighteenth-century literature, see F. Felsenstein, *English Trader, Indian Maid: Representing Gender, Race and Slavery in the New World: An Inkle and Yarico Reader* (Baltimore, 1999), esp. pp. 9–27.

5. East Sussex Record Office, SAS/RF, 18/04, Rose Fuller's (undated) notes for a draft speech about Boston. Internal evidence suggests that the speech came amid the Tea Party crisis of 1773–74. For discussion of the popular support for government imperial policy in the era of the American Revolution, see E. Gould, *The Persistence of Empire* (Chapel Hill, 2000), chapters 4 and 5.

Bibliography of Manuscript Sources

A. British Archives

1. Bowood House, Wiltshire
   Countess of Shelburne's diaries

2. Bristol
   i. Arts and Social Sciences Library, University of Bristol
   DM58   Pinney Collection
   ii. Bristol Record Office
   SMV/8/2/2   Steadfast Society papers

3. East Sussex Record Office, Lewes
   SAS-RF 17-21   Raper and Fovargue papers (Fuller correspondence)

4. Essex Record Office, Chelmsford
   D/DM/01   Mildmay papers
   D/DQ10   Beckford letters

5. Hampshire Record Office, Winchester
   COPY/814/1-2   Edward Morant diaries
   9M73   Harris papers

6. London
   i. The British Library, St. Pancras
   Additional Mss
      12418-19   Long (Knight) papers
      12422   Long (Barham) papers
      12431   Long papers
      15154–57   Free British Fishery Society papers
      22676   Long papers
      27968   Long papers

30001	Ricketts papers
30867	Wilkes papers
32695, 32735–37, 32860–61, 32867, 32888, 32898, 32920–21, 32946–57, 32972–74, 32988	Newcastle papers
34181	Jamaican wills
38334	Liverpool papers
40776	Vernon papers
41346–58	Martin papers
42081	Hamilton and Greville papers
57827	Grenville papers

Egerton Mss

3490	Moore papers

Sloane Mss

4050, 4052	Hans Sloane papers

ii. The College of Arms

Grants of Arms

Norfolk Pedigrees

iii. Guildhall Library

951–2	Vestry papers, St. George Botolph Lane
1239–40	Vestry papers, St. Mary-at-Hill
1703	Book of rules, Fellowship of Billingsgate Porters
2480	Jewer monumental inscriptions
6647	Butchers' Company papers
11316	Tax assessments
16967	Ironmongers' Company records

iv. Hoare's Bank, Fleet Street

Ledgers B–D

Money Lent book 1743–73

Private Letters 1758–71

v. Institute of Commonwealth Studies Library

M915	Minutes of West India merchants' committee

vi. London Metropolitan Archives

CLA/002/02/01	Orphans' Inventories
COL/AC/13/003/18	Papers regarding troop movements
COL/CHD/FR/07	Freedom certificates
Misc mss/65/12	Beckford statue papers
Q/WIL/26	Willis collection

vii. Royal Bank of Scotland Archives, Islington

EB/1	Edward Backwell, customer ledgers

viii. The National Archives, Kew

C5–12	Chancery papers
C24	Chancery depositions
C107	Chancery Masters' Exhibits
CO1	Colonial Office
CO137–40	Colonial Office, Jamaica papers
CO388	Board of Trade papers
CO700	Colonial Office, Jamaica maps
PRO30/8	Pitt papers
PRO30/24	Shaftesbury papers
PRO30/47	Egremont papers
PROB	Prerogative Court of Canterbury wills
SP34	State papers
T1	Treasury papers
T70	Royal African Company papers

ix. Westminster City Archives

Parish records	St. Anne Soho; St. George's, Hanover Square

7. National Records of Scotland, Edinburgh

GD110/529	Hamilton-Dalrymple papers

8. National Monuments Record, Swindon

BF060059	Fonthill Splendens file
BF061770	Fonthill church file
Red Box files	34 Great Tower Street, London

9. Oxford

i. Balliol College, Oxford

Battels books

Clark's annual lists of members

ii. Bodleian Library, Oxford

Beckford mss

Bowood mss (microfilms)

Boyd Alexander mss

Clarendon deposit (Barham-Vassall papers)

North mss

Rawlinson mss

iii. Keble College, Oxford

File Bonham 930	Wilson papers

10. Somerset Heritage Centre, Taunton

DD\HY	Dickinson papers (Fuller materials)

11. Warwickshire County Record Office, Warwick

L6/1336	Lucy papers

12. Wiltshire and Swindon History Centre, Chippenham

D1/60–1	Fonthill Gifford parish papers
File 9/34–5	Savernake papers
413/277	Fonthill deeds
1990/2/3	Fonthill deeds

13. Worcestershire Record Office (County Hall), Worcester

Lyttelton papers (on deposit from Hagley Hall)

B. AMERICAN AND CARIBBEAN ARCHIVES

1. Beinecke Library, Yale University

General mss 102	Beckford papers

2. Jamaica Archives, Spanish Town

1A/3	Chancery Court libers
1B/11/1	Land patents
1B/11/3	Inventories
1B/11/4	Crop accounts
1B/11/24	Powers of Attorney

3. Library of Congress, Washington

Peter Force Papers (Vernon-Wager materials)

4. National Library of Jamaica, Kingston

B/N	Biographical files, Beckfords
Maps	Beckford estates
Ms 306	Trelawny papers
Ms 472	Trelawny papers
Ms 1021	Agent letter
Ms 1027	Beckford letter
Ms 1579	Beckford legal case
Ms 1792	Beckford letters
P/592	Album of Beckford materials

5. University of San Diego, California

Hall papers

Index